The most *fearless*
and *gallant* soldier
I have ever seen

The most *fearless* and *gallant* soldier I have ever seen

The story of Martin O'Meara,
Australia's only Irish-born Victoria
Cross recipient of the First World War

Ian Loftus

Published by the Author
2016

Published by the Author

PO Box 58, Applecross WA 6953, Australia

www.ianloftus.com

ianloftus@gmail.com

+61 417 674 974

National Library of Australia Cataloguing-in-Publication entry:

Creator: Loftus, Ian, author.

Title: The most fearless and gallant soldier I have ever seen: the story of Martin O'Meara, Australia's only Irish-born Victoria Cross recipient of the First World War / Ian Loftus.

ISBN: 9780646949987 (paperback)

Notes: Includes bibliographical references and index.

Subjects: O'Meara, Martin, Private. 1885-1935.
  Soldiers--Western Australia--Biography.
  Victoria Cross--Biography.
  World War, 1914-1918--Participation, Australian--Biography.

Dewey Number: 355.134092

They were gained in Gallipoli's gullies,
In the orchards of green Armentieres,
And where the foul German shell sullies,
The outskirts of battered Pozieres.
Unafraid of the scrimmage and scurry,
First in the wild forlorn hope –
Martin O'Meara and Murray,
Throssell and Carroll and Pope.

Five little Crosses for Valour,
Each won by a man amongst men.
Gained where the bravest may pallor,
Not knowing the where or the when.
When they calculate victories and losses,
When the eagle's replaced by the dove.
Five little bronze-coloured Crosses,
Will shine like our Star-Cross above.

Five little bits of gun-metal,
Five little ribbons and bars;
Five little chips of gunmetal,
Worth all the garters and stars,
And as Ireland reveres ancient Tara,
And the Welsh in St. David give hope,
We'll immortalize Carroll, O'Meara,
Throssell, Murray and Pope.

Five V.C.'s by 'Coo-ee' (*Australian*, 26 September 1917, p.1)

Contents

Foreword

I respectfully beg to draw your attention to the conduct of Pte O'Meara during the recent operations of this Bttn. Pte O'Meara is the most fearless and gallant soldier I have ever seen.[1]

Lieutenant Bill Lynas of the 16th Battalion of the Australian Imperial Force (AIF) penned these words in mid-August 1916, shortly after the battalion had withdrawn from fierce fighting near the small French village of Pozières, on the Western Front. Bill Lynas was no stranger to fearlessness and gallantry. He had enlisted in September 1914 and had served with the 16th Battalion at Gallipoli and in Egypt during 1915 and 1916. He survived the war with the Military Cross (MC) and two bars, the Distinguished Service Order (DSO), and had been mentioned in dispatches. The official Australian war historian, Dr Charles Bean, later described Bill Lynas as 'one of the finest fighting leaders that Australia produced'.[2] The conduct of Martin O'Meara must have been exceptional to have been noticed by Bill Lynas.

Accounts of Martin O'Meara's life prior to his enlistment in August 1915 tell of similarly good personal qualities. One report records that:

He was highly respected by all with whom he associated. Although of a reserved nature, when his heart thawed to one whom he felt he could confide, he was a most genial character – a warm, true-hearted Celt, charitable and fair-minded, and, above all, a devout Catholic, a staunch Hibernian – he belonged to St. Canice's branch, Cottesloe – and a strict total abstainer.[3]

---

[1] AWM28: 2/101, Recommendation file for honours and awards, AIF, 1914-18 War 4th Australian Infantry Brigade 1916.
[2] Bean, 1942, pp.588-9.
[3] *Kalgoorlie Miner*, 19 September 1916, p.3.

The picture of Martin O'Meara painted by Bill Lynas (and many others) was, however, not to last very long. A little over two years later, in December 1918, O'Meara was described as:

> suffering from Delusional Insanity, with hallucinations of hearing and sight, is extremely homicidal and suicidal, and requires to be kept in restraint.[4]

The contrast with 1916 could not appear to be any greater. So what happened to Martin O'Meara in those two or so years?

I first encountered Martin O'Meara in mid-2013 after writing a piece on the Western Front for the travel section of a newspaper. Shortly after the article was printed I received a letter from one of the newspaper's readers, asking if I was aware that Martin O'Meara had received a Victoria Cross for bravery near Mouquet Farm, which I had mentioned in my article.

I had not heard of Martin O'Meara at that time, but became fascinated by his story after doing a little reading. The more I found out about him, the more intrigued I became, as it became obvious that very little had been published about him, and a fair chunk of what had already been published was not entirely accurate. This triggered a journey of discovery in search of the 'real' Martin O'Meara.

Martin O'Meara, Australia's only Irish-born Victoria Cross recipient of the First World War, remains an elusive and enigmatic character some eighty years after his death. He has been viewed as many things over the years: a compassionate hero, a hard-working loner, a peace-loving stretcher-bearer, an Irish nationalist, a committed trade unionist, a pious Roman Catholic, an unlucky bachelor, a tragic victim of the war, a model of manhood, and a dangerous lunatic. Some of these views are undoubtedly correct, but the range of different portrayals (and some apparent contradictions) demands a greater examination of his life in order to peel back the 'O'Meara myth' and to identify the 'real' Martin O'Meara.

My investigations into his life show that the image of Martin O'Meara that evolved through the popular media since 1916, and which persists today, inadequately describes the real Martin O'Meara.

---

[4] NAA: B2455, Martin O'Meara.

Sadly, this inaccurate portrayal can be found in a wide range of books and articles, and propagated by a wide range of authors and scholars alike.

Rather than being a pacifist who served as a stretcher-bearer with his unit in order to save (rather than take) lives, the evidence shows that Martin O'Meara was involved in combat: he trained and served as a machine gunner in Egypt, and then as a sniper, observer and scout in France and Belgium. Yes, Martin O'Meara saved many lives, but it is very likely that he also killed and wounded German soldiers. His exemplary service record during the war suggests that he was a diligent, willing and obedient participant in the war.

The link between his wartime service and his post-war mental health has also been subject to the 'O'Meara Myth', with the popular portrayal being that the stress of his service (particularly at Pozières and Mouquet Farm in August 1916) was the main factor that caused his breakdown in November 1918, and that he suffered 'shell shock', or perhaps something akin to the currently diagnosed condition of Post-Traumatic Stress Syndrome (PTSD). Whilst his wartime experiences were undoubtedly a contributing factor to his breakdown in November 1918, the evidence suggests that a range of other factors also played an important part in his breakdown.

My journey into the life of Martin O'Meara has turned up much previously unreported (or, at the least, under-reported) evidence and information, and this opens up several interesting aspects to his life.

His relationship with Mary Murphy in County Kilkenny prior to him leaving Ireland is one area that has not previously been fully explored, with most accounts simply mentioning her existence and speculating about who she might have been. Being able to identify her and verify that she had ongoing contact with Martin O'Meara during 1916, 1917 and 1918 adds an extra dimension to our understanding of his life.

Although claimed by the Western Australian town of Collie as one of their own (correctly, given that he enlisted there in 1915), Martin O'Meara spent a relatively short time in the Collie area. His time in South Australia between 1912 and 1914 has not been fully explored nor reported, although alluded to in newspaper reports during the First World War, and his time in the Pinjarra area south of Perth has been under-reported. In particular, his time at Port August and

McLaren Vale in South Australia adds interesting perspectives to his life. If anything, my exploration of his time in South Australia and Western Australia highlights his relatively nomadic lifestyle.

The circumstances of his return to Australia in 1918 also provide interesting additional perspectives on his life. His reluctant return to Australia to assist in AIF recruitment has been previously unreported. Also underreported[5] have been the circumstances surrounding his mental illness and his time in mental hospitals in Perth.

Recent research has questioned a commonly held (but unproven) view about the nature of his mental illness, and we can be reasonably confident that there was more to his descent into mental illness than a simple after-the-fact diagnosis of either 'shell shock' or PTSD provides for.

Despite my own (and others') extensive research into the life of Martin O'Meara over several years, several areas of interest remain yet unanswered.

Firstly, we do not know exactly when and how O'Meara arrived in Australia. We can narrow down his probably arrival in Australia to the early part of 1912, but no trace of his name has been found in shipping and immigration records. It is possible that he was a ship's crewman (rather than a passenger), and in the absence of definitive evidence this remains a possibility.

Secondly, his time in the town of McLaren Vale in South Australia during the second half of 1913 and the first few months of 1914 remains a mystery. He arrived in the area as a railway construction worker, but a possible link to the sale of a boarding house in the town offers some intriguing possibilities.

Thirdly, we do not know exactly why he chose to enlist in the AIF in August 1915. It is possible that he was motivated by a desire to do his duty and serve, although it is also possible that he was looking for a way to return to Ireland. The poor state of the timber industry in late 1915 suggests a possibility that he enlisted for economic reasons; again, another possibility.

---

[5] I must note the work done by Dr Philippa Martyr and Dr Sophie Davison in the last few years to examine O'Meara's mental illness.

Fourthly, Martin O'Meara's relationship with his family in Ireland during 1917 remains an area of interest. He made significant changes to his will after visiting them in late 1917, and this seems to have been the result of a breakdown in this relationship. It is possible that the backdrop of Irish politics may have played a role, as he was from a family of Irish nationalists (and was one himself, as well as being a staunch Roman Catholic) but was fighting for the British Empire.

And, fifthly, we still do not have a definitive picture of exactly what led to his mental illness. It is likely that his wartime experience was a contributing factor, but other factors were likely involved.

Some of these knowledge gaps might be filled as additional information is unearthed over the coming years, but it is unlikely that we will ever be able to answer every remaining question about the life of Martin O'Meara.

And finally, some notes on place names and measurements. As most readers will be aware, the names of some places have changed since the First World War, particular in Belgium where Flemish names are frequently used in place of the French names used a century ago. To avoid confusion, I have adopted the spelling of place names used by the Australian official war historian, Dr Charles Bean, in his official history. No disrespect is intended to those who use more current spellings; I just needed a consistent way of spelling places, and Bean's writings provide such a consistency. Obviously Australia no longer uses the old Imperial system of measurements (such as inches, miles, acres and tons), but most wartime sources mostly do (despite continental Europe using the metric system during the war). For consistency, I have provided in-text metric conversions where Imperial sources are cited, and used metric measurements in my own work.

1   A Tipperaryman

The village of Lorrha lies in northern County Tipperary close to the geographical centre of Ireland. It is a land of rolling green hills and pastures, peat bogs, dry-stone walls and whitewashed cottages. There are newer, more substantial, houses in the main street of the village along with a school, a hairdresser, a post office, a Garda Siochana (Police) Station, a Roman Catholic Church, the ruins of two old abbeys and, unsurprisingly, a pub. The village is surrounded by the civil parish of Lorrha, an administrative (rather than religious[6]) land division within the Barony of Lower Ormond [another type of historical Irish administrative land division. The civil parish of Lorrha is itself subdivided into a series 'townlands', the smallest of Irish administrative land divisions.

The Lorrha area has a rich history. Saint Ruadhán, also known as Saint Rodan and Saint Rowan, is believed to have established a monastic settlement in the area in the sixth century, and a church was established by the eleventh century.

The village of Lorrha developed around these religious settlements. The Normans established a fortress in the twelfth century and around the same time a group of Augustinian priors had established the Augustinian Priory that lies to the east of the village adjacent the current Saint Rodan's Church of Ireland (Anglican) building which dates back to circa 1815 and is itself an expansion of a fifteenth century church. A Dominican Friary was established by Walter de Burgo, the Earl of Ulster, a prominent local Anglo-Norman landowner and noble, in 1269 and it was located adjacent to the current Saint Ruadhan's Roman Catholic church to the village's south-west (which itself dates back to circa 1813).

By 1841 the civil parish of Lorrha had a population of 4,742 but this had dropped to 2,860 by 1851 (a loss of around forty percent of the population), as a result of the Great Famine.[7]

---

[6] The Roman Catholic parish is 'Lorrha and Dorrha.'
[7] House of Commons, 1852, p.285.

The Great Famine was the result of the failure of several successive crops of potatoes, the staple diet of much of the Irish population. The crop was poor in 1845, with around half the expected harvest occurring, and the crop of 1846 was worse. Things were still bad when the 1847 potato crop was harvested. The famine resulted in the decline in the population of Ireland by around a quarter of its population, some two million people. Of these, around a million died of starvation or related illnesses, and around a million emigrated.

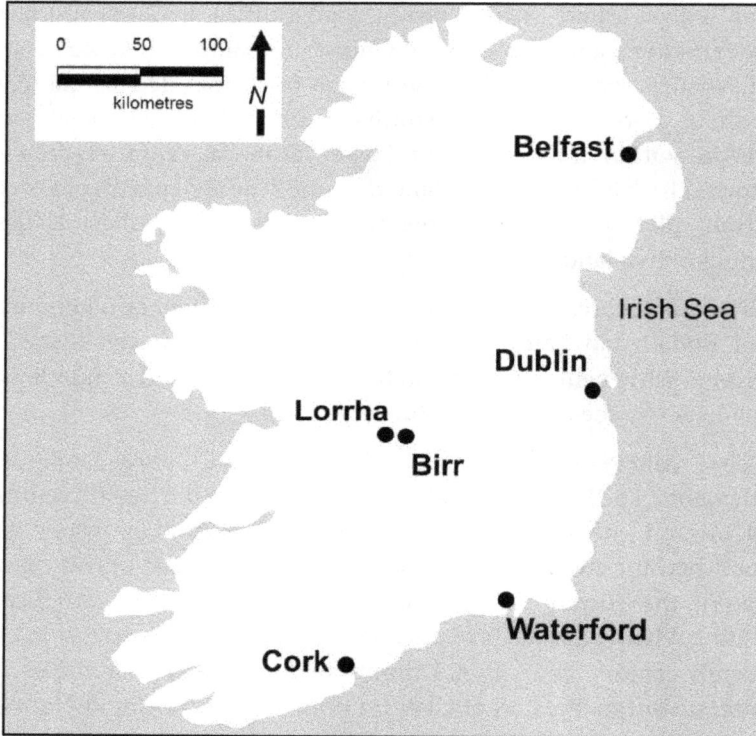

Ireland, showing major cities and places relevant to the life of Martin O'Meara.

In the mid-nineteenth century Lorrha had two churches (a Roman Catholic church at the south-west of the village and a Church of Ireland church to the east), and old Ordnance Survey maps show that it also had a smithy, a Royal Irish Constabulary barracks, a National School, a court house, a post office, and a dispensary.

Martin O'Meara's family farmed in the agricultural townland of Lissernane within the parish of Lorrha, around six kilometres west of

Lorrha village. The townland of Lissernane (variously described as Lishernan, Lisserrane and Lishenane in earlier days) has existed as an identifiable place since ancient times. Despite the establishment of Anglo-Norman estates dating back to the twelfth and thirteenth centuries in some parts of County Tipperary, it seems that the area now forming Lissernane and surrounding townlands in the Barony of Lower Ormond was still, despite Anglo-Norman influence, subject to traditional Gaelic land ownership that was little changed from the medieval period.[8]

In 1641 an uprising by the Irish Roman Catholic elite against the established administration occurred, and led to a decade of turmoil which saw Ireland caught up in the English Civil War from early 1642 onwards. This turmoil continued until the early 1650s when forces loyal to Oliver Cromwell finally put down the remaining resistance by monarchist forces. The conflict descended into a state of insurgency as Cromwell's forces pursued the remnants of Irish Catholic resistance. Lissernane was impacted by this, with a later account noting that 'This land is totally wast.'[9] The Cromwellian settlement of Ireland followed, with large parts of the Ireland being settled by former soldiers and 'adventurers' who had subscribed funds for the war. This process saw County Tipperary being divided amongst the soldiers and the adventurers, with the Barony of Lower Ormond (containing Lissernane) being divided amongst the soldiers.

Two surveys were subsequently commissioned to determine the value of land in Ireland so that the soldiers and adventurers could be rewarded. The Civil Survey was conducted in 1654-66 and the Down Survey was conducted from 1656-68; this second survey resulted in Ireland being mapped thoroughly, and a townland called 'Lisserrane' clearly appears on the Down Survey map of the Barony of Lower Ormond. The Civil Survey of Ireland described Lissernane as having an area of 370 Irish (plantation) acres, which converts to around 592 English acres.[10] It identified the Lissernane lands as being owned by:

---

[8] Simms, 1989, p.27.
[9] Simington, 1934, p.314.
[10] A survey conducted in 1852 indicated that the size of Lissernane was 609 acres, so it is reasonable to assume that the townland of Lissernane was virtually unchanged

The sd. Bryen Hogan and Donagh Kenedy being equal pprietors in fee by descent from their Ancestors and Tennant in common of the said pld [ploughland] of Lishernane. The said pld. Of Lishernane is not clearly devided between the afforsed pprietors whereby each pprietos pportion may be pticularly meared and bounded.[11]

Both Hogan (or O'Hogan) and Kennedy (or O'Kennedy) were described as 'Irish Catholics' and lived nearby. The Kennedy family was one of the most important of the Gaelic landowners in Tipperary with an account from 1600 recording that 'the three O'Kenedies' were the inhabitants of Lower Ormond.[12] Kennedy was the last of the Chieftains of Ormond, and Donagh O'Kennedy surrendered Lackeen Castle to Cromwell's forces in 1653 and was subsequently transported to Galway. The restoration of the English monarchy on 1660 did not fully restore land ownership to its pre-1641 state, and most of those who had received land during the 1650s appeared to have retained their holdings. It seems that the Kennedy family reclaimed some of their estate after the restoration, but the majority of the land appears to have been retained by soldiers loyal to Cromwell.

By the nineteenth century the largest landowners in the Lissernane area included the Hackett and Egan families, although it is not known whether they became land owners as the direct result of the Cromwellian settlement or whether they acquired the land during the seventeenth or eighteenth centuries. The Hacketts seem to have descended from Anglo-Norman settlers whilst the Egans seem to have been of Irish stock.

The northern part of County Tipperary was home to a large number of separate O'Meara[13] families during the nineteenth century, some of which were directly related to each other. The O'Mearas were

---

in the intervening 200 years. The Civil Survey estimated, rather than accurately measured, land areas.

[11] Simington, 1934, p.314.

[12] Hogan, 1878, p.208.

[13] Whilst the rendering 'O'Meara' is used for Martin O'Meara, it must be remembered that the spelling of the surname varied, and included the variations 'Meara', 'O'Mara' and 'Mara'. Martin O'Meara's family were typically known as Meara during the nineteenth century. The dropping of the 'O' seems to have occurred from the seventeenth century onwards.

typically engaged in agricultural pursuits, usually as tenant farmers, although some of the wealthier families did own land in their own right. Martin O'Meara's family were not landowners, and farmed as tenants on estates owned by landholders who had mostly gained estate during the mid-seventeenth century as a result of the Cromwellian settlement of Ireland. Although tenants rather than landowners, Martin O'Meara's family do not seem to have been at the very bottom rung of rural Irish society as they were able to rent (and retain) a modest parcel of land upon which was (according to a later census) a stable, a cow house, a piggery, a fowl house and a barn.[14]

The Tithe Applotment Books, compiled in 1824 in order to determine the amount which occupiers of agricultural holdings of over one acre should pay in tithes to the Church of Ireland, record two individual entries for Mara families living in Lissernane: they were James Mara and Martin Mara who both leased land from Terence Cornelius John Egan. The Egan family had owned land in County Tipperary since at least prior to the mid-eighteenth century. Howard E. Egan had died in England in 1809 and left land to his sons Howard N. Egan (born in 1803) and Terence C.J. Egan (born in 1804), and both boys lived in London during their younger years. Howard N. Egan seems to have actually lived in Ireland later in his life, farming at Sharragh adjacent to Lissernane. Terence Egan seems to have pursued several unsuccessful ventures in England and declared bankruptcy in 1844. The lands at Lissernane where the O'Meara families lived seems to have been sold by the Egans to the Hackett family sometime in the first half of the nineteenth century.

The Great Famine would have directly impacted the O'Meara family at Lissernane. Statements included in a report to the House of Commons by the Scarcity Commission in April 1846 noted that in the Barony of Lower Ormond (which contained Lissernane and surrounding townlands), the situation was 'disease extensive and increasing' and 'that inhabitants of barony are suffering severely from failure of potato crop ... distress daily arising.'[15] This would undoubtedly resulted in a significant impact on the local population

---

14 NAI: 1911 Census.
15 Scarcity Commission, Weekly Report, for March 1846, House of Commons sessional paper No.201, 1846, HMSO London.

and stories of the famine's hardships were undoubtedly told to Martin O'Meara by his relatives when he was a young boy.

Lissernane was never densely populated. By 1841 its population had risen to 183, but this had fallen to 140 in 1851 as a result of the Great Famine, with the number of occupied houses dropping from 34 to 24 over the same period.

The economic impact of the famine meant that many landholders were unable to meet their financial obligations. Debt was particularly compounded for landowners by mortgages that bound them to repay loans, which was made very difficult because of the economic impact of the famine. The *Encumbered Estates Acts* of 1848 and 1849 allowed for the sale of estates in Ireland which were burdened with debt, but offered no protection for the tenants on the estates. The 1849 Act allowed the state to assume ownership of encumbered estates and to sell them. The sale required a petitioner, either the landowner or a person holding an encumbrance (such as a mortgage), to apply for the sale. The volume of land that became available for purchase as a result of this process forced down the value of land, and many speculators took advantage of this to acquire for themselves extensive Irish landholdings. This often resulted in the poor treatment of tenants, including evictions and rent increases.

Some of the Egans' landholdings in Tipperary were sold off under this process. On 13 May 1853 the Encumbered Estates Commission held a public auction of land at Lissernane and Sharragh, close to where James Meara lived.[16] The auction was successful in selling some of the estate, but the land at Lissernane did not sell despite an offer of £3,000.[17] Those two parcels of land that failed to sell were re-auctioned by the Commission on 24 June and were sold to solicitor Frederick Hamilton,[18] possibly in trust for a third party.

It seems that the land owned by Thomas Hackett, where Martin O'Meara's family lived, was not sold through the unencumbered estates process and this would tend to indicate that the Hacketts' estate remained profitable.

---

16 *Nenagh Guardian,* 16 March 1853, p.3.
17 *Nenagh Guardian,* 18 May 1853, p.1.
18 *Nenagh Guardian,* 28 May 1853, p.3, and *Freeman's Journal,* 25 June 1853, p.4.

The returns of the primary land valuations for County Tipperary, published in 1853, show that Lissernane still had two separate O'Meara households; one headed by a Patrick O'Meara and the other headed by a James O'Meara, who was probably Martin O'Meara's grandfather. The household headed by James O'Meara occupied two separate land parcels (around fourteen acres) leased from Thomas Hackett.[19] The household headed by Patrick O'Meara, who is not known to be closely linked to Martin O'Meara's family, occupied two separate land parcels (around 82 acres) leased from Howard N. Egan.

Martin O'Meara's grandfather, James O'Meara, had married Alice (surname unknown) sometime before 1835 and they had several children, including at least two sons, Michael and Daniel, and possibly others: Thomas and John. According to civil death records, James Meara died on 3 June 1868 of 'constipation' that he had suffered for ten days without medical attention. He was aged 79. Civil death records also indicate that Alice died of 'old age' on 17 February 1871, aged 85.

Their son Michael Meara, who had been born around 1835 and who continued to farm in the area, married Margaret Connors (the daughter of Thomas Connors, a farmer of Carrigahorig, about three kilometres south west of Lorrha village) on 30 April 1870 in the parish church at Terryglass near Lorrha.

Michael and Margaret's first child, Hugh O'Meara, was born in 17 May 1871, little more than a year after they married. He was followed on 16 November 1872 by another son, James O'Meara. A native of the area later noted the 'dark complexion of the family, with the exception of the V.C.'s brother James, who was fair.[20] As there were a number of separate O'Meara families in the Lorrha area, Martin's family was

---

[19] Thomas Hackett (1798-1869). These Hacketts lived near Birr in Co. Offaly and were a branch of the family that included Sir John Winthrop Hackett who was ultimately the first Chancellor of the University of Western Australia, a member of the Legislative Council and owner of the *West Australian* newspaper. One of Thomas Hackett's sons, Lieutenant-Colonel Thomas Hackett had won the Victoria Cross during the Indian Mutiny in 1857.

[20] James O'Meara was recorded as having blue eyes and brown hair when he registered for the US Army draft in 1918 in Hudson NY. All photographs of Martin are characterized by a dark complexion and piercing dark eyes.

referred to locally as the 'black O'Meara's' because of their dark complexions.[21]

The ruins of the old O'Meara farm at Lissernane, Lorrha, taken in 2014. This is where Martin O'Meara was born in 1885. (Noreen O'Meara)

Michael and Margaret's first daughter, Mary O'Meara, was born at Lissernane on 15 April 1874. Another son, Patrick O'Meara, was born on 5 March 1876, but died of 'debility' 15 hours after his birth. Patrick was followed by Thomas O'Meara who was born on 28 August 1877.

A second daughter, Alice O'Meara, was born on 28 August 1879 and another son, John O'Meara, followed on 10 June 1881. On 24 June 1883 another son, Peter O'Meara, was born (but died on 29 June 1883 of 'convulsions') and another son, Michael O'Meara, was born on 14 June 1884; he also died of 'convulsions' on 29 July 1884.

Martin O'Meara himself was born at Lissernane on 3 November 1885 and baptised at the Roman Catholic Church at Lorrha on 20 November 1885.[22] It has been suggested that a Pat and Bridget Connors were the sponsors at Martin's baptism, and if this was

---

[21] Noreen O'Meara, pers. comm., 4 February 2015.

[22] An alternative baptism date is possible: 6 November 1885.

accurate then they would probably be relatives of Martin's mother Margaret.[23]

On 2 August 1889 a heavily pregnant Margaret Meara of Lissernane appeared before the Court of Petty Sessions in neighbouring King's County (now County Offaly) on a charge that she 'did cruelly illtreat abuse and torture a jennet [a small horse or mule] by working same in an unfit state contrary to law' in Birr on 27 July 1889. She was convicted and fined one shilling.[24] Shortly afterwards, on 3 September 1889, another (second) son named Michael O'Meara was born. He did not survive his first year and died of croup on 2 August 1890.

Newspaper reports would later record that Martin O'Meara 'was a bright, lively boy, full of frolicsome fun. He was a keen lover of sports but an excellent workman nevertheless.'[25] In this respect he was probably similar to other young men of his generation in the county, and those newspaper comments are probably generic in nature and reflect the need to say something flattering in the absence of any specific knowledge about his childhood. It was later reported that Martin O'Meara's brothers were 'great hurlers'[26] so it is quite possible that Martin O'Meara was involved in hurling himself.

The O'Meara family (and many of the local population) tended to support home rule for Ireland; a Michael Meara of Lissernane, probably Martin O'Meara's father, donated 2s to the Irish National Fund in early 1897. His neighbour John Kelly donated 1s 6d and the local Roman Catholic Priest, the Rev R. Kennedy who was President of the Lorrha and Dorrha Branch of the Irish National Federation, contributed £1. At the time the Rev Kennedy wrote:

the people contributed with great spirit and unanimity ... we unanimously adopt and endorse resolutions of Irish Race Convention, particularly "Majority Rule."[27]

---

[23] King, 2012, p.47.

[24] Margaret Meara was was convicted of a similar offence in August 1911.

[25] *Nenagh Guardian*, 30 September 1916, p.5.

[26] *Daily News*, 15 September 1916, p.7.

[27] *Freeman's Journal*, 25 March 1897, p.5.

The Irish National Federation was a breakaway nationalist group that split from the Irish National League in 1891 and later became part of the Irish Parliamentary Party. It advocated 'home rule' for Ireland and was strongly supported by the Roman Catholic clergy.

The 1901 census tells an interesting picture of the area that Martin O'Meara would know as a young man. Lissernane now had 69 residents, comprising around a dozen separate households. All of the residents were Roman Catholics, and all were engaged in agricultural pursuits as farmers, agricultural labours or servants, or members of the families of those engaged in such pursuits. When the census was taken on 31 March 1901, Martin O'Meara was a 'scholar', and was living at Lissernane with his father, Michael Meara (a farmer), his mother Margaret, his brothers Hugh, Thomas and John, and his sisters Mary and Alice. The O'Meara's house was small; it had only three rooms and the farm had several outbuildings. Martin's brother James was unmarried and was working as a domestic coachman for William Henry O'Meara at the nearby Abbeville House.

Martin O'Meara would have attended one of the nearby National Schools, probably at Lorrha or at Gurteen (near Rathcabbin). A former Lorrha resident, who later emigrated to Western Australia, claimed to have attended school with O'Meara and his brothers at Lorrha,[28] whilst stories recalled by the O'Meara family suggest that he attended the school at Gurteen.[29] Regardless of the school he attended, it is likely that he walked the several miles to school each day from the farm at Lissernane.

Other aspects of life for that would probably have occupied young Martin O'Meara would have involved helping his family with the running of the farm, his attendance at the Roman Catholic church at Lorrha, the sport of hurling, and Irish politics (particularly relating to the matter of home rule). The O'Meara family was later described as 'very industrious, honest people, and small farmers.'[30]

The O'Mearas of Lissernane remained tenant farmers into the twentieth century, and were still renting from the Hackett family in October 1902 when Colonel Charles Hackett sued Margaret O'Meara

---

[28] *Daily News*, 15 September 1915, p.7.
[29] Noreen O'Meara, pers. comm., 29 March 2015.
[30] *Daily News*, 15 September 1915, p.7.

to recover some £13 in overdue rent. Hackett's estate office had alleged that the amount due was two years at £6 per year and an additional £1 that was owing previously. Margaret O'Meara responded that an agreement with the Hacketts dating back some fourteen or fifteen years (to around 1887) had fixed the rent at £5 per year and that she had previously (in 1900) attempted to pay £5 but that it was rejected and that she ultimately mailed the Hacketts the money. Margaret O'Meara's statement about the reduction was rejected by the Hacketts.[31]

Martin's father, Michael Meara, died on 29 January 1902 of bronchitis of seven months' duration, having not received medical attention during that time. He left his widow, Margaret, and several of their children on the farm at Lissernane. Michael Meara was subsequently buried at Lorrha cemetery, but it seems that his grave had no headstone as the family could not afford one.

On 19 April 1903 Martin's brother James O'Meara boarded the steamer *Campania* at Queenstown (now Cobh) in County Cork and sailed to New York, arriving there on 25 April 1903. His United States arrival records note that he was heading for the city of Hudson in New York state where a cousin, James Meara, was living. He had paid his own passage to the United States and arrived with $20. James O'Meara was known as James Meara (or sometimes Mara) after his arrival in the United States, and shortly after arriving in Hudson met Mary Grace who was also from Tipperary.[32] Mary had worked at a mill in Hudson in 1900, and by 1910 was describing herself as a 'manicurist'. James worked as a coachman for a number of years after arriving in Hudson and then found work as a chipper at a nearby foundry. Mary Grace died in 1921 (and was buried as Mary Meara at the Hudson City Cemetery) and James probably died between 1930 and 1940 (he is buried in the same plot as Mary, but no date of death

---

31 *Nenagh Guardian*, 22 October 1902, p.4.

32 It is not certain that James Mara actually married Mary Grace. She is referred to as Mary Mara in the 1910 and 1920 US censuses and in James' 1915 US Army draft papers, but as Mary Grace in US immigration records for her arrival in at New York in September 1910 following a visit to her mother in Ireland. There is also some confusion as to when Mary Grace was born; her headstone at the Hudson City Cemetery says 1857 but census and immigration records suggest either 1870 or 1866 (1870 seems more likely).

is given on the headstone). James and Mary lived at 416 Diamond Street in Hudson, and it seems that Mary had lived with her uncle at 414 Diamond Street prior to meeting James.[33] After Mary died, James moved and boarded with his neighbours at 414 Columbia Street.

Martin's sister Mary O'Meara left Ireland in 1906, sailing from Queenstown on the *Campania* (the same ship that her brother James had left Ireland on) on 13 May 1906 and arriving at New York on 19 May 1906. United States arrival documents record that she was travelling to join her brother James O'Meara at 416 Diamond Street in Hudson, New York. Mary married a German immigrant, Bernhard Rohmer in Hudson on 6 February 1912 and lived with him at North 6th Street, Hudson.[34]

Land rental was still a problem for the O'Meara family when the Land Commission met at nearby Borrisokane on 14 December 1906. It determined that the 'fair rent' for the farm (an area of 11 acres) that Margaret O'Meara rented from Colonel Hackett was £4 12s per annum, a good deal less than the previous rent of £6. The Land Commission also found that the Poor Law valuation of the land was £5 15s.[35] Colonel Charles Hackett later died in 1909 and left his estate in trust for his children Charles Bernard Hackett and Ethel Alice Hackett.[36]

Margaret also had other financial problems. On 24 March 1909 the *Nenagh Guardian* reported that the Court of Quarter Sessions at Nenagh had recently heard a case in which William H. O'Meara of Somerset House, Lorrha (who was not directly related to Martin O'Meara's family) was taking action against Margaret O'Meara to recover the sum of £7 9s 'for the hire of horses, hay sold and delivered, grazing of cattle, and service of a bull.' Margaret claimed to have offered him 8s ('I only owe him 8s'), which she claimed he refused to

---

[33] Diamond Street (known as Columbia Street after 1926) was noted for its bars and brothels.

[34] Bernhard was a 42 year old kiln burner whose first wife had died prior to him leaving Germany. Mary died in 1927 and was buried at the Hudson City Cemetery. Bernhard died some years later and was buried at Hudson.

[35] *Nenagh News*, 27 April 1907, p.4.

[36] It seems that Charles Hackett's estate was eventually broken up by the Land Commission process in the years preceding the First World War, with the O'Meara's purchasing the lands they occupied at Lissernane.

take. The court subsequently ordered Margaret to pay £7 9s and she is reported to have responded 'It is all the same, I owe only 8s (laughter).'[37]

Martin O'Meara seems to have remained at Lissernane until at least 1901 (when he was aged 16), and it was later reported that during 'all the earlier part of his manhood he worked in his native district and was very popular there'.[38] The Hoctor family that has farmed at Sharragh near Lissernane for many generations recalls that their ancestors employed Martin O'Meara as a labourer on their farm when he was a young man, and that he also worked on other nearby farms before moving away from the area.[39] The Hoctors' farm was close to the farm at Sharragh where Martin's brother John O'Meara later farmed. He left Lissernane sometime between 1901 and 1911 (when he was aged 26), and nothing more is known about his life during that period.

Martin O'Meara as a young man, probably taken several years before he left Ireland (perhaps around 1910).

This photograph was published in at least one Irish newspaper in September 1916 following the announcement of his Victoria Cross.
(Noreen O'Meara)

When the next Irish census was taken on 2 April 1911, Martin O'Meara was living in the southern part of County Kilkenny, close to the port city of Waterford. Martin's mother Margaret was a widow and only two of her children, Thomas and Alice O'Meara, remained

---

[37] *Nenagh Guardian*, 24 March 1909, p.3.
[38] *Nenagh Guardian*, 30 September 1916, p.5.
[39] Noreen O'Meara, pers. comm., 7 May 2015.

on the farm at Lissernane. Martin's brother Hugh was working as a farm servant for John Brennan at Dary in County Tipperary, and his brother John O'Meara was living at on a farm several kilometres north of Lissernane, where he was working as a farm labourer for the Liffey family.[40] Martin O'Meara, now aged 26, was living as a boarder in the house of John Steacy, a 69-year old mill hand, at Skeard in County Kilkenny, north of Waterford city on the Blackwater River, close to the villages of Kilmacow Upper and Kilmacow Lower. He was described as a native of County Tipperary, his occupation as 'wood worker', and that he was a Roman Catholic who could read and write. Also living at same dwelling were two other boarders, Peter Skelly and William Skelly who were both wood workers.[41]

Martin O'Meara's occupation is consistent with later reports that he was a 'tree-feller' before leaving Ireland[42] and later newspaper reports that also noted he was working as a timber-feller at Greenville in Skeard, on the estate of John Brown, who owned a flour (later a corn) mill.[43] The Greenville Mill was one of a number powered by water directed from the Blackwater River through a series of channels and sluices to the mill.

Whilst living at Skeard, Martin O'Meara developed friendships with a number of local people, including with Mary Murphy, a young lady (born on 4 February 1890) who lived on a farm in the townland of Dangan, at Kilmacow on the western side of the Blackwater River, only a few kilometres to the east of where Martin lived. Mary was living with her brother Bob (a farmer aged 26) and another brother, William (aged 10). Bob Murphy had been living in Dangan since around 1897, initially with his uncle and aunt, John and Catherine Walsh. Mary had joined him at Kilmacow in her teenage years and was helping her brother work the farm.[44] Mary's parents were Michael Murphy, a farmer, and his wife Mary Anne Murphy. They farmed at Mooncoin several kilometres to the west of Dangan.

[40] NAI: 1911 Census.
[41] NAI: 1911 Census.
[42] *Sunday Times*, 4 August 1918, p.3.
[43] *Munster Express*, 30 July 1937, p.8.
[44] Margaret Clews, pers. comm., 8 March 2014.

Mary Murphy's daughter later recalled an account from her mother that Mary and Martin O'Meara 'were probably friends ... and belonged to a pleasant group of young neighbours who met mainly for dances and cycling, all very rural pursuits.'[45]

It has been suggested that Martin O'Meara lived and worked in Liverpool in England prior to travelling to Australia. One newspaper account records that 'The call of the wilds was in his blood and, as stated, after staying some time in Liverpool he emigrated to Australia.'[46] The same article records that he worked in Liverpool, although no evidence has been found to confirm this. If he did work in Liverpool, the limited time between his appearance in the April 1911 Irish census and his appearance in South Australia during 1912 indicates that it cannot have been for any significant period of time. However, given Liverpool's importance as a port, it is quite possible (or even likely) that he passed through Liverpool on his way to Australia. The other major departure port for ships to Australia was London, and it is also possible that he sailed from London, or perhaps spent time living and working there.

It is also quite possible that Martin O'Meara returned to visit his family at Lissernane before leaving for Australia, as he was later reported as being quite close to his mother and is most unlikely to have left Ireland without making a final visit to her. An account, published in a Lorrha parish newsletter in 1985, records that Martin O'Meara:

> set out from Lisernane [sic] with his kit on his back to seek his fortune in the world. "I am thinking of heading for Australia" he told a neighbour on the road at Abbeyville [sic].[47]

Whilst no evidence exists to corroborate this account, it is certainly feasible that he bid goodbye to friends and family and that this story was retold by local people. The same newsletter records that he obtained work as a stoker on a ship headed for Perth, and that he later said 'The hardest task in my life ... was shovelling coal to the boilers

---

[45] Margaret Clews, pers. comm., 8 March 2014.
[46] *Nenagh Guardian*, 30 September 1916, p.5.
[47] Lorrha parish newsletter, undated 1985.

on that three months voyage.'[48] In a similar vein, the *Collie Mail* reported on 23 September 1916 that:

> The hero spent much of his life at sea, and during his sea-roving history saw much of the great wide world.[49]

No evidence has been located to confirm that he actually was a seaman, although as there appears to be no record of Martin O'Meara either leaving the United Kingdom as a passenger or arriving in Australia as a passenger, the possibility that he did serve as a seaman cannot be ruled out.

Several factors are likely to have contributed to Martin O'Meara's decision to leave Ireland and to make a new life in Australia. The economic situation in Ireland was not good and many people left Ireland and settled overseas (in places such as England, Scotland, Australia, Canada and the United States of America) during this period. Mary Murphy's family later recalled accounts from her that O'Meara had been interested in marrying Mary Murphy but that nothing came of the relationship so he moved to Australia. Mary Murphy, so the story goes, was not interested in marrying, settling down and remaining in rural Ireland.[50]

Evidence that he was in Ireland in April 1911 and in South Australia in March or April 1912 indicate that O'Meara left Ireland during this period; probably in late 1911 or early 1912.

---

[48] Lorrha parish newsletter, undated 1985.

[49] *Collie Mail*, 23 September 1916, p.2.

[50] Roy Clews, pers. comm., 27 February 2014, and Margaret Clews, pers. comm., 8 March 2014. Mary Murphy's family have suggested that O'Meara was interested in marrying her.

2   South Australia

On 29 March 1911 Australia's High Commissioner to the United Kingdom, Sir George Reid, announced that the South Australian Government had established a scheme for assisted passage immigration to that State. He noted that there were significant developments underway there, including the new trans-Australian railway that would link Western Australia with the eastern states.[51]

The Irish were not unfamiliar with emigration. Many had left their homeland from the 1840s onwards as a result of the famine and had travelled to other places. Martin's own brother James and his sister Mary had themselves emigrated to the United States in the early twentieth century.

In an interview given in November 1918 shortly after he had returned from France, Martin O'Meara said:

> "I was born in Tipperary 34 years ago this month," he said, "and I came out here in 1911 like a lot of other young Irishmen had done before me, to try my luck in Australia."[52]

Martin O'Meara probably arrived in South Australia around March or April 1912 and his journey (whether as a passenger or seaman) is likely to have taken somewhere around six weeks, via either South Africa (stopping at Cape Town and/or Durban) or the Suez Canal (stopping at Aden and Colombo). Either route is most likely to have taken him via Fremantle in Western Australia.

Martin O'Meara is most likely to have arrived at Port Adelaide, and probably spent his first few nights in Australia in lodgings at Port Adelaide or in Adelaide itself before heading north. It seems quite likely that Martin O'Meara first worked for the Lyons family at Wild Horse Plains, approximately 70 kilometres north of Adelaide. One of Martin's companions, Sid Williams, sent a postcard from Wild Horse

---

[51] *Freeman's Journal*, 30 March 1911, p.10.
[52] *West Australian*, 8 November 1918, p.7.

Plains to Sadie (Sarah) Lehane whose family was a close neighbour of the O'Meara family at Lissernane.[53] The postcard reads:

> No doubt you will be surprised to hear from a boy in South Australia. Mr. Martin O'Meara is working here with me, that's how I got your address. Well dear, I hope to come home to Ireland with Martin in a few months to see you all and the other girls or colleens as you are called. I have never been over there so will be pleased if you will write back to me. This is a lovely place Adelaide, and if I come over you may want to come back with me. I should like you to send me over some views of Ireland. Well dear if you care to answer this my address is, Sidney Williams, c/o J Lyons, Wild Horse Plains, Via Adelaide, South Australia.[54]

Wild Horse Plains was not a large place. It had a population of 26 (and seven houses) in 1912, consisting primarily of people who provided services to support the local farmers and associated workers. The township had a post office, a store, and a school, and was linked to Adelaide by a daily coach service.[55] It is likely that the J. Lyons noted in the postcard was John Alexander Lyons, the son of Henry Alexander Lyons, an Irish immigrant from County Monaghan who had settled in the Wild Horse Plains area north of Adelaide during the 1880s. John Lyons served with the 9th Light Horse Regiment in the First World War and was elected to the South Australian House of Assembly in 1926, representing the district of Stanley and later the district of Rocky River until his death 19 December 1948.[56]

Sid Williams' postcard's text is also interesting as it suggests that Martin O'Meara was intending to return to Ireland, perhaps on a permanent basis. It is quite possible that his time in Australia was

---

[53] Sarah (Sadie) Lehane later married Martin's brother John O'Meara in late 1913.

[54] Undated postcard in Noreen O'Meara's possession. As Sarah (Sadie) married John O'Meara between October-December 1913 the postcard was most likely sent prior to that time.

[55] Sands & Dougall, 1912, p.446.

[56] *Advertiser*, 20 December 1948, p.2.

intended to be temporary, and that he wanted to return to Ireland and resume farm work.

John Lyons advertised in Adelaide newspapers during May 1912 for 'White Malee Fencing Posts, Shed Forks, and Bails, cut to order',[57] and white mallee probably refers to *Eucalyptus dumosa*, a small tree found in the semi-arid lands from South Australia through north-western Victoria and south-western New South Wales. White mallee was extensively cleared to create agricultural land for many years, and it is possible that Martin O'Meara was employed in land-clearing for John Lyons.

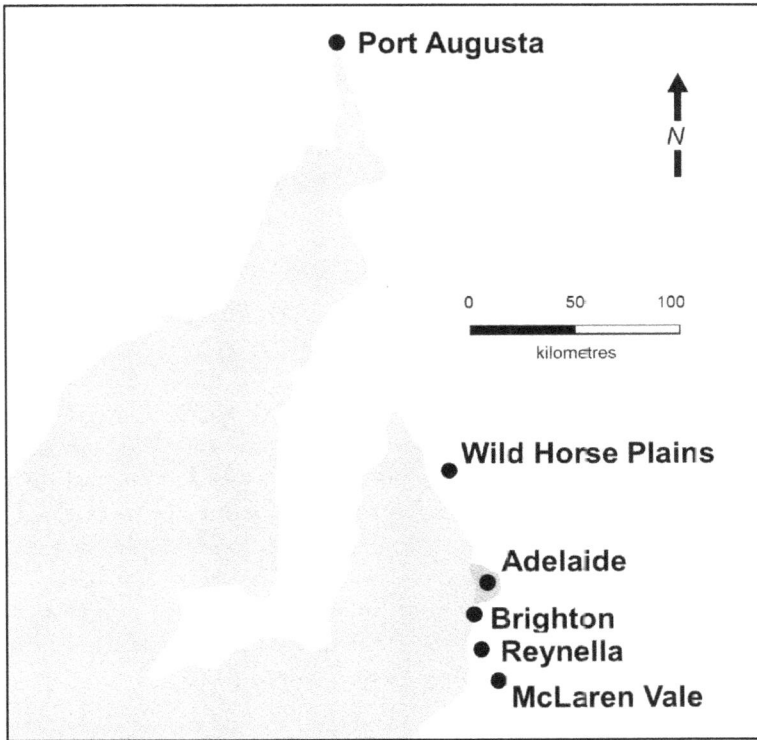

South Australia, showing places relevant to the life of Martin O'Meara.

Martin O'Meara does not seem to have stayed very long at Wild Horse Plains, and it seems likely that he made his way north to Port Augusta during the second half of 1912. It is not known if Sid Williams

---

[57] *Advertiser*, 16 May 1912, p.15, and Chronicle, 18 May 1912, p.28.

also travelled to Port Augusta, or what ultimately became of him. The lure of railway construction work may have been the main lure for many immigrants, rather than agricultural labouring, and Port Augusta is likely to have attracted him as a place of prospective employment. The *Kalgoorlie to Port Augusta Railway Act 1911* had passed through the Australian Parliament during 1911 and received Royal Assent on 12 December 1911. This Act authorised the construction, by the Australian Government, of a standard gauge railway line between Kalgoorlie in Western Australia and Port Augusta in South Australia. In early February 1912 it was reported that:

> Fifteen hundred men will be required to construct the Western Australian railway according to the estimates framed by the Home Affairs Department. The Minister (Mr. O'Malley) was asked whether strict preference should be given to unionists in connection with this work. Mr. O'Malley contented himself with the remarks that he had never found non-unionists good workers.[58]

Another South Australian newspaper, the Adelaide *Register* reported later that month that:

> About 1,800 men will be required, 900 of whom will be engaged at the Western Australian starting point, and 900 at Port Augusta. The work is to be conducted by day labour, but the Commonwealth reserves the right of letting out contracts if it is thought advisable.[59]

It was later reported in Ireland that Martin O'Meara had worked on the railways after emigrating from Ireland to Australia,[60] and this is likely to refer to railway construction work.

Initially settled in the 1850s, by the early twentieth century Port Augusta was starting to develop as an important railway town, and it became the eastern base for construction of the Transcontinental Railway, as well as for the South Australian Government Railways. In

---

[58] *Chronicle*, 10 February 1912, p.39.
[59] *Register*, 24 February 1912, p.16.
[60] *Nenagh Guardian*, 23 September 1916, p.3.

1912 the town had a permanent population of less than a thousand people, and was linked to Adelaide by daily railway services and a weekly steamer service.

The first sod of the new Transcontinental Railway line was turned at Port Augusta on 14 September 1912 by the Governor-General, Lord Denman, and at the opposite end of the line in Kalgoorlie in Western Australia on 12 February 1913.

The Governor-General turns the first sod of the Transcontinental Railway at Port August in September 1912. Martin O'Meara may have been amongst the crowd. (SLSA PRG280/1/17/31)

Martin O'Meara's move to Port Augusta may have been prompted by a shortage of work at Wild Horse Plains, rather than by higher wages. Wages for workers on the Transcontinental Railway at Port Augusta were consistent with wages for workers in other parts of South Australia, with labourers in September 1912 being paid 10s per day whilst day gangers and carpenters were paid 13s per day.[61]

---

[61] *Register*, 13 September 1912, p.9.The Reserve Bank of Australia's inflation calculator website <www.rba.gov.au/calculator> shows that 10s per day in 1912 would have the purchasing power of $58 in 2015 and 13s per day in 1912 would have the purchasing power of $75 in 2015.

There seems to have been a rapid increase in the number of labourers at Port Augusta in September 1912 as the United Labourers' Union sent an official to that town in mid-September to organise those men who were working on the Transcontinental Railway line.[62] When the official returned to Adelaide, he reported that there were more than one hundred men who had travelled to Port Augusta who had not yet found work with the possibility of some men with work losing their jobs because 'the Federal Government have not sufficient plant there. The men have been fooled for weeks past in regarded to the expected arrival of more plant.'[63]

The first sod on the new line, however, was only turned on 14 September 1912, so it seems likely that many of the men who travelled to Port Augusta had done so in anticipation of work being available rather than work actually being available. Martin O'Meara could have been one of those men who travelled to Port August as early as September, but he was definitely working at (or near) Port Augusta as a labourer in mid-December when he nominated Michael O'Rourke from Kilbane in County Clare, Ireland, as an assisted passage migrant under the South Australian Government's immigration scheme.[64]

As a sponsor, Martin O'Meara paid the South Australian Government a contribution of £7 for O'Rourke's passage.[65] O'Rourke was an agricultural labourer aged 24 years and was described by Martin O'Meara as his 'comrade'. This suggests that they had worked together in Ireland previously, and it is possible that O'Meara felt that he was doing well in South Australia and thought that his friend Michael O'Rourke could join him. In his nomination submitted to the South Australian Crown Lands Office (which administered the state's immigration schemes), Martin O'Meara offered two referees who could report on his own character (Charles Myers and J.A. Magee, both of Port Augusta) and two referees who could report on Michael O'Rourke's character (M. Larken of Leitrim, County Clare, and M. Mulroney, also of Leitrim, County Clare). It is possible that O'Meara

---

[62] *Daily Herald*, 18 September 1912, p.8.

[63] *Daily Herald*, 27 September 1912, p.2.

[64] SRSA: GRG7/2, Application by nominee for assisted passage previously paid for by nominator in South Australia.

[65] SRSA: GRG7/2, Application by nominee for assisted passage previously paid for by nominator in South Australia. £7 had the purchasing power of $812 in 2015.

worked with Michael O'Rourke in County Clare, but no evidence has been found to confirm this.

Charles Myers was a railway ganger and secretary of the Port Augusta section of the United Labourers' Union.[66] It seems likely that Martin O'Meara had joined this union, probably in order to make it easier to secure work on the railways. No evidence has been found as to identify J.A. Magee.

Whilst living at Port Augusta Martin O'Meara attended services at All Saints' Roman Catholic Cathedral, and he became acquainted there with the Rev John O'Rourke, the local priest. O'Rourke was himself Irish and had arrived in South Australia in December 1905, taking up parochial duties in Pekina (85 kilometres southeast of Port Augusta) in early 1906. He subsequently took up duties at Port Augusta. Later newspaper reports of Martin O'Meara's time in Port Augusta record that he:

> was a frequent visitor at the [Roman Catholic] Presbytery. He loved to denounce the disgraceful treatment of the working classes at home and to express his views on the Irish question in general. As a Catholic he was practical and a credit to the land of his birth.[67]

The befriending of local Roman Catholic clergy was to become a recurring theme in Martin O'Meara's life, and references to the working classes and 'the Irish question' are consistent with his later membership of trade unions and his position as an Irish nationalist.

Martin O'Meara was still living and working in the Port Augusta area on 1 March 1913 when he wrote to the Crown Lands Office in Adelaide on behalf of a friend, Denis Brosnan, who wanted to nominate his sister as an assisted passage immigrant. No clues remain as to who Denis Brosnan actually was, or how he was acquainted with O'Meara. Martin O'Meara also took the opportunity to query the status of Michael O'Rourke's travel to Adelaide, indicating that 'you can let me know as soon as possible as I might move to the West'.[68]

---

[66] *Daily Herald*, 27 September 1912, p.5.

[67] *Southern Cross*, 4 January 1918, p.11.

[68] SRSA: GRG7/2, Application by nominee for assisted passage previously paid for by nominator in South Australia.

Again, it seems that moving to Western Australia was being considered, possibly with the aim of securing work on the Western Australian portion of the Transcontinental Railway east of Kalgoorlie.

Martin O'Meara is recorded on the 1914 electoral roll for the Commonwealth division of Grey (subdivision of Port Augusta) as a labourer living in Port Augusta, suggesting that he did not update his electoral registration after leaving Port Augusta.

It seems likely that Martin O'Meara left Port Augusta in March or April 1913 and travelled to Brighton, south-west of Adelaide. His move was probably work-related, as the South Australian Government was expanding the State's network of railway lines and the railway line between Adelaide and Willunga was under construction at this time. Brighton was located along this railway line. Contractor Joseph Timms had been awarded the contract to build the Willunga railway in late 1912, and quickly moved to recruit the labour he needed to do the work. On 14 February 1913 he advertised for 'a further ONE HUNDRED NAVVIES' to work on constructing the Goodwood to Willunga railway line, and that men should apply in-person at Brighton.[69] It seems most likely that Martin O'Meara obtained work as a labourer on this line, and quite probably around this time.

Martin O'Meara was living and working at (or near) Brighton on 29 April when wrote to another letter to the Crown Lands Office, again querying the status of Michael O'Rourke's travel from the United Kingdom. His stay at Brighton seems to have been relatively short, as he moved further south to Reynella, probably following the construction of the railway line, during mid-1913. A newspaper article of May 1913 records that many labourers, perhaps including Martin O'Meara, were involved on constructing the railway line south of Brighton at this time:

> Along the earthworks to Hallett's Cove [between Brighton and Reynella] six hundred navvies and a hundred horses and drays are in engaged in the cuttings … At every three or four miles of camps of navvies are pitched. I was informed it costs each

---

[69] *Advertiser*, 14 February 1913, p.7.

navvy 17/ a week for board and lodging, or 12/ to 15/ if the men choose to "batch" amongst themselves.[70]

Martin O'Meara again wrote to the Crown Lands Office in Adelaide from Reynella, on 14 July 1913, seeking information on Michael O'Rourke.

Railway workers' camp near Pedler's Creek west of McLaren Vale. (National Trust of South Australia, Willunga Branch)

Construction of the Willunga railway appeared to be progressing at a good pace, with the *Southern Argus* newspaper reporting on 25 September that 'Gangs of men are now at McLaren Vale, and the contractor, Mr. J. Timms, hopes that the work may be proceeded with'.[71] Martin O'Meara may have been in one of these gangs, for by December 1912 he had moved again, to McLaren Vale, south of Reynella and further along the new railway line to Willunga. McLaren Vale was a small rural hamlet in a primarily agricultural district in 1913, with a population of 200 and was served twice daily by coach from Adelaide.[72]

On 8 December he wrote, from McLaren Vale, yet another letter to the Crown Lands Office seeking any information on Michael

---

[70] *Advertiser*, 17 May 1913, p.20.
[71] *Southern Argus*, 25 September 1913, p.2.
[72] *Southern Argus*, 3 July 1913, p.4.

O'Rourke's whereabouts. The Crown Lands Officer replied on 23 December, stating that if Michael O'Rourke did not arrive in South Australia shortly his nomination would expire, as the nomination certificate had been issued on 20 December 1912 and was valid for twelve months.

In an unusual and interesting case, it seems quite likely that Martin O'Meara had some sort of involvement (apart from possibly being a resident) with the McLaren Vale boarding house run by Mrs Jane Cook. Long-time McLaren Vale resident Alf Martin recalled in 1995 that:

> a storekeeper at Aldinga, built a new stone house and store across from Sylvan Park gates ... East of the store was Charlie White's paint shop and the "Klondyke" boarding house run by Mrs Jane Cook, whose son Victor was a prominent Vale footballer. Mrs Cook also had a small shop where she sold sweets and icecreams, but the place has long since been demolished.[73]

In February 1913 the *Advertiser* advised that Jane Cook's McLaren Vale boarding house was for sale.[74] Jane Cook kept advertising her boarding house for sale until July when she withdraw it from sale.[75] As it seems that O'Meara was in the McLaren Vale area in the second half of 1913, it is possible that these events were connected. South Australian Land Titles records indicate that Jane Cook owned land along McLaren Vale's main street (Main Road) between Main Road and the new railway line, and this coincides with the location of the boarding house described by Alf Martin. Mortgages registered over parts of this land in 1912 and 1913 suggest that Jane Cook was carrying debt, and that she was looking to sell the land to repay debt.[76]

Shortly afterwards, on 22 July, another advertisement appeared in the *Advertiser* advising that tenders would be received for the

---

[73] National Trust of South Australia (Wilunga Branch), pers. comm., 22 February 2016. Mrs Jane Cook was born circa 1865 and died in 1947. She had married Thomas E Cook in the 1880s, and later separated from him.

[74] *Advertiser*, 8 February 1913, p.12.

[75] *Advertiser*, 22 July 1913, p.2.

[76] SA Land Title Certificate of Title Volume 987 Folio 101.

purchase of three acres of land at McLaren Vale with a dwelling suitable for use as a 'boarding house or private hospital.'[77] The timing of these advertisements seem to suggest that it is the same property. According to Sands and McDougall's South Australian Directory for 1913 and 1914, Jane Cook was the only boarding house keeper in McLaren Vale so it is reasonable to assume that the newspaper advertisements referred to her boarding house. In any case, it seems too coincidental for this not have been the case. On 10, 12 and 13 January 1914 advertisements appeared in Adelaide's *Advertiser* newspaper, advising 'For sale, good Boardinghouse, cooking utensils, in good order. Apply M. O'Meara, McLaren Vale'.[78] It is not known for sure whether this refers to Martin O'Meara, or which particular boarding house, but the timing seems more than simple coincidence. No other M. O'Mearas have been identified in the McLaren Vale area during 1913-14. By another coincidence of timing, just under three acres of land in the same location appears to have been sold by Jane Cook to local farmer James Bigg on 12 March.[79]

---

[77] *Advertiser*, 22 July 1913, p.16.
[78] *Advertiser*, 10 January 1914, p.24, 12 January 1914, p.7, and 13 January 1914, p.16.
[79] SA Land Title Certificate of Title Volume 987 Folio 101.

3   Moving to the West

According to a newspaper interview he gave in 1918, Martin O'Meara left South Australia and travelled to Western Australia during 1914.

It seems that he probably left South Australia around February 1914 and, as the Transcontinental Railway linking Western Australia to South Australia (and the other mainland states) was not completed until October 1917, he would have travelled by ship. Newspaper advertisements in the Adelaide *Advertiser* in early January show that one-way third class steamer tickets between Adelaide and Fremantle were available at £3 13s and £3 18s[80], which would have been around eight days' wages for a labourer on 10s per day.

Regardless of the date or ship, it is probable that O'Meara arrived in Fremantle and found lodgings there, or took the train from Fremantle to Perth and found lodgings in Perth. Either way, he would have travelled through Perth at some stage.

On 10 March the Crown Lands Office in Adelaide wrote to Martin O'Meara at McLaren Vale, advising that the South Australian Government's immigration agent in London had been asked to return his nomination certificate as it had now expired [81] O'Meara was advised that his £7 would be refunded once the nomination certificate was returned to the South Australian Government's representative in London. O'Meara, however, did not receive this correspondence as he had already left South Australia and travelled to Western Australia.

Martin O'Meara seems to have known at least one person in Perth, and later newspaper reports suggest that Timothy Michael Quinlan, a land and estate agent, was one of them. A fellow Tipperaryman (he had been born in Abbeville near Lissernane around 1878), Quinlan was the nephew of Timothy Francis Quinlan, a businessman and former member of the Western Australian Legislative Assembly who

---

[80] *Advertiser*, 12 January 1914, p.1. £3 13s would have the purchasing power of around $409 in 2015.
[81] SRSA: GRG7/2, Application by nominee for assisted passage previously paid for by nominator in South Australia.

had been born in Borrisokane in Tipperary, and who had arrived in Western Australia in 1863 as an infant. It was later reported by Timothy Michael Quinlan that Martin O'Meara had visited his office at suite 23 on the second floor of 'Eagle Chambers', 624 Hay Street in Perth several times during 1914, but that he had been interstate.[82] On his return, Quinlan reported that Martin O'Meara had left a message that he was going to Collie.[83]

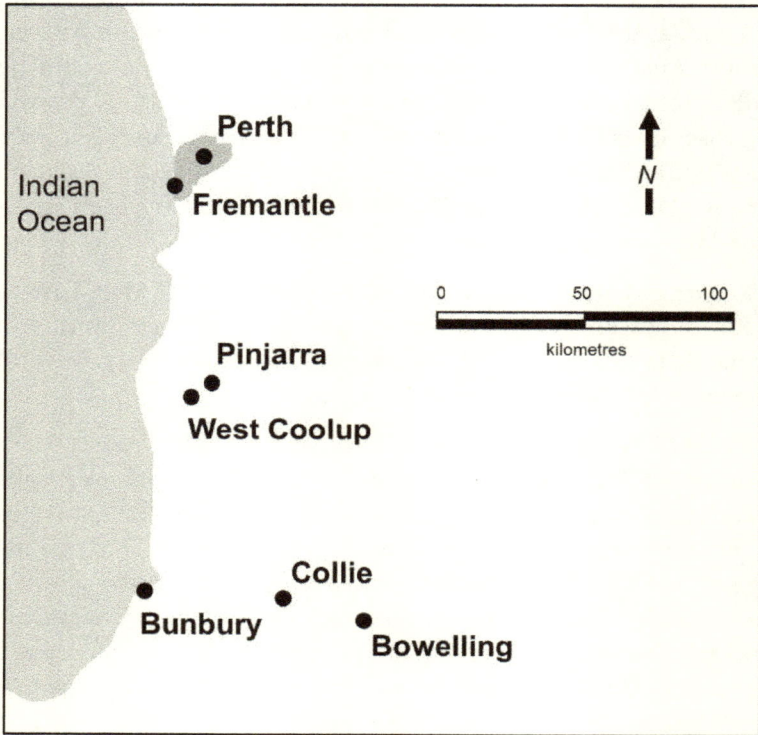

Perth and surrounding region, showing places to the life of Martin O'Meara during 1914-15.

It seems that Martin O'Meara made his way south from Perth and ended up in the Pinjarra area working at Creaton, an early pioneer

---

[82] Eagle Chambers at 624 Hay Street was demolished in 1919 and replaced with a three-store department store, Robertson and Moffat's Successors, which later became Ahern's and is now the location of the David Jones department store.
[83] *Daily News*, 15 September 1916, p.7.

property. Pinjarra is located some 85 kilometres south of Perth, and the area was first settled as a farming district during the 1830s. Creaton was located some three and a half kilometres north of the Pinjarra township, and was occupied by the Paterson family during the first half of the twentieth century.[84] In 1914 it was owned by brothers William and George Paterson. According to reports citing the Paterson brothers, Martin O'Meara:

> was in our employment for some months, and left only a short time before he enlisted. Like most Irishmen, he was very responsive to any kindness which was shown to him, and generous to a fault. No obstacle or difficulty which confronted him in connection with any work upon which he was engaged caused him to "side track" in the slightest degree.[85]

Ruins of Creaton farmhouse, 2015. (Author)

The electoral roll for the State Electoral District of Murray-Wellington of 8 September 1914 records that Martin O'Meara was

---

[84] The old farmhouse at Creaton now lies in ruins.

[85] *Kalgoorlie Miner*, 19 September 1916, p.3.

living at Creaton and was a labourer.[86] Under Western Australia's *Electoral Act 1907*, the qualifications for enrolment as a voter for Legislative Assembly elections were that the person had to have resided in Western Australia for six months continuously, and have resided in the electoral District (in this case Murray-Wellington) for a continuous period of one month. Based on this, it seems likely that Martin O'Meara arrived in Western Australia prior to mid-March and was living in the Pinjarra area south of Perth prior to mid-August.

The small township of Pinjarra had a Roman Catholic church, St Augustine's, and it is likely that Martin O'Meara attended this church whilst he lived at Creaton. The priest responsible for this area was the Rev John Fahey, a Tipperaryman who was based at nearby Yarloop. Martin O'Meara became friendly with other Irish Roman Catholics whilst worshipping at St Augustine's, and these probably included John and Anne Foley from West Coolup near Pinjarra. The Foleys had arrived in Western Australia from Ireland in 1902, and Foley was reported as having donated some fencing for the new church building when it was constructed during 1913.[87]

Rev Fahey was transferred to Kalgoorlie in early 1914, and his final service at Pinjarra was held on 22 February.[88] It is quite possible that O'Meara met him at Pinjarra during February.

Later accounts suggest that Martin O'Meara lived with the Foleys at their property, Inistoge, at West Coolup south of Pinjarra sometime prior to his enlistment,[89] but no information exists to suggest whether this was before or after his employment by the Patersons at Creaton. The Foleys farmed at West Coolup and Anne Foley was also a teacher, in charge of the West Coolup School.[90] It has also been suggested that O'Meara worked for Edward McLarty at Edenvale, near Pinjarra,

---

[86] The State electoral roll for 31 March 1916 records the same information, as does the Commonwealth electoral roll for the Division of Fremantle that was prepared for the 28 October 1916 conscription referendum.

[87] *South Western Advertiser*, 4 April 1913, p.5.

[88] *South Western Advertiser*, 20 February 1914, p.2.

[89] *South Western Advertiser*, 8 December 1916, p.2.

[90] John Foley died 1947 and was buried at Pinjarra. Anne Foley taught at West Coolup between 1912 and 1919.

sometime prior to enlisting,[91] but no corroborating evidence has been found to confirm this.

It seems likely that Martin O'Meara moved from the Pinjarra area to the Collie area further south in mid to late 1914, probably in search of work as a sleeper cutter cutting the iconic jarrah trees that are characteristic of the area. In an article published in the *Collie Mail* in 1916 it was reported that:

> Emigrating from Ireland to Western Australia about four years ago, he worked we understand at Patterson's farm at Pinjarrah. From Pinjarrah he migrated to Brunswick Junction and Collie districts.[92]

This account is consistent with that given in an interview given in November 1918, in which O'Meara is reported as saying:

> "I spent a couple of years in South Australia, but in 1914 I came to the West and settled in the bush about 34 miles out from Collie."[93]

Collie is located just over 200 kilometres south of Perth and about 60 kilometres inland from the port city of Bunbury. The area around Collie was first explored in 1829, and the town that developed took its name from the river of the same name, which was in turn named by Dr Alexander Collie, a Royal Navy surgeon who explored the area. Originally an agricultural, pastoral and timber harvesting area, Collie grew quickly after the discovery of coal in 1883. Timber, however, remained an important part of the local economy.

The iconic jarrah (*Eucalyptus marginata*) of south-western Western Australia grows up to 40 metres in height and has a girth of up to three metres in diameter. Jarrah is termite-resistant and resilient, making it a good timber for railway sleepers and other construction purposes. Because of this, the jarrah forests of south-western Western Australia became home to a strong timber industry. Prior to the

---

[91] Richardson, 2003, p.156. Edward McLarty was a Member of the Legislative Council and his son Ross (later Sir Ross) was a Member of the Legislative Assembly and Premier of Western Australia from 1947-53.

[92] *Collie Mail*, 23 September 1916, p.2. Pinjarra was often referred to as Pinjarrah during the late nineteenth and early twentieth centuries.

[93] *West Australian*, 8 November 1918, p.7.

mechanisation that occurred from the 1920s, these trees were felled by either axe or cross-cut saw. The trees were then hewed in situ, or dragged over a saw pit and cut, although the use of saw pits had largely been replaced by sawmills by the early twentieth century.

A Western Australian sleeper cutter. (SLWA 022072PD)

Manual hewing, however, continued to be used for railway sleepers into the 1930s and involved the splitting and squaring of the sleepers (and other types of timber product) which were then transported (by dragging or carting) to a storage and loading site (typically a railway siding).[94] This type of manual labour was undoubtedly physically demanding and would have required great stamina and strength. The timber axemen have been described as the 'glamour men of the industry' and were either employed by a company or for a contractor who supplied timber to one of the companies.[95] The timber industry also employed other types of workers, such as labourers and carters.

The early part of the twentieth century saw an increasing demand for railway sleepers, with the expanding network of Western Australian Government Railways as well as the Commonwealth Government's Transcontinental Railway between Port August in South Australia and Kalgoorlie in Western Australia. As he had

---

[94] Heberle, 1997, p.204.
[95] Mills, 1988, p.276.

previously worked on the construction of the Transcontinental Railway whilst living at Port Augusta, O'Meara would have been very familiar with the project.

The sleeper hewing industry was going through a relatively unstable and uncertain period when Martin O'Meara arrived in the Collie area. In August 1913, the Commonwealth Government[96] had entered into a contract with the Western Australian Government for the supply of 1,400,000 karri sleepers for the Transcontinental Railway. Sleeper supply was due to commence in November and continue for several years, but in mid-November Premier John Scaddan advised the Commonwealth that supply would be delayed. The Commonwealth then cancelled the contract and recommenced negotiations. Premier Scaddan subsequently revoked timber hewing licences so that the Commonwealth could not purchase railway sleepers on the private market.[97] The Scaddan Labor government had established state-owned sawmills and was attempting to constrain competition from private timber suppliers.

Sleeper hewers also faced pressure from State Government forestry policy during 1913-14 when they were excluded from hewing sleepers in virgin forest and only permitted to hew sleepers in 'cut-out bush', being those areas that had already been logged by sawmillers, because 'the waste and destruction of valuable timber by sleeper hewers in virgin forest was enormous.'[98] The State Government's policies were not popular with timber workers and on 18 February 1914 sleeper hewers met in Collie to protest against the State Government's decision to cease issuing further licences to hew sleepers on Crown land.[99]

Martin O'Meara, like many of his colleagues in the timber hewers' camps, was a member of the Amalgamated Timber Workers' Union.[100] A branch of the Union had been formed at Bowelling Pool in mid-

---

[96] The Commonwealth Liberal Party, an ancestor of the current Liberal Party, was in Government under Prime Minister Joseph Cook.

[97] *Sydney Morning Herald*, 7 March 1914, p.23.

[98] Woods and Forests Department, *Annual Report for the Year Ended 30th June 1914*, Perth, p.9.

[99] *West Australian*, 23 February 1914, p.8.

[100] *Daily News*, 28 March 1917, p.8.

1914, where O'Meara later worked, and Ernest McManus (another sleeper hewer) was an early union steward.[101] It is quite possible that McManus was the union steward who recruited O'Meara, and (at the very least) it is likely that the two knew each other. J. Young was appointed steward at Bowelling in March 1915.[102]

A state election was held on 21 October 1914 and Premier John Scaddan's Labor Government was re-elected, albeit with a reduced majority. State Government forestry policy continued to be erratic following the election. The onset of the First World War itself also contributed to the decline in the timber industry, as the overseas export market for timber shrank significantly and commercial shipping was difficult to obtain for both the overseas and interstate transport of timber. On 22 March 1915, the Collie Branch of the Amalgamated Timber Workers' Union met to protest the closure by the State Sawmills Department of the sleeper dumps to sleeper hewers, like Martin O'Meara, on the railway line between Collie and Bowelling. The closure was reported as being likely to affect 'several hundred men' who would now have to transport their sleepers to Collie or travel to Bowelling to cut their sleepers.[103] This suggests that a relatively large number of men remained employed in sleeper cutting at this time. On 4 August the poor state of the timber industry was raised by the Labor Party Member for Forrest, Peter O'Loghlen MLA, in the Legislative Assembly:

> There is not in Australia, to-day, I believe, an industry of any magnitude that has been paralysed to the same extent as the timber industry ... Of sleepers along the State enterprise [State-owned sawmills] has over 900,000, stacked at the various sidings ... The people working the sleeper trade at present secure small orders ...[104]

It is not known who first employed Martin O'Meara in the Collie district, or exactly where he first lived and work, but it is almost

---

[101] *Westralian Worker*, 10 July 1914, p.4.

[102] *Collie Mail*, 20 March 1915, p.2.

[103] *West Australian*, 28 March 1915, p.13.

[104] Legislative Assembly of Western Australia, Hansard, 4 August 1915, p.153.
  O'Loghlen had been associated with the Union. See Mills, 1986, p.53 and p.71.

certain that by mid-1915 Martin O'Meara was living at a timber hewers' camp near the small township of Bowelling. It is also not known whether O'Meara was an actual sleeper hewer, or whether he was simply a labourer working with hewers.[105] Bowelling, some 32 kilometres east of Collie, (originally known as Bowelling Pool, a pool on the nearby Collie River) lies at the junction of the Wagin-Bowelling railway line and the Collie-Narrogin railway line. The Collie-Narrogin railway had reached Bowelling in 1906 and a siding, known as Siding Number 2, was established. Bowelling Pool was formally shortened to Bowelling in December 1907, and was gazetted as a townsite in 1908.[106]

During mid-1915 O'Meara was working for £3 a week for Thomas (also known as Charlie) James, who had been sleeper hewing and carting in the district for several years and who had maintained a camp near Bowelling Pool since around 1911.[107] The *Westralian Worker* reported in 1913 that Thomas James had 22 men working for him at a camp at Muja east of Collie and that all were trade unionists,[108] and reported in July 1914 that 16 men from James' Camp had voted in Union elections.[109]

It was later reported that Martin O'Meara 'is well known down there [Collie], although he is a very quiet chap and a teetotaller. He was always sending all the money he could spare home to his mother.'[110] O'Meara's relatively quiet and 'ordinary' life as a sleeper cutter, however, was soon to end and be changed forever.

---

[105] Some accounts describe O'Meara as a labourer whilst other describe him as a sleeper hewer or cutter.

[106] Bowelling gradually declined in population during the course of the twentieth century. The school closed in 1948 and the post Office closed in December 1973. The railway station ceased being used in 1967 and the railway later closed to freight traffic.

[107] *Westralian Worker*, 26 February 1915, p.4. O'Meara noted his former employer on a Repatriation Department registration form that he signed in September 1918. £3 per week equates to 10s per day based on a six-day working week.

[108] *Westralian Worker*, 12 September 1913, p.4. Muja is a little more than half way between Collie and Bowelling, and it is not clear whether the Muja camp and the camp near Bowelling were the same camp, or whether Charlie James had more than one camp.

[109] *Westralian Worker*, 24 July 1914, p.9.

[110] *Daily News*, Tuesday 12 September 1916, p.4.

4   Off to War

The assassination of Archduke Ferdinand of Austria by a Serbian nationalist in June 1914 at Sarajevo triggered a series of events that profoundly changed the course of Martin O'Meara's life. Austria had suddenly found itself at war with Serbia, Russia then sided with Serbia, Germany declared war on Russia, and France supported Russia. The United Kingdom soon found itself supporting Belgium and France against German aggression.

Australia had joined with the United Kingdom in declaring war on Germany in August 1914, and had formed a special expeditionary force, the Australian Imperial Force (AIF), as it did not have a standing military force that could be committed to war. The AIF was an all-volunteer force based on an original commitment of 20,000 personnel, but which later grew to more than 330,000 men and women. The initial standards for AIF recruits were high: men had to be aged between 18 and 35 years and have a minimum height of 5 feet 6 inches. Martin O'Meara would have met these requirements if he had applied to enlist in the early years of the war. These standards were relaxed as the war dragged on and further recruits were sought.

The AIF was involved in the disastrous Gallipoli campaign from 25 April 1915 onwards, and was still active at Gallipoli when Martin O'Meara decided to enlist. His views on the war were likely to have been influenced by his views as an Irish Roman Catholic who held nationalist sentiments. Irish nationalist leader John Redmond had, in September 1914, six weeks after the start of war (and shortly after the Irish home rule bill had been passed by the British Parliament), pledged his support to the Allied war effort and urged the Irish to enlist in the British army. Many of them did, but Martin O'Meara did not respond initially.

Sergeant Michael O'Leary, the first Irish Victoria Cross recipient of the First World War, took an active role in calling for his countrymen to enlist. An article in the *West Australian* in July 1915 reported that he had been feted at a dinner in London and:

O'Leary afterwards received a tremendous ovation in Hyde Park, when appealing to Irishmen to enlist. When addressing the crowd, Sergeant O'Leary said: "I have only done my duty. There are many fellows as good as myself. I happened to be lucky. Don't stand cheering me; that's no good. We want more men to pull down the German hordes."[111]

In Australia, organised enlistment campaigns were staged during late 1914 and into mid-1915, with the result being that monthly enlistments significantly increased. For example, Western Australian enlistments rose from 208 during April 1915 to 689 in May 1915, 806 in June 1915, 1,485 in July 1915 and 1,903 in August 1915 when Martin O'Meara enlisted.[112] The push for further recruits grew during mid-1915 as the need to replace men killed and wounded at Gallipoli escalated. The *Collie Mail* reported on 19 June 1915 that:

Although no new units may at present be under organization, it is vitally important that there should be no shortage of recruits for reinforcements. There may be some ideas abroad that enlistment for reinforcements is not so necessary nor nearly so important as enlistment for a definite unit. This is quite incorrect ... Reinforcements are urgently required to maintain units already at the front at their normal strength.[113]

Martin O'Meara applied to enlist in the AIF at the Collie municipal offices in July 1915, although the reasons why he enlisted are not clear. There seems to have been a great deal of pressure on men to enlist during this time; on 19 August the *Collie Mail* reported that:

The Defence Department wish to deny the rumours current in some districts to the effect that it is relaxing its efforts in the matter of securing recruits, as every available man is to be pressed to join. As far as Collie is concerned the denial is hardly necessary seeing that almost every medically fit single man has enlisted, and two recruiting sergeants are now working to see

[111] *West Australian*, 12 July 1915, p.7.
[112] Bean, 1941a, p.8.
[113] *Collie Mail*, 19 June 1915, p.3.

that as many married men as possible into camp, or give their reasons why.[114]

On second anniversary of the start of the war, the Perth *Daily News* published an editorial encouraging a patriotic and practical response to the war:

> This war, which is being conducted by Great Britain and her Allies, is solely in the interests of civilisation of humanity, and at all costs it must be prosecuted until victory is assured. To bring this about some must fight, fight, fight, others must work, work, work, others must do, do, do, and the rest must pay, pay, pay.[115]

Those applicants who met the minimum requirements would be given railway tickets for travel to a training camp. The conditions of service were not particularly attractive; daily pay rates started at five shillings per day for private soldiers whilst in Australia, and six shillings per day after embarkation for active service,[116] hence the term 'six bob-a-day tourists' that later emerged. Daily rates increased following promotion to Lance-Corporal and beyond. Having met the AIF's initial enlistment requirements, Martin O'Meara travelled to the Blackboy Hill Camp in the foothills east of Perth, and formally enlisted there on 19 August. The Blackboy Hill Camp was established shortly after the start of war and had already trained many officers and men for overseas military service, including many of those who had sailed with the first AIF convoy from Albany in December 1914.

His enlistment papers provide some basic information about Martin O'Meara. He was aged 29 years and nine months, was a sleeper cutter/hewer, was 5 foot 7 inches (about 170 centimetres) tall,

---

[114] *Collie Mail*, 19 August 1915, p.2 .

[115] *Daily News*, 4 August 1915, p.4. O'Meara's employer, Charlie James, seems to have left the sleeper cutting business and was (according to his February 1917 marriage certificate) a teamster. This may have been the result of a combination of the economic downturn and the State Government's forestry policies.

[116] *Daily News*, 17 August 1915, p.9. Six shillings in 1914 would have the purchasing power of just under $30 in 2015. Six shillings is just over half of the 10s daily (or 60s weekly) wage that O'Meara had been earning working for Charlie James; the average male weekly income in Western Australia was 62s 10d at this time.

weighed 140 pounds (about 63.5 kilograms) and had a dark complexion with brown hair and brown eyes. He was a Roman Catholic, and he nominated his sister, Alice O'Meara in Ireland, as his next of kin.[117]

Martin O'Meara undertook the first part of his recruit training from 19 August to 13 September with the No. 24 Depot Company at the Blackboy Hill Camp. O'Meara's initial recruit training would have included physical training and fitness, the use and proficiency in using the Short Magazine Lee-Enfield (SMLE) .303 rifle, bayonet fighting, grenade throwing, drill, and trench digging.

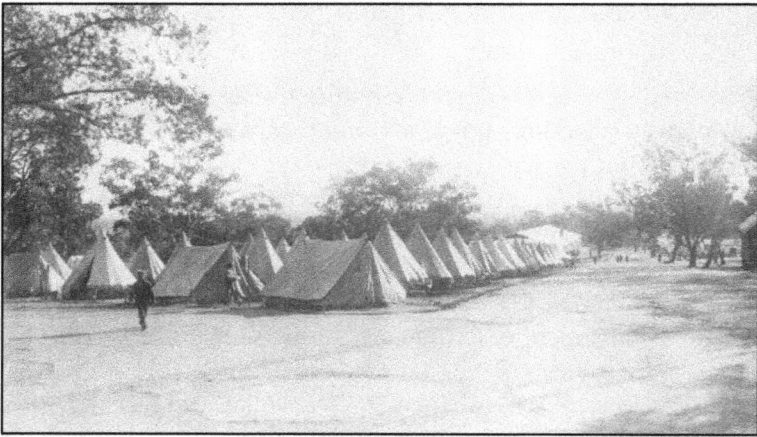

Tent lines at the Blackboy Hill camp. The men were accommodated in both tents and huts. (AWM A02874)

The camp routine was strenuous, but probably not much different to that which a working man like Martin O'Meara would have been used to. The men were woken at 5am and trained between 5.45am and 5.15pm, with breaks for breakfast at 8am and lunch at 12.30pm. Lights out ('tattoo') was at 9.30pm.[118]

During August 1915 the Department of Defence changed its approach to the training of new AIF recruits, and replaced the network of smaller Depot Companies with larger Depot Battalions.

---

[117] NAA: B2455, Martin O'Meara
[118] *Camp Chronicle*, 9 December 1915, p.4.

On 14 September the newly-established No. 2 Depot Battalion moved from the Blackboy Hill Camp to a new camp established at the Belmont Racecourse, two kilometres north-east of the Perth city centre.[119] Martin O'Meara was a member of the No. 2 Depot Battalion and moved to Belmont with his unit. Newspaper statements made in September 1916 and attributed to a Captain Aidan Bryan,[120] indicate that, 'O'Meara occupied his spare time with attending to our wants as officers' batman, so I had exceptional opportunities of studying his uncommon character.' Bryan added, 'After several months' training, the men were drafted to the various units in which they embarked, and during that time O'Meara, I believe gave away to his mates interests in several camps he had near Collie.'[121]

Portrait of Martin O'Meara, probably taken at a studio somewhere in Perth (perhaps near Blackboy Hill) shortly after he enlisted in August 1915.

Note the absence of badges or insignia on the uniform. His relatively youthful appearance can be compared with later photographs. (AWM H12763)

Whilst based at the Belmont Racecourse Camp (and, to a lesser extent, the more distant Blackboy Hill Camp), Martin O'Meara was able to travel within the Perth area, and in September 1915 he joined the St Canice's branch of the Hibernian Australasian Catholic Benefit

---

[119] *Western Mail*, 27 August 1915, p.17 and West Australian, 14 September 1915, p.7.

[120] Captain Aidan Hugh Bryan was a Captain of Cadets who served as Mayor of Cottesloe in the 1920s, and then served with the Volunteer Defence Corps during the Second World War.

[121] *Daily News*, 13 September 1916, p.1.

Society, a benevolent society for Roman Catholics of Irish ancestry, at Cottesloe. The branch president later noted:

> He joined this society in September of last year. I was the president of the branch at the time, and I congratulated Private O'Meara on the step he had taken in joining the society, and wished him a safe return. I said at the time that I was sure that the honour of the society would be safe in his keeping. In reply, he thanked me and members for our good wishes, and said that speech making was not much in his line.[122]

Martin O'Meara also had several friends in Perth. Horace Holland Payne of 19 Charles Street, West Perth, claimed that O'Meara 'spent all of his leave whilst in Blackboy down with me and the missus [Hilda Payne], and he was never better pleased than when he was taking my little girl out.'[123] Payne said that he had cut sleepers with O'Meara together at Collie, and this is quite possible, as Payne's entry in the 1910 Commonwealth electoral roll indicates that he was living at Busselton (south of Bunbury) at that time, and that he was a carpenter.

A newspaper article published in 1917 provides an interesting perspective on Martin O'Meara's thoughts in the period leading up to his embarkation for overseas service:

> War, according to one of his few friends in Australia, did not appeal to him; frequently had he expressed reluctance at the idea of killing, but sought consolation in the fact that the Empire wanted eligible men and that he was eligible to go. While in training at the camp he became friendly with one of the reverend fathers at St Brigid's Church and just before embarking asked whether it was not possible to join some other branch of the service, and be excluded from the actual fighting force. He received the reply that he was doing splendidly where he was, and should give his services in the direction they were most required. When nearing the time of his embarkation he received news of his mother's illness, and lost considerable interest in his soldiering duties. He even confided to a comrade

---

[122] *Kalgoorlie Miner*, 19 September 1916, p.3.
[123] *Daily News*, 12 September 1916, p.4.

that he blamed himself for the change in his mother's health, and he felt he should not go on active service. Subsequently, however, his friend vouches that he made use of the following expression: "As I am going, I will do the best I can to bring back the Victoria Cross."[124]

The article continued:

O'Meara is foremost a strict teetotaller and a staunch Roman Catholic. He is seemingly a man who seeks friends, but who is most discriminate in their selection. He is a fine stamp physically, hardened by work in the open, and weighs on the vicinity of 12 or 13 stone. Apart from his other relatives in Ireland he has a brother in America.[125]

It is not possible to corroborate all the points raised in the article, but it does contain enough known facts to give us confidence that the overall 'flavour' is probably accurate. Some embellishment is possible; for example, the reference to O'Meara stating that he would bring back the Victoria Cross, which could have been a 'throw-away' statement of a general nature.[126]

In either late September or early October 1915 O'Meara wrote (care of the Young Men's Christian Association (YMCA) at the No. 2 Depot Battalion at Belmont) to the South Australian Government's Crown Land Office, seeking a refund of his £7 for the nomination of Michael O'Rourke as an assisted passage immigrant. He wrote:

On making inquiries with regard to Michael O'Rourk whom I got nominated for a passage to South Aus in 1911 so far as I can learn he was away from home and I can't definatly [sic] learn of his whereabouts but one thing I do know he never come to this Continant [sic] and although I know it is necessary to produce the sailing order before the £7 pounds I paid is refunded still I think I am entitled to it when I tell you I did my

---

[124] *West Australian*, 13 September 1916, p.7.

[125] *West Australian*, 13 September 1916, p.7.

[126] James O'Boyle, another Roman Catholic AIF enlistee was reported as saying in a farewell speech that 'He hoped that he would be adorned with the Victoria Cross...'. See *W.A. Record*, 31 July 1915, p.8.

best to get it but it must have been Mislaid or destroyed. So as I am in the Military Camp here and not knowing when we might be sent on active service there is nothing for me to do only hand what papers I have in my possession over to a leagel [sic] advisor that is if I don't get a satisfactory answer to this.[127]

The context of the letter suggests that O'Meara was tidying up his affairs before he was sent to war. It seems that contact was lost between O'Meara and O'Rourke, and that O'Rourke never returned his nomination certificate to the South Australian Government's London representative. The Crown Lands Office wrote back to O'Meara on 7 October advising that the £7 would be refunded, and presumably it was refunded to him at a later stage.

On 15 October 1915 Martin O'Meara finished his recruit training and left the No. 2 Depot Battalion, and on 16 October he returned to Blackboy Hill and joined the 12th Reinforcements of the 16th Battalion.

2th Reinforcements of the 16th Battalion at Belmont Racecourse Camp, December 1915. Martin O'Meara is somewhere amongst this group (Ian Gill)

---

[127] SRSA: GRG7/2, Application by nominee for assisted passage previously paid for by nominator in South Australia. £7 would have had the purchasing power of about $685 in 2015, so it is understandable that O'Meara would want it refunded.

The Western Australian men of the 12th Reinforcements (another group came from South Australia), O'Meara's colleagues, were a diverse group of men who reflected the makeup of Western Australia where they had been recruited. Ranging in age from (officially) 18 to (officially) 44, they came from both urban and rural backgrounds, from a range of religious faiths, and trades and occupations of a broad nature. The group included those engaged in rural and agricultural endeavours (such as farming and forestry, including loggers, labourers and sleeper cutters), urban occupations (such as clerks, storekeepers, butchers, bakers, and a hairdresser) and a small number of professional men (teachers, accountants and a Methodist minister). A small number of miners and prospectors were also represented, as well as a camel driver. A large proportion of the men nominated next of kin in other states or the United Kingdom, reflecting the transient and immigrant-based population of Western Australia.

The 16th Battalion had been raised in September 1914, not long after the start of the war, and consisted of men from Western Australia and South Australia. It formed part of the 4th Brigade. The 16th Battalion had originally sailed from Australia in December 1914 and had trained in Egypt before fighting at Gallipoli between April and December 1915 when it was evacuated from Gallipoli to Egypt. Successive groups of reinforcements for the battalion had been already been sent from Australia to replace those killed and wounded.

Like many of the men who were about to embark for overseas service, Martin O'Meara made a will (on 15 November 1915), the importance of which will become evident later; it was witnessed by YMCA representatives at the Blackboy Hill Camp. The YMCA social hall (also referred to as the Garrison Hall) at the Blackboy Hill Camp was an important part of camp life, and had been opened by Sir John Forrest MP on 16 October 1915. It featured a wide range of recreational facilities for the men of the camp.[128]

During his time in training and before his departure, Martin O'Meara remained in contact with his family in Ireland, and it was later reported that:

---

[128] *Western Mail* (War Souvenir), 25 December 1915, p.35.

Prior to his departure from here [Perth] he received the news that his mother was in very delicate health, a fact which caused him much anxiety. He was a most faithful son, and his one wish was that he might see his mother before she died.[129]

At 11.00am on 12 December 1915 some 500 Roman Catholic officers and men from the Belmont and Blackboy Hill Camps attended Sunday morning Mass at Perth's Roman Catholic Cathedral. The men had arrived at Perth railway station and had then marched, led by the Western Australian Police Band, to the Cathedral. Mass was celebrated by the Rev Creagh and was also attended by several dignitaries, including the Hon Hugh Mahon MP (Minister for External Affairs) and the Hon Michael Troy MLA (Speaker of the Western Australian Legislative Assembly.[130] As a practising Roman Catholic, it is most likely that Martin O'Meara attended.

The men were given several days of leave prior to their departure, and Martin O'Meara is likely to have used this time to tidy up his affairs. This would have included dealing his interests in sleeper hewers' camps (as noted by Captain Aidan Bryan previously) and visiting his friends around Perth. Timothy Michael Quinlan claims that Martin O'Meara approached him a few days before the *Ajana* sailed (which would have been around 20 December 1915) but that he did not recognise him.[131] Some men were known to have travelled from Perth back to their own hometowns to visit friends and family, but it is not known whether Martin O'Meara visited Collie at this time.

[129] *Kalgoorlie Miner*, 19 September 1916, p.3.
[130] *West Australian*, 13 December 1915, p.6.
[131] *Daily News*, 15 September 1915, p.7.

5   Egypt

On 22 December 1915, Private Martin O'Meara departed from Fremantle's Victoria Quay on the troopship *Ajana*, which then sailed to Egypt. The *Ajana* was owned by the Australind Steamship Company Ltd and displaced 7,760 gross tons; she had previously served as a refrigerated passenger and cargo vessel used primarily for long distance voyages such as those between Australia and Europe.

The troopship Ajana. (AWM PB0075)

Martin O'Meara was one of 197 troops (consisting of two officers and 195 men) of the 12th Reinforcements of the 16th Battalion who sailed from Fremantle that day.[132] The *Ajana* also sailed with an officer and 70 men of the 12th Reinforcements of the 12th Battalion who had embarked at Fremantle, and an officer and 133 men from the 7th Reinforcements of the 26th Battalion who had joined the *Ajana* in Melbourne, and 12 men from the 12th Reinforcements of the 2nd Field Ambulance, as well as a chaplain and a medical officer, who had both embarked at Melbourne. According to a report in the Perth *Daily News* (which, in accordance with security regulations, mentioned nothing

---

[132] Another contingent of the 12th Reinforcements for the 16th Battalion had sailed from Adelaide on the *Malwa* on 2 December 1915.

of the ship's role as a troop transport), the *Ajana* had arrived at Fremantle on 20 December and would be taking on flour and wool in Fremantle.[133] The *Ajana* had sailed from Melbourne on 13 December, bound ultimately for the United Kingdom.

The *Ajana* arrived at Port Suez at the southern end of Egypt's Suez Canal on 13 January 1916 but the men were unable to disembark until 15 January due to congestion caused by other vessels already in port. The *Ajana* disembarked seven officers, two warrant officers and 411 other ranks, with the commander of the ship's troops reporting that the 'conduct and discipline of the Troops has been excellent throughout the voyage'.[134] The *Ajana* then sailed through the Suez Canal and on to London, arriving there on 2 February.

Private Billy Rickards, who had trained with Martin O'Meara at Blackboy Hill and Belmont and who had sailed with him to Egypt on the *Ajana*, wrote to his family in Victoria shortly after arriving, describing his initial impressions of Egypt:

> What we saw of Suez was not much; it is a very dirty port. We were pestered with the natives trying to sell different articles. The best bargain we made with them was cigarettes.[135]

An earlier 16th Battalion arrival in Egypt, Private Henry Jones of the 10th Reinforcements, gave a similar report of his arrival at Suez in late 1915 after the voyage from Australia:

> The novel surroundings were most interesting, as to most of us it was our first experience of foreign soil … Suez is only a small place, but is evidently destined to fill a more important role in the future. It has plenty of trees, gardens and nice residences, but the business portion is unpretentious and the native quarters squalid. The boys were all agog with excitement to see the country as we steamed out of Suez station.[136]

---

[133] *Daily News*, 20 December 1915, p.1.
[134] AWM7: Ajana2.
[135] *Echuca and Moama Advertiser and Farmers' Gazette*, 14 March 1916, p.3.
[136] *West Australian*, 4 March 1916, p.7.

Martin O'Meara and the rest of the 12th Reinforcements (and probably the rest of the officers and men from the *Ajana*) then departed Suez by train at 2pm on 15 January, travelling 'third class [with] one small loaf of bread, bottle of tea, and a tin of bully [beef].'[137] They then travelled across the desert from Suez to Cairo arriving at Cairo's Helmieh (now El Helmiah) railway station at 5.30am on 16 January. The men then marched to nearby Zeitoun (now the Cairo district of El Zaytoun) where they settled into one of the AIF's training camps.[138] Zeitoun was located just over 11 kilometres from central Cairo near Heliopolis where the Australians had established a Field Hospital at Luna Park, a former amusement park.

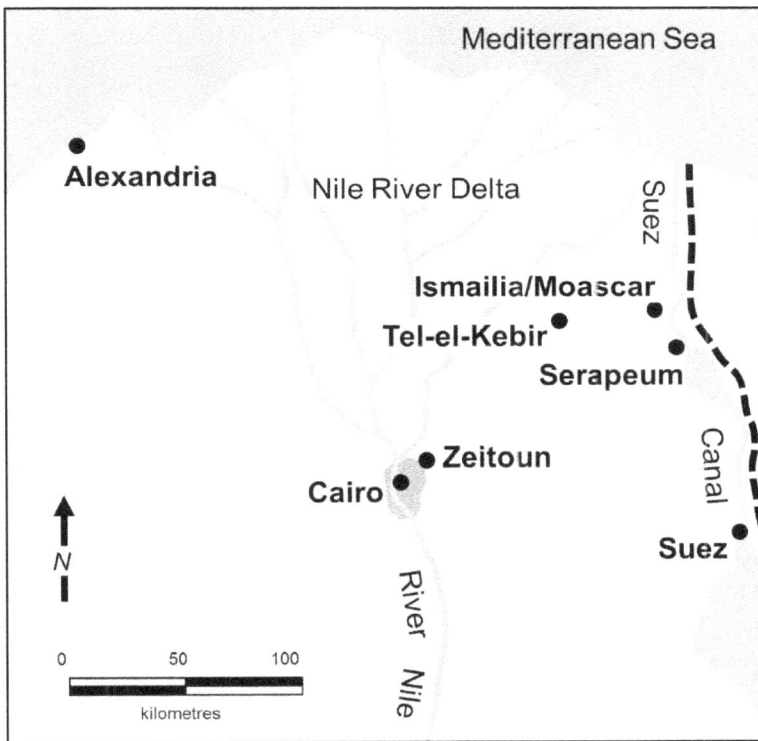

Egypt, showing locations where Martin O'Meara served.

---

[137] *Echuca and Moama Advertiser and Farmers' Gazette*, 14 March 1916, p.3.
[138] *Echuca and Moama Advertiser and Farmers' Gazette*, 14 March 1916, p.3.

Northern Egypt, particularly the Cairo area, was an important staging area for Australian (and other Empire) troops, with many men already based there and thousands more added following the evacuation of Gallipoli in late 1915 and the constant arrival of new recruits. Training was an important activity for these men. The war diary of the 4th Brigade noted that 'considerable time [was] being devoted to Musketry as new Re-inforcements from Australia appear to have had very little training in this.'[139] This is hardly surprising given the relatively short recruit training that the men had been given in Western Australia prior to embarkation, and the relatively short period of training provided by the training battalions in the Cairo area. Dr Charles Bean also noted the state of the reinforcements, later writing that 'the large drafts from Cairo were of very raw material.'[140]

The 16th Battalion's Henry Jones described the training in a letter to his family in Australia:

> We have worked hard to start with: Bayonet fighting, musketry, extended order work, artillery formations, infantry in attack, outposts, route marches, etc., form part of the curriculum. We work an hour before breakfast, then from 9.15 to 12 o'clock, and from 2.15 to 4.30 in the afternoon, with night marches twice a week.[141]

Whilst in the Cairo area many Australia soldiers took the opportunity to visit the historical sights of the area, and Martin O'Meara visited the pyramids during this time. It was later reported in the press that he had written to a friend in Perth from Egypt, and that the 'atmosphere and history of the land of the Pharaohs seemed to have made a great impression upon him, giving him apparently a much wider, deeper, and stronger conception of life and its responsibilities.'[142]

On 7 March 1916 the men of the 12th Reinforcements left the Cairo area and joined the rest of the 16th Battalion at Tel-el-Kebir (about 110 kilometres north-west of Cairo) and commenced battalion and

---

[139] AWM4: 23/4/6, 4th Brigade War Diary, March 1916.
[140] Bean, 1941a, p.50.
[141] *West Australian*, 4 March 1916, p.7.
[142] *Kalgoorlie Miner*, 19 September 1916, p.3.

brigade-level training. The battalion's Routine Order No. 136 issued that day noted that eight officers and 484 men had joined the battalion from reinforcements that day.[143] Tel-el-Kebir was a major training camp for Australian troops, and the 16th Battalion had been at Tel-el-Kebir since 26 February 1916 following its evacuation from Gallipoli.

The 12th Reinforcements of the 16th Battalion camped in Egypt in 1916. (AWM C00644)

Just prior to the arrival of the 12th Reinforcements, the 16th Battalion had been split in half with the new 48th Battalion being formed in early March with a nucleus of 16th Battalion men. This was the result of a significant expansion and reorganisation of the AIF at this time. Reinforcements from Australia were later used to bring both the 16th and 48th Battalions up to full strength. Brigadier-General John Monash, commanding the 4th Brigade, wrote from Tel-el-Kebir on 5 March that:

About 1,600 [of my] men were sent to form the nucleus of the 12th Brigade, which is to be commanded by Glasfurd. I keep 2,000 men – all my own C.O's – Tilney, Dare, Cannan, and Pope – and most of my own staff. I am getting and shall get, steady

---

143 AWM25: 707/9 Part 240, 16th Battalion Routine Orders.

drafts of reinforcements already in Egypt, from Heliopolis and Zeitoun.[144]

The 4th Brigade was transferred from the Australia and New Zealand Division (which had fought at Gallipoli) to the new 4th Division, which had been formed in Egypt in February, at this time. The 4th Division was commanded by a British officer, Major-General Herbert Cox.

Martin O'Meara, however, did not spend much time with the 16th Battalion in March 1916, as he was transferred to the newly-formed 4th Machine Gun Company. The company had been formed in early March when the four Vickers and Maxim machine guns from each individual infantry battalion in the 4th Brigade were separated and placed under the command of the 4th Brigade headquarters. Each battalion's machine gun section was to replace their existing Vickers and Maxim guns with the newly-introduced Lewis guns. It is not certain exactly when Martin O'Meara joined the 4th Machine Gun Company, as his name does not appear on a list of men transferred from the 4th Brigade's infantry battalions from 9 March onwards.[145]

On 22 March the 4th Brigade, which included both the 16th Battalion and the 4th Machine Gun Company, was inspected by HRH the Prince of Wales, and 4th Brigade sports day was held on 23 March. On 24 March the 4th and 5th Divisions received orders from Lieutenant-General Sir Alexander Godley, Commander of the II ANZAC Corps, to move from Tel-el-Kebir to Serapeum to assist with the defence of the Suez Canal against possible Turkish incursions. The two divisions spent 25 March preparing for the move.[146]

The 4th Brigade was with the first group leaving on 26 March, with the last group of 4th and 5th Division troops arriving at the Suez Canal on 3 April. Most of the men were to march from Tel-el-Kebir to the Suez Canal area, although the men of the 16th Battalion were fortunate to have missed out on the march, as they (and the whole of

---

[144] AWM: 3DRL/2316, War Letters of General Monash: Volume 1: 24 December 1914 to 4 March 1917.

[145] AWM25: 707/9 Part 562, 4th Machine Gun Company Routine Orders.

[146] AWM4: 1/48/1, General Staff, HQ 4th Australian Division War Diary, March-April 1916.

the 8th Brigade) had been sent ahead from Tel-el-Kebir to Serapeum by train on 26 March as an advance party.[147] It is likely that those men selected to attend upcoming training courses in the Cairo area did not proceed to Serapeum at this stage, but remained at Tel-el-Kebir or travelled back to Cairo, and it is probable that Martin O'Meara was one of the men who remained.

Portrait of Private Martin O'Meara taken in a studio in Egypt, between January and May 1916.

He is wearing the AIF tunic and breeches with leather boots and puttees, and a fur felt ('slouch') hat with the brim down.

He is also wearing 1908 pattern webbing, consisting of a belt, shoulder straps and ammunition pouches and stands with the Small Magazine Lee Enfield (SMLE) .303 rifle with bayonet fixed.

It is likely that O'Meara sent the original of this photograph to soembody in WA after it was taken. (Army Museum of WA)

The march from Tel-el-Kebir to the Suez Canal by the remainder of the 4th and 5th Divisions was later remembered in the popular folklore of the AIF, with a former serviceman writing, some ten years later, that:

Many diggers will remember the distressing march from Tel-el-Kebir to Serpaeum [sic], undertaken, so we afterwards heard, on the suggestion of one Australian general, to test the

---

[147] Bean, 1941a, p.290.

stamina and training of the various units. The author of this brilliant suggestion was afterwards returned to Australia ...[148]

The 16th Battalion set up a camp after arriving at Serapeum and then, after a day of rest, resumed training. It was also involved in an aquatic sports carnival in the Suez Canal on 12 April.

Martin O'Meara was, meanwhile, still in the Cairo area and was to undergo machine gun training. A machine gunners' course was held at the Imperial School of Instruction at Zeitoun near Cairo from 3-22 April, with NCOs and men required to arrive (fully equipped and with blankets) at Zeitoun prior to noon on 1 April. Those men selected to attend the machine gunners' course were required to 'have some aptitude for the work, be of good physique, keen and intelligent.'[149]

Men of the AIF preparing to fire a Vickers machine gun on a firing range in Egypt in early 1916. Martin O'Meara trained on this type of machine gun. (AWM P00851.012)

The men trained on the Vickers machine gun, a water-cooled, tripod mounted weapon capable of firing some 450 rounds of .303 inch ammunition (the same as used by the infantry's Small Magazine

[148] *Sunday Times*, 28 February 1926, p.7.
[149] AWM25: 877/1, Courses of Instruction at Imperial School of Instruction, Zeitoun January-May 1916.

Lee Enfield rifles) per minute. The gun's team consisted of one man firing, one man feeding the ammunition belt into the gun, and several other men who were responsible for carrying ammunition and supporting the gun's movement.

Martin O'Meara was one of 57 Machine Gun Company men who attended the three-week machine gun course, passing the course as a first-class machine gunner.[150] The 4th Division war diaries record that on 22 April sixteen officers and 131 other ranks returned to the 4th Brigade from the Imperial School of Instruction at Zeitoun. The 4th Division was headquartered at Serapeum at this time, and this group probably included the machine gunners, amongst whom was Martin O'Meara. The men travelled by train from Cairo to Serapeum where the 4th Brigade was stationed and involved in defending the Suez Canal from possible Turkish attack. Sergeant Harry Leake of the 16th Battalion, a Gallipoli veteran, wrote to students at a school in Victoria in Australia April 1916 noting that:

Just at present our battalion is camped right on the banks of the Suez Canal at a place called Serapium [sic], and when we see the mail-boats passing through bound for Australia, we feel like taking one big jump right on to the deck and sailing away home. However I don't think it will be so very long now before we are all able to go home again; I hope so, at all events. I was right through the Gallipoli campaign, so have no wish to see any more fighting.[151]

The 4th Brigade was involved in constructing and manning a sector of defences along the eastern side of the Suez Canal during April, May and June. Defensive positions were established up to 10 kilometres east of the Canal to protect against possible Turkish incursions. The 4th Division was responsible for the defence of 'A' Subsector of No. 2 (Central) Sector of the Canal defences, which was the area to the east of Serapeum and the Canal. The I ANZAC Corps was responsible for this sector which had its headquarters at Ismailia.

On 25 April, the first anniversary of the Australians' landing at Gallipoli, commemorative church parades were held in the morning

---

[150] AWM25: 707/9 Part 562, 4th Machine Gun Company Routine Orders.
[151] *Grenville Standard*, 3 June 1916, p.1.

with a 4th Division sports (with athletic and aquatic events) carnival being held in the afternoon. An AIF man wrote to his family in Australia describing the events of the day:

> being Anzac Day, it was decided to celebrate it in some way or other, and the weather of late being exceptionally hot, a swimming carnival was decided on. There were four or five sprint races before the principal race, the Anzac Derby, was run. The Derby was a race in boats made by the competitors, and attracted great attention. After a very close race, the Ascot, manned by men of the 16 Battalion, won ...[152]

Meanwhile, in Ireland an uprising was being staged in Dublin by a small group of the 'Irish Volunteers', radical republicans who had broken away from John Redmond's 'home rule' nationalist movement. The 'Easter uprising', as it was to later known, saw Patrick Pearse lead around 1,800 Irish Volunteers in taking control of the General Post Office and other buildings in central Dublin. The uprising was quickly put down, but the execution of a number of the uprising's leaders saw an increase in support for more radical nationalist actions at the expense of the more pragmatic nationalism of John Redmond. Initially derided by many Irish nationalists, the executed leaders were soon to be regarded as heroes and martyrs by many Irish, both in Ireland and in Australia, within a few months.

Although the O'Meara family was known to support the Irish nationalist cause generally, it is not known how they responded to the Easter uprising.

---

[152] *Forbes Times*, 16 June 1916, p.6.

6   The Western Front

On 23 May 1916 Martin O'Meara left the 4th Machine Gun Company and returned to the 16th Battalion, and was posted to B Company.[153] The 16th Battalion was located at Serapeum at this time, and engaged in military training in the desert from 25-26 May ahead of its pending deployment to the Western Front. At 8.40pm on 31 May the 16th Battalion departed its camp at Serapeum and travelled overnight by train to Alexandria on Egypt's Mediterranean coast, arriving before dawn the next morning.

The men then boarded the troop ship *Canada* which sailed that day for Marseilles in southern France. The 16th Battalion's history noted that 'The voyage through the Mediterranean ... was uneventful. The weather was fine, the sea calm and the usual troopship routine was adopted'.[154] The usual troopship routine included having men on submarine guard, as German U-boats presented a serious threat to allied shipping at that time.

The *Canada* arrived at Marseilles at 10.00am on 7 June, and the men of the 16th Battalion disembarked, marched through the town, and boarded trains that took them north through France to Bailleul near the Belgian border. Although the trip would have been interesting to the Australians, most of whom had never travelled to France previously, it was not a comfortable experience. Lance-Corporal Marshall Way of the battalion's D Company, writing to his family at Unley in South Australia on 13 June, described the journey as '3 days on the train in closed in cattle trucks travelling towards Paris'.[155] Of the journey, the battalion's historian recorded that:

> Before the 16th arrived at its destination, the men had plenty of evidence that they were nearing the scene of fierce fighting. Trains passed them laden with battered guns for the repair

---

[153] AWM25: 707/9 Part 241, 16th Battalion Routine Orders.
[154] Longmore, 1929, p.111.
[155] AWM: 2DRL/0280, Marshall Way.

shops, with wounded men for the hospitals, and with muddy French and English soldiers en route for the rest areas.[156]

After arriving at Bailleul in northern France the men then marched to their billets, generally farm buildings, where they remained until 16 June. Lance-Corporal Marshall Way, who had joined the 16th Battalion at Gallipoli in November 1915, described Bailleul as 'a town some 10 miles from the firing line'[157], and this area was known as 'the nursery sector' as it was relatively quiet, and therefore a good area to familiarise the Australian troops with trench warfare on the Western Front. The Bailleul area in northern France was relatively close to the opposing lines of trenches where the attacking Germans had been stopped and had dug in during late 1914 and through early 1915, well before the Australians had arrived in the area. The fortified lines now extended from the North Sea on the coast of Belgium in the north to the Swiss border in the south, and the British Empire's forces were garrisoning the lines in northern France and Belgium.

The portion of the fortified line in the Bailleul area was not strictly a trench system, as many of the defences were built above ground level rather than dug below ground level. They were described by official war historian Dr Charles Bean as:

> a rampart of sandbags and earth of from nine to fourteen feet in thickness. In most parts a back wall or parados also had been provided, the effect being to create a sunken passage, which, although it appeared to those who were between its walls to be little different from a trench, was in reality piled above the surface of the surrounding fields. Behind this breastwork, in most part forming its parados, were rectangular shelters for men and officers ...[158]

It seems that Martin O'Meara's mother had died at Lorrha in County Tipperary around May 1916, whilst he was serving in the Suez Canal area, and it is unlikely that he received news of her death until June when he arrived in France. She was buried at Lorrha cemetery. On 14 June, whilst in the Bailleul area, Martin O'Meara wrote a letter

---

[156] Longmore, 1929, p.111.
[157] AWM: 2DRL/0280, Marshall Way.
[158] Bean, 1941a, pp.102-103.

to a friend in Western Australia (whose identity remains unknown) in which he described hearing of his mother's death. O'Meara wrote:

> I heard from the old country a couple of weeks back, and learned of my mother's death. I thought I would be able to see her once again in this world. Well, dear friend, don't forget to look after your mother while she is with you, for when she is gone your best friend is lost. Don't ever think yourself above taking mother's advice. We may be going into action any day now, so don't forget to say a prayer for all the fine lads in the trenches, all our fine Australian men in particular. We have plenty of work in front to do, but particularly pray that if we have to die that we get the assistance of God's Grace and the intercession of His Holy Mother to die bravely and honourably, but above all, purely and then, by doing that in place of dying we shall commence to live a new life.[159]

Characteristics of O'Meara, the letter reveals something of his Roman Catholic faith, of his affection for his mother, and of his camaraderie with his fellow soldiers.[160]

The battalion's initial tasks in the nursery sector during this time included providing fatigue parties involved in digging and maintaining trenches, breastworks and other defences. On 15 June 1916 the men were issued with their steel helmets and gas respirators, which would become essential items of kit for the trench warfare they were to experience. Marshall Way wrote a letter to his family several days later:

> We have all got steel hats now to minimise the danger of getting hurt by shrapnel pellets & gas helmets to secure us against gas & I can tell you we look queer when we are rigged out for the various attacks.[161]

---

[159] *Daily News*, 21 September 1916, p.6.

[160] The letter also demonstrates significantly better spelling and grammar than earlier writing by Martin O'Meara, and may have been improved by the reporter or newspaper editor to improve its readibility.

[161] AWM: 2DRL/0280, Marshall Way.

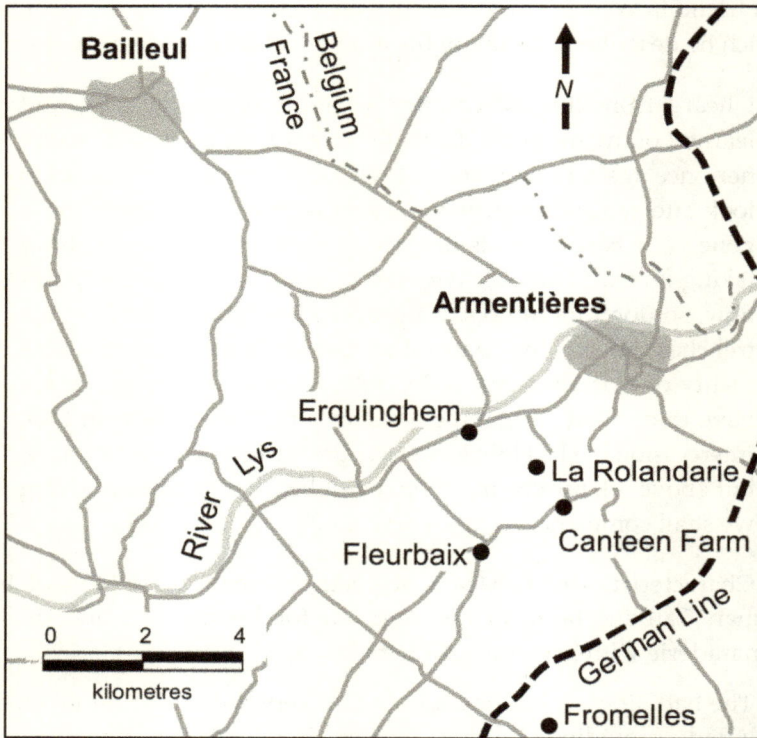

The 'nursery sector' (or 'Bois-Grenier sector') during June-July 1916 showing locations where the 16th Battalion operated.

On the same day the 4th Brigade had received orders to relieve the 7th Brigade on 17 June, and on that day 4th Brigade relieved the 7th Brigade in the Erquinghem area, around ten kilometres south-east of Bailleul and around three kilometres south-west of Armentières, on the southern side of the River Lys. On 20 June the 4th Brigade received orders to move to the front line to gain experience in trench warfare, and to occupy the lines held by the 3rd Brigade. The brigade was also engaged in specific training in trench warfare, including training raiding parties.

The 16th Battalion's first taste of the war in Europe was in June when several platoons were sent forward to the front-line trenches to gain experience. The 16th Battalion's exposure to actual fighting was, however, very limited and the 16th Battalion lost only one man during June when, on 23 June, a very heavy thunderstorm passed over the area occupied by the battalion and a lightning strike killed Private

Alfred Brooke and injured several other men from B Company.[162] As Martin O'Meara was serving with B Company at this time, it is likely that he knew Alfred Brooke, and possible that he was close to the area where the lightning struck. Brooke was buried at Erquinghem on 24 June, and it is likely that Martin O'Meara attended the funeral. Brooke was the first member of the 16th Battalion to die in France during the war.

On 27 June the 4th Brigade took over the front line at Bois-Grenier, with the 13th and 14th Battalions in the front line trenches and the 16th Battalion remaining in reserve at Canteen Farm, some three kilometres behind the German front line.

Unidentified Australian soldiers walking along a duckboard track on their way to the front line trenches in the Bois-Grenier area in June 1916. Breastworks reinforced with timber and sandbags can be seen behind the men. (AWM EZ0048)

Although located some distance the front line, the area occupied by the battalion was not necessarily safe. On 20 June a German shell had struck Canteen Farm resulting in the deaths of five officers and men from other battalions who were billeted there. A further 14 were injured.[163]

The type of warfare encounter by the Australians on the Western Front was very different to that encountered at Gallipoli and in Egypt.

---

[162] AWM: 2DRL/0280, Marshall Way.
[163] AWM: 1DRL/0428, 2878 Esric Montague Dowling.

The existence of fixed friendly and enemy lines of trenches separated by a 'No Man's Land' meant that some fighting would require quite different skills to those being taught to ordinary infantrymen. British and Canadian infantry had been serving on the Western Front for around eighteen months when the Australians joined them in 1916, and the Australians were able to learn from their earlier experiences. In particular, the presence of a well-defined No Man's Land separating lines of trenches meant that scouting and patrol work would become important, yet there was a recognition that scout and patrolling work conducted during the earlier parts of the War had been less than fully effective as many of the men were inadequately trained and equipped.[164]

This problem was to be addressed by establishing separate groups of scouts within the individual infantry battalions, and the scouts themselves were to be specially selected for their sound physique, good condition and powers of endurance, their courage and self-reliance, their good eye-sight and powers of observation, and their confidence and skill with weapons. The Australian battalions established scouting sections shortly after arriving on the Western Front in 1916, and these men were provided with specialist training and much was expected of them:

> No man can be considered a trained scout until he has been proved under fire and in the face of the enemy, and the further training of the scouts must continue when the Battalion goes into the trenches ... Any man who proves himself unreliable when facing the enemy must be immediately returned to his company.[165]

The initial training was provided within the battalion themselves and was conducted by the Scouting Officer who was also the battalion's Intelligence Officer.

One of the most useful authorities on the role of scouts, observers and snipers during the First World War was the improbably named

---

[164] AWM25: 741/1, Precis of a Lecture on Organisation and System of Training and Scouts and Patrols for Trench Warfare.

[165] AWM25: 741/1, Precis of a Lecture on Organisation and System of Training and Scouts and Patrols for Trench Warfare.

Major Hesketh Hesketh-Prichard of the British Army; writing after the war in his book *Sniping in France*, he noted that:

> The work of the scout was, of course, to dominate the enemy in No Man's Land, and to this end he was continually patrolling it during the hours of darkness.[166]

Official Australian war historian Dr Charles Bean noted that the men in the scouting platoon were exempt from the battalions' ordinary fatigue duties and that 'this was the chief inducement to remain in it.'[167] The justification for Bean's position here is not known, and it remains uncorroborated.

An Australian scout dressed ready to enter No Man's land.

In addition to his standard uniform and steel helmet, his equipment includes box respirator, revolver, prismatic compass and wire cutters.

Some scouts also carried various types of clubs for use in hand-to-hand fighting in the confined spaces of trenches.

This is Private George Watkins of the 39th Battalion. (AWM P10885.006)

The scouts were involved in a variety of activities, as noted by Major Hesketh-Prichard:

> A scout may, in a single two hours of his life, be a sniper, an observer, and the old-fashioned scout who has to go out and

---

166 Hesketh-Prichard, 1920, p.193.
167 Bean, 1941a, p.119.

find out things at close range. He has to be essentially an individualist capable of seeing and seizing the opportunity.[168]

The actual practice of deploying the scouting section probably varied between the different battalions, with each battalion's Scouting Officer would have had slightly different approaches. Whilst it is very likely that each man carried the necessary skills to function as a scout, observer or sniper, it is probable that men were deployed in roles that suited their own particular skills. Actual tactical deployment involved those men operating as observers and snipers working in pairs in forward trenches and along parapets, with other men operating as actual scouts in an intelligence-gathering role in No Man's Land. A scout from the 36th Battalion, Private Harry Smith wrote in early 1918 that:

> Scouting is awfully interesting work. Many a night I have crawled out over our parapet with my little party of six and scouted 'No Man's Land' for hours at a stretch, covered with mud from head to foot, and only a couple of bombs and a knob-stick for weapons. We have crept right up to Fritz's parapet and could hear them talking and plainly see their faces when a Verey light was sent up. I often felt like dropping a bomb or two amongst them, but as our job was purely reconnaissance work we left them alone …[169]

The order for the 16th Battalion to establish groups of scouts reached the Commanding Officer shortly after 17 June 1916, when the 4th Division Headquarters issued orders for the formation of groups of battalion scouts, 'consisting of expert observers, snipers and scouts, all of whom will be men specially chosen for this work.' Each battalion was ordered to establish a scouting section consisting of an officer and thirty men. Martin O'Meara was to serve with the scouts throughout the war. The function of the battalion scouts was described in the Divisional Order:

> When a battalion is in the trenches those observers and snipers will work in pairs, either in the front line trench or from supports of other positions slightly in rear and will be

---

[168] Hesketh-Prichard, 1920, p.202-203.
[169] *Young Witness*, 10 May 1918, p.1.

independent of the ordinary trench garrison. Their special work will be the location and subduing of enemy snipers, the location of enemy M.G's and observing posts, general observation and reporting of the progress or otherwise of work on the enemy's front and support trenches. The patrol men will be about 6 in number and will be volunteers from among the battalion Scouts. Their special task will be to gather all information concerning the enemy up to and including his parapet, including precise topographical details, frequent reports on enemy's wire, location of enemy's observation posts, M.G. emplacements, listening posts, etc. Permanent, well concealed and protected observation posts may be constructed with the sanction of the C.O. at the direction of the Scout Officer for the use of himself and his observers, if he thinks that adequate observation cannot otherwise be obtained. The Scouts may be required to remain in the trenches after the Battalion has been relieved, in order to carry on and hand over all information to the next Battalion. [170]

The 16th Battalion's scouting section was formally established on 27 June when a group of men selected from across the battalion paraded at Canteen Farm south of Erquinghem at 9.00am. Martin O'Meara and five of his colleagues from B Company joined the section along with eight men from A Company, six men from C Company, five men from D Company and one man from the battalion signallers.[171]

The first Scouting Officer was Lieutenant Bill Lynas, the battalion's Intelligence Officer. Originally from New Zealand and of Irish stock, Bill Lynas had been working at a mine near Marble Bar in Western Australia's remote north when he enlisted in September 1914. He had served with the 16th Battalion at Gallipoli and in Egypt and had been commissioned after the battalion had withdrawn from Gallipoli to Egypt. Bill Lynas was later described as eagerly participating in his new role, and was 'never happier than when he was out in No Man's Land patrolling along the enemy wire in search of scalps.'[172] The scouting section sergeant was George Hough from Bunbury in

[170] AWM4: 1/48/3, General Staff, HQ 4th Australian Division War Diary, June 1916.
[171] AWM25: 707/9 Part 241, 16th Battalion Routine Orders.
[172] Longmore, 1929, p.4.

Western Australia, one of the men transferred from A Company. Gough was originally from Lancashire in England but had been living in Collie, where he was a teacher, when he had enlisted in September 1914. He had served with the battalion at Gallipoli, and was later commissioned and was killed in action in December 1916. As a former resident of Collie, it is possible that he had contact with Martin O'Meara before the war.

On 1 July 1916 the Battle of the Somme was launched by the Allies as a massive attack on the German lines that had been on place since the two sides had reached a stalemate earlier in the war. The Allies were now determined to break the stalemate, and the area around the Somme River near of the town of Albert was chosen as the place for this to occur. The scale of the offensive, which became known as 'the Big Push', was immense. The British committed thirteen divisions with a further five French divisions active south of the Somme River.

The day is now widely regarded as a British failure. Most of the German units took shelter in deep bunkers and dugouts during the week-long artillery bombardment that preceded 1 July, and had emerged from these bunkers in time to repel the Allied attacks. The British (including Empire) forces suffered nearly 60,000 casualties that day and the anticipated advances into German-held territory did not, apart from a few small examples, occur. Australian forces were not involved in the Somme offensive 1 July but quickly joined the offensive later in July.

The 4th Brigade remained in the Bois-Grenier sector during the first part of July, and was headquartered at La Rolanderie, just to the north of Canteen Farm. Training continued during the early part of July. The 16th Battalion was relieved in the Bois-Grenier sector by the 32nd Battalion (part of the 8th Brigade) on 10 July. After its relief, the battalion moved north-west across the River Lys to billets at L'Hallobeau and then to billets near Bailleul on 11 July. The battalion remained near Bailleul until 13 July when the men woke early and boarded a train at Bailleul West station at around 7.30am, and travelled south to Doullens. After arriving by train at Doullens, the 16th Battalion (apart from D Company which remained on fatigue duty at Doullens) marched to Saint-Ouen. The march must have been difficult for the battalion, as its war diary noted that the 'Mens feet in very bad condition', and that they were ordered to conduct route marches to 'harden men up.'[173] D Company rejoined the rest of the battalion on 15 July and on 16 July the whole battalion marched to Naours. The battalion was involved in training whilst at Naours, and remained there until 25 July. The men then marched some 15 kilometres east to Toutencourt. The battalion was then involved in specialist training until 27 July, when the men marched with other 4th Brigade units to Warloy (a march of around seven kilometres) and continued training.[174] The time at Warloy was spent preparing the men for their coming move into the trenches east of Albert.

On 1 August the entire 4th Brigade conducted attack training in the morning around two kilometres south of Warloy, and this was repeated in the evening after dark and included scouts fixing small electric torches at position's in No Man's Land guide the attacking troops. The 16th Battalion's training continued on 3 August, with practice attacks in both daylight and night-time conditions conducted and this included paying special attention to the roles of the specialist troops which included the scouts.[175]

---

[173] AWM4: 23/33/8, 16th Battalion War Diary, July 1916.
[174] AWM4: 23/33/8, 16th Battalion War Diary, July 1916.
[175] AWM4: 23/4/11, 4th Brigade War Diary, August 1916.

7   Pozières and Mouquet Farm

The village of Pozières is located some seven kilometres north-east of the town of Albert in the Somme region of France, and was a key German stronghold at the start of the Allied Somme offensive on 1 July 1916. The area had been in German hands since September 1914 when the French 10th Army had failed to push back the attacking German 6th Army. Its capture had been one of the goals of the British 8th Division on 1 July 1916, but it was not captured that day and allied forces faced a protracted (and bloody) struggle to push the German forces from the earlier front line positions, near the village of La Boisselle to the west, beyond Pozières.

The Australians had been involved in repeated assaults on Pozières between 23-27 July when the 1st Division had wrested control of the village from the Germans, and between 28 July and 6 August when the 2nd Division captured the ridge to the north of the village, sometimes referred to as the 'Pozières Heights'. Pozières had suffered almost total destruction during July when Dr Charles Bean wrote in his diary 'I don't want to go through Pozières again I have seen it now once – it was a quiet day. It is far worse than Fricourt or Boiselle or Contalmaison. There is nothing left of it more than an ash heap …'[176] The 4th Division, which included the 16th Battalion, was the next Australian division to be brought into action at Pozières. The Division's objective was to continue to push the German lines back towards the village of Thiepval to the north-west of Pozières along the western extension of the 'Pozières Heights' ridge.

In the evening of 4 August, following a morning spent training, the 16th Battalion left the Warloy area and moved to the Brickfields area just north of Albert (a march of about eleven kilometres), arriving there at around midnight. The men then spent the rest of the night there and rested for most of 5 August. The stay at the Brickfields area was not pleasant, with Private Jim Mundy of D Company later writing in his diary 'camped in open in rain and under shell fire.'[177]

---

[176] AWM38: 3DRL 606/54/1, Bean papers – Diary, July-August 1916.
[177] SLSA: D7167(L), Letter and Diary of J.W. Mundy.

At 8.30pm on 5 August the battalion received orders to move closer to the front line as a reserve for the 2nd Division which was already active in the front line near Pozières. The 16th Battalion then moved east to Tara Hill, located south of the main road running east between Albert and Bapaume. The men overnighted in the nearby Tara Gully area, the battalion's war diary noting that the area was shelled overnight, but that many of the shells were 'duds' and that did not cause any casualties. At noon on 6 August the 16th Battalion's A and B Companies moved out to report to the commander of the 12th Brigade for carrying duties, whilst C Company moved out to report to the commander of the 7th Brigade and D Company moved out to report to the commander of the 6th Brigade on carrying duties.

Photograph captioned 'All that was left of La Boiselle', probably taken during the first week of August 1916. This is how La Boisselle was when the 16th Battalion passed through the area. (AWM P07670.010)

One of Martin O'Meara's comrades from the battalion's 12th Reinforcements, Private Billy Rickards, was wounded in action in the area on 6 August. He later wrote:

Along with a mate I was returning from headquarters when we took shelter in a dug-out for the night. About midnight Fritz disturbed our slumber by sending over three charcoal boxes – 9.2 shells. The first one went very close to our little home; the second closer still. My mate suggested getting out. I was not having any of it. The third shell was the one that did the damage. All I remember was the dug-out falling in on me.[178]

Billy Rickards survived the war but, sadly, his mate did not.

At 10.00am on 7 August 1916 the 16th Battalion's headquarters, together with A Company and D Company, moved to Wire Trench on the low ridge around 400 metres north-west of La Boisselle, with B and C Companies moving in later. At 1.40pm the battalion sent two Lewis gun detachments to the 15th Battalion headquarters to assist with that battalion's operations north-west of Pozières.

The 16th Battalion's men were starting to move into areas that were recently subject to fierce fighting, and the evidence of war would have been readily apparent to them. Dr Charles Bean later wrote:

The reader must take for granted many of the conditions – the flayed land, shell-hole bordering shell-hole, corpses of young men lying against the trench walls or in shell-holes; some – except for the dust settling on them – seeming to sleep; others torn in half; others rotting, swollen, and discoloured. He must also take for granted the air fetid with their stench or at times pungent with the chemical reek of high explosive.[179]

A large proportion of the battalion had joined as reinforcements after the evacuation from Gallipoli and would not have previously experienced the conditions that Bean described. It was into this environment that Martin O'Meara and his 16th Battalion comrades had their first real taste of Western Front trench warfare. Those of the battalion who had served at Gallipoli would have noticed the different nature of European warfare, but perhaps not the horrors of violent death. It is likely that Martin O'Meara, as a battalion scout, would experience this ahead of most of the other men in the battalion.

On 8 August 1916, at 6.00pm, the 16th Battalion's A Company under Captain Ross Harwood moved off to support the 15th Battalion. The 15th Battalion was to mount an attack the line from the Brind's Road (or Ovillers-Courcellete Road) trench line towards the 5th Avenue/Ration Trench/Park Lane trench system to the northwest

[178] *Echuca and Moama Advertiser and Farmers' Gazette,* 10 October 1916, p.4.
[179] Bean, 1941a, p.728.

of Pozières in the direction of Mouquet Farm, a distance of around 200 metres) at 9.20pm that evening following an artillery barrage.

The 7th Battalion of the British Army's Suffolk Regiment was to attack the same trench system on the left (southeast) flank, including an assault on some German strongpoints near 'Point 78' close to the current Pozières-Thiepval Road.

At 10.40pm on 8 August, the battalion headquarters received a message from the 4th Brigade headquarters asking about the position of A Company, and the battalion replied that A Company was under the control of the 15th Battalion in K Trench (which ran north-south to the west of Pozières) and that D Company was ready to move at short notice if required. At 12.30am on 9 August the 16th Battalion was ordered to have a third company ready to support the 15th Battalion, and C Company was warned and made ready. Despite ferocious German artillery and machine gun fire against the attackers, the 15th Battalion managed to reach their objectives at Park Lane trench by around midnight on 8 August. Some 15th Battalion men advanced up to 150 metres beyond their objectives, but later pulled back.

The men of the Suffolks, however, failed to reach their objectives on the left flank, leaving several German machine gun positions at 'Point 78' intact. The Suffolks suffered greatly. The Suffolks' war diary recorded that, on the night of 8-9 August, their right assault (which would have been on the flank adjacent to the 15th Battalion) on the German positions involved three waves (six platoons) of men, and 'was well carried out, but the [British trench mortar] bombardment had been insufficient and all three waves were destroyed by M.G. fire, only one Officer 1 N.C.O. and 12 unwounded men came back.'[180] A sergeant of the Suffolks had reported to his battalion headquarters at 1.14am on 9 August that 'When reconnoitring the trench he saw the Germans on their parapet ... he saw many of our men lying and several of them wounded. These are coming in now.'[181]

It seems likely that Martin O'Meara was working alongside the 16th Battalion's A Company in support of the 15th Battalion

[180] TNA: WO 95/1852/2 7 Suffolks War Diary, 1916.
[181] TNA: WO 95/1852/2 7 Suffolks War Diary, 1916.

overnight, as Captain Ross Harwood, commanding the 16th Battalion's A Company, observed that:

> On the night of the 8/9th I saw No.3970 Pte. O'Meara, M., out into "No Man's Land" where it was being severely shelled and remove wounded men to places of safety where he rendered first aid and thence subsequently he assisted to carry them down to the Dressing Station. I personally saw him remove not less than 6 men mostly of the 15th Battalion A.I.F. and the Suffolk Battalion. One of the wounded whom I saw him remove in this is Lieut Fogarty of the 15th Battalion A.I.F.[182]

One of Ross Harwood's platoon commanders, Second Lieutenant Frank Wadge, noted:

> I am able to identify Lieut Fogarty of the 15th Bn to whom he rendered first aid and whom he subsequently brought into trench. This Officer was wounded and had been lying in No Man's Land for almost four hours the enmy fire at this point was so dense that it had been impossible to make a search for wounded but such conditions did not deter O'Meara.[183]

According to the 15th Battalion's published history, Second Lieutenant Neville Fogarty was commanding one of the platoons in the 15th Battalion's A Company's during the attack on the German positions the evening of 8 August, and that all of the 15th Battalion's A Company officers were casualties.[184]

Neville Fogarty was probably located by O'Meara in the vicinity of the Park Lane trench, and it is likely that the four-hour period noted by Frank Wadge indicates that O'Meara rescued Fogarty sometime just before dawn (between 4am and 5am) on 9 August 1916. The 15th Battalion history also records that a troublesome group of German

---

[182] AWM28: 2/101, Recommendation file for honours and awards, AIF, 1914-18 War 4th Australian Infantry Brigade 1916.
[183] AWM28: 2/101, Recommendation file for honours and awards, AIF, 1914-18 War 4th Australian Infantry Brigade 1916.
[184] Chataway, 1948, pp.123-128. A Company was the centre left of their line, with D Company on the left, C Company on the right, and B Company at centre right.

machine gunners surrendered at around 4am on 9 August 1916,[185] and this probably provided an opportunity for Martin O'Meara and other Australians to be more active in No Man's Land that morning. Neville Fogarty was subsequently evacuated with gunshot wounds to his left hand.[186]

Based on the location of the operations of the 15th Battalion and the Suffolks, it is likely that Martin O'Meara was rescuing men from the area of No Man's Land between Brind's Road and the Park Lane trenches, as far west as the Pozieres-Thiepval Road, and assisting them move south, probably along K Trench towards the Chalk Pits area were medical facilities were located.

The 15th Battalion was forced, in part due to the failure of the Suffolks, to retire to its original positions at Brind's Road on the morning of 9 August 1916. Commonwealth War Grave Commission records indicate that 81 15th Battalion officers and men were killed on 8-9 August, with 65 missing with no known grave. The Suffolks suffered 56 killed and missing during the same period. This number would have certainly been higher had it not been for Martin O'Meara. Second Lieutenant Frank Wadge, a platoon commander with A Company, noted:

I saw O'Meara on a number of occasions attending to or bringing in wounded men from the area over which the Battn had advanced and from No Man's Land. I estimate that a number of men rescued by him is not less than 20. At times when he was carrying out this work of mercy the H.E. Shrapnel and Machine Gun fire was intense beyond description. I cannot state who these men were – they were mostly members of the 15th Battn A.I.F. and the Suffolk Battn.[187]

On morning of 9 August 1916, the 4th Division headquarters issued orders for another attack on the Park Lane trenches, this time directly involving the 16th Battalion. During the course of the day the

---

[185] Chataway, 1948, p.127.

[186] Second Lieutenant Neville Fogarty was an accountant from Dalby in Queensland. He was wounded in action on 8 August 1916 with a gunshot wound to his left hand, and later evacuated to England.

[187] AWM28: 2/101, Recommendation file for honours and awards, AIF, 1914-18 War 4th Australian Infantry Brigade 1916.

16th Battalion's officers and senior NCOs were involved in reconnaissance of the trenches that were to be attacked and occupied that night. As a scout and a man with knowledge of the area, it is very likely that Martin O'Meara assisted in this reconnaissance work.

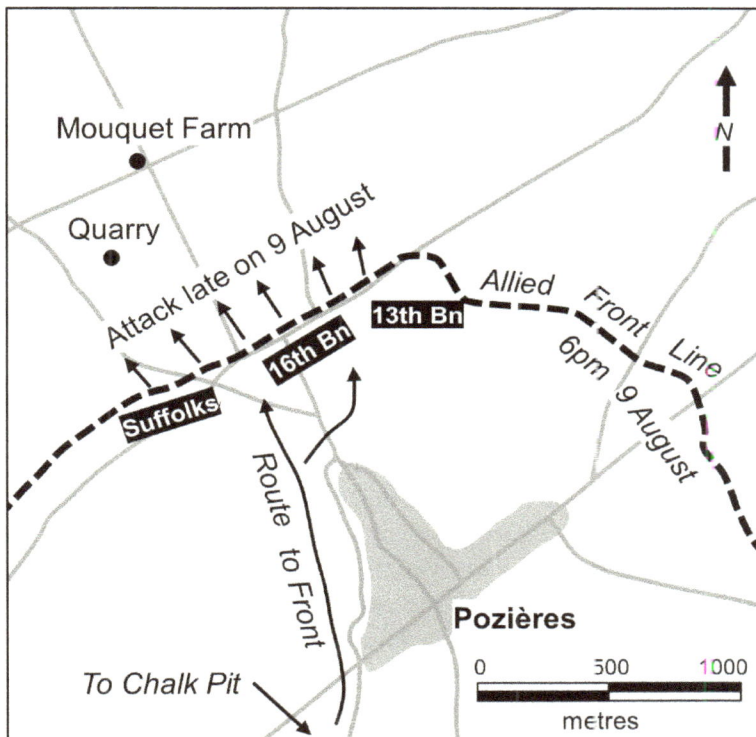

The Pozieres/Mouquet Farm area showing approximate Allied lines as at 6pm on 9 August. That evening the 16th Battalion attacked the same area that had been attacked by the 15th Battalion the previous evening. O'Meara was active in No-Man's Land to the north of the 16th Battalion positions.

At 8.30am D Company moved to the front line near Brind's Road, but by 10.00am had returned from supporting the 15th Battalion as it was no longer required. It then joined the other companies (less A Company, which was still in the front line with the 15th Battalion) located in Wire Trench near La Boisselle. These companies remained at Wire Trench during the day, and at 7.00pm they moved from Wire Trench up to the front line to relieve parts of the 15th Battalion who closed to their right (north) flank, and part of the Suffolks who closed to their left (south flank).

The 16th Battalion frontage was now along the Brind's Road trench system, from where the 15th Battalion had launched the previous night's attack. At this time the 16th Battalion's headquarters was located just over a kilometre to the south, just south of the ruins of Pozières, close to the point where Dead Man's Road (leading to the Chalk Pits) meets the Centre Way trench system.

Around midnight on 9 August 1916, following a five-minute artillery barrage, the 16th Battalion launched an attack on the same trench systems that the 15th Battalion had attacked the previous night.

Dr Charles Bean noted that the battalion's scouts played an important role in this attack, 'even directing the flanks of the several companies by placing in No-Man's Land electric torches shaded from the enemy by being embedded in scooped-out earth, with a different light for each company.'[188] Martin O'Meara was probably involved in these activities, which meant that he was in No Man's Land again.

Several hours later, at 2.50am on 10 August, the 16th Battalion reported to the 4th Brigade headquarters that an objective known as Circular Trench had been captured, and that twenty-two German prisoners were already in custody at the battalion's headquarters with a further fifty prisoners also taken.[189] At 3.50am the battalion reported that the operation had been successful and that they had captured fifty enemy prisoners, three machine guns and a gas plant (probably gas cylinders or dispensers) and fire plant (probably a flame-thrower). The battalion headquarters also asked the 4th Brigade headquarters for 10,000 sandbags to assist with consolidating their positions, as well as 500 tins of water and 200 shovels.[190]

Despite the success of the operation, the 16th Battalion sustained many casualties. Major Percy Black[191], the B Company commander, later noted that:

---

[188] Bean, 1941a, p.741.
[189] AWM4: 23/33/9, 16th Battalion War Diary, August 1916.
[190] AWM4: 23/33/9, 16th Battalion War Diary, August 1916.
[191] Percy Black was awarded the Distinguished Service Order and French Croix de Guerre for service at Pozières and Mouquet Farm, and was killed in action at Bullecourt on 11 April 1917.

During the advance of the Bn on the night of 9-10th a number of men were wounded and left lying on the ground [north of Brind's Road] over which the advance had been made …[192]

At noon on 10 August, the battalion headquarters reported that it had taken over a portion of the western end of the Ration Trench/5th Avenue/Park Lane system as far as the Pozières-Thiepval Road) from the Suffolks. At around 5.00pm on 10 August the Germans started shelling the 16th Battalion's new forward positions along Park Lane, in preparation for a counter-attack. The battalion asked for four Vickers machine guns and crews to assist with its defences, and these were provided by the 4th Machine Gun Company.

At 5.00pm a conference of the 16th Battalion's company commanders was held to discuss coming overnight activities, which involved another attack to take further ground and to consolidate earlier gains. This next attack by the 16th Battalion was launched at 1.00am on 11 August, and at 2.50am it reported that it had made good several objectives and that the men were constructing several communications trenches.

At 4.50am the battalion reported that it had established new strong points at the front line. The enemy subsequently placed a heavy artillery barrage in the rear of the ground just captured, and the maintenance of the communication trenches between the front line and battalion headquarters to the rear became difficult. A message from the battalion to the 4th Brigade headquarters later advised that enemy shelling had been constant from 1.30am but was abating.[193] After sunrise on 11 August the left flank trenches which were occupied by D Company were subject to heavy German shelling. Martin O'Meara remained active as a scout in No Man's Land, in front of the battalion's forward positions during this time, as later noted by Major Percy Black who commanded B Company:

On the morning of the 11th Aug O'Meara was on scouting duty in No Man's Land. At this time some three machine guns were firing over the section of ground which he was examining and

[192] AWM28: 2/101, Recommendation file for honours and awards, AIF, 1914-18 War 4th Australian Infantry Brigade 1916.
[193] AWM4: 23/33/9, 16th Battalion War Diary, August 1916.

it was also being very heavily shelled by H.E. shells. About ten minutes after I saw him go over the parapet into No Man's Land I saw him return carrying a wounded man whom he had found lying in a shell hole in No Man's Land. Having dressed the wounds of this man he returned to No Man's Land in pursuance of his duties as a scout.[194]

At 1.00pm on 11 August the 16th Battalion garrison was withdrawn from parts of the trenches in the vicinity of Park Lane but the area was constantly patrolled during daylight, probably by the battalion scouts. Preparations were made for a quick re-occupation of this area in case of a German counter-attack. Shortly afterwards, at 1.40pm, reports were being received from the front line that German soldiers were emerging from Mouquet Farm in small groups and fanning out around the farmhouse. Immediate orders were given for the reoccupation of the trench and Lewis gunners were sent to assist.

At about 2.45pm a counter-attack was staged by those German soldiers and was met with heavy rifle fire from the Australians. The Lewis gunners brought machine gun fire on the Germans and it was particularly devastating. Eighteen-pound field guns also assisted in repelling the attack. The battalion subsequently reported that the enemy suffered heavy casualties, and at 3.05pm the enemy troops were completely demoralised and had scattered. About ten Germans surrendered and were taken prisoner, and about thirty more were seen going towards the 13th Battalion lines on the right (northern) flank.

A number of enemy soldiers took refuge in the dugouts near the quarry to the south of Mouquet Farm in No Man's Land, and artillery shelling of the quarry was requested and this resulted in the Germans running 'from place to place to find shelter'. The 16th Battalion asked that artillery continue intermittently shelling No Man's Land overnight in front of the battalion's positions to dissuade the Germans from launching further attacks. After dark on 11 August the 16th Battalion, together with one company from the 13th Battalion, was engaged in completing communications trenches between the newly-taken locations and the rear positions.

---

[194] AWM28: 2/101, Recommendation file for honours and awards, AIF, 1914-18 War 4th Australian Infantry Brigade 1916.

The Mouquet Farm quarry was located in this group of trees. Martin O'Meara rescued men from the area of No-Man's Land to the right of these trees. (Author)

At 7.45pm the battalion's commanding officer, Lieutenant-Colonel Edmund Drake-Brockman, reported to 4th Brigade headquarters that the 16th Battalion positions on the left flank were again being subjected to heavy German shelling and that the battalion's casualties were heavy. Counter-battery shelling was requested to stop the German shelling. The heavy enemy shelling threatened to cut off supply routes between the front line and the rear positions to the south and the men at the front were running short of supplies. Lieutenant Bill Lynas, commanding the battalion scouts, later noted that Martin O'Meara made two trips to the ammunition dumps at the rear to bring vital supplies to the front:

> During Friday [11 August] night's operations I required more ammunition and bombs on the left section. most of the reserve stocks having been buried owing to there being no communications saps, and the perfect hail of shells that were blowing the parapets to pieces. I would not detail anyone for this job. O'Meara went of his own initiative to the Bn Dump twice, returning with S.A.A. [ammunition for rifles] and bombs [grenades]; on his second return he managed to guide a fatigue party across and relieved us of our shortage. During these trips he located wounded men and carried three of them back to the

Dressing Station. This man has been responsible for the evacuation of at least 20 men under conditions that are indescribable.[195]

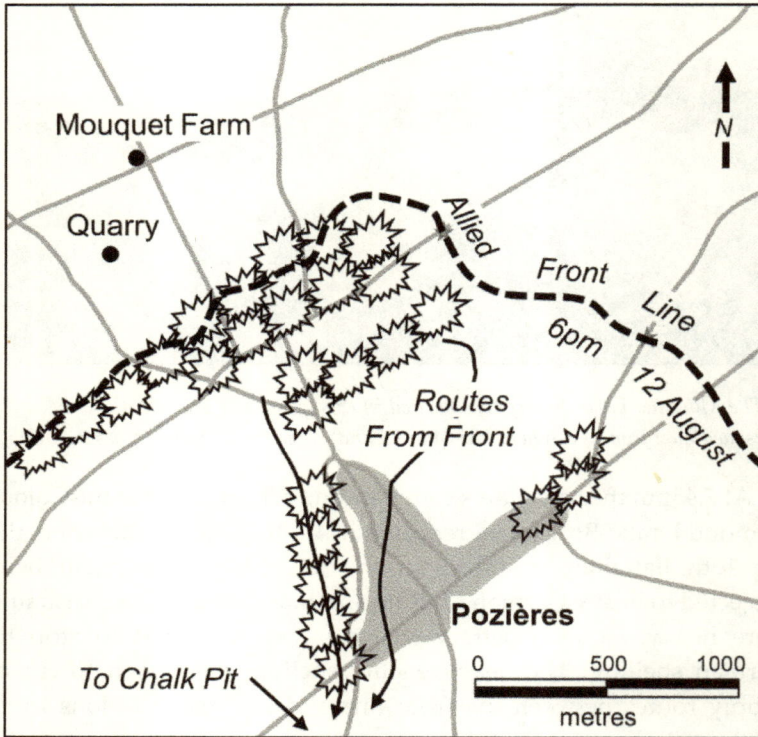

The Pozieres/Mouquet Farm area showing approximate Allied lines as at 6pm on 12 August, after the 16th Battalion had withdrawn and been replaced by the 50th Battalion. It shows the areas that were subject to heavy German artillery bombardment on 11-12 August. O'Meara carried supplies and wounded men through these areas during this period.

Lieutenant Robert Somerville, a platoon commander with D Company, also attested to Martin O'Meara's actions during this period:

On the night of 11-12th Inst. that section of the front line occpied by "D" Coy was intensively shelled. All

---

[195] AWM28: 2/101, Recommendation file for honours and awards, AIF, 1914-18 War 4th Australian Infantry Brigade 1916.

communication trenches were blown in as well as a considerable portion of the Front system of trenches. It was discovered that the supply of S.A.A. was very short and that all bombs and flares for signalling purposes had been buried; and Infantry assault was expected to succeed the barrage. O'Meara volunteered to go down to the Regimental Dump and precure bombs and flares. He made this trip twice and on both ocassions staggered back under a heavy load of the munitions required.[196]

At 8.45am on 12 August the battalion reported to the 4th Brigade headquarters that its bombers had advanced along the remains of trenches in the area between Park Lane and Mouquet Farm. These trenches had been virtually obliterated as a result of heavy German shelling the previous night. At 9.00am the battalion headquarters received a report from the left flank that Ration Trench (also known as 5th Avenue) was unoccupied for a distance of around 200 metres and had apparently been abandoned by British troops the previous evening because of the heavy enemy shelling.

The 16th Battalion received orders at 9.27am on 12 August for its relief by the 50th Battalion (which was part of the 13th Brigade) during the course of that afternoon. The battalion was to withdraw to the south via Centre Way, the Chalk Pits and then on to the Brickfields area near Albert.

The Commanding Officer of the 50th Battalion, Lieutenant-Colonel Frederick Hurcombe, arrived at the front line ahead of the rest of his troops at 11.30am, and arrangements were made for the relief. The first men from the 50th Battalion (A Company) arrived at around 1.30pm, but heavy German shelling of the 16th Battalion's positions (particularly K Trench, 1st Avenue and Centre Way leading down to the Chalk Pits area south of Pozières) slowed the relief, which was eventually completed by 4.00pm. The 50th Battalion's war diary entry for 12 August recorded that 'Enemy heavily bombarded trench leading up, and extra heavy barrage immediately on arrival in front

---

[196] AWM28: 2/101, Recommendation file for honours and awards. AIF, 1914-18 War 4th Australian Infantry Brigade 1916.

line ... Casualties fairly heavy, and work of removing same to Dressing Station very difficult ... '[197]

An unidentified soldier surveys the shell shattered battlefield in front of the village of Pozières, seen from the Centre Way trench. The 16th Battalion withdrew through this type of environment on 12 August 1916. The photograph was taken in late August 1916. (AWM EZ0099)

Sergeant Percy Nuttall of the 50th Battalion was part of this relief and made the following notes, which further illustrate the severity of the German artillery barrage, in his diary on 12 August:

We marched off at 6am for Pozières to await final instructions. Poor old Pozières completed razed. Dead bodies smelling awful. Went into firing line, after a march of 4 miles through trenches razed to the ground. Fritz spotted us, turned his artillery on us and cut our battalion up, we lost a big crowd, reaching our line. Dead bodies all the way up ... On reaching the line we were told to advance over one of Fritz's trenches and make another trench 250 yards ahead ... The day passed quickly, their artillery never ceased. Dead, dying and wrecked were lying all over the place. Fritz never counter attacked on

---

[197] AWM4: 23/67/2, 50th Battalion War Diary, August 1916.

our front. But he got in a bit to the right but did not stay long before he was dug out.[198]

Major Percy Black of B Company commented favourably on Martin O'Meara's work in rescuing men wounded by the German artillery barrage that day:

> My notice was again drawn to this man on the morning of the 12th when the section of trench was occupied by my Coy was being Heavily bombarded by H.E. [high explosive] and Shrapnel. I withdrew the garrison to either flank from one portion that was in the process of being completely obliterated which subsequently happened; one man failed to get out in time and was buried. O'Meara despite the overwhelming fire at once rushed to the spot extricated the man concerned and therefore undoubtedly saved his life [and] and subsequently on the 11-12th runners and carriers who had occasion to cross this area were wounded there. I saw O'Meara on many occasions on the 10-11-12th Aug: searching the ground for wounded to whom he rendered first aid and whom he subsequently brought in or assisted to bring in.[199]

Dr Charles Bean later speculated that the appearance of the 50th Battalion's men in the area between the Pozières cemetery and the Australian lines may have been noticed by German observers, and that this triggered the heavy artillery bombardment. Bean also noted that the incoming men of the 50th Battalion passed the outgoing men of the 16th Battalion in Park Lane trench and that the '16th gradually dribbled out, their officers telling them where to go, and the men finding their own way.'[200] Martin O'Meara was one man who did not withdraw. Captain Albert McLeod, commanding the 16th Battalion's C Company, noted that Martin O'Meara continued his brave actions later into the afternoon of 12 August:

---

[198] <http://www.australiansatwar.gov.au/stories/stories_war=W1_id=181.html> [Accessed 12 December 2015].

[199] AWM28: 2/101, Recommendation file for honours and awards, AIF, 1914-18 War 4th Australian Infantry Brigade 1916.

[200] Bean, 1941a, p.752.

Late in the afternoon of the 12th inst after my Coy had been relieved in the front firing line I noticed Lieut [Arthur Ronald 'Ron'] Carse of the 4th Machine gun Coy lying wounded in a sap which was at that time cut off from the rear by a heavy barrage. In order to go to the assistance of this Officer Pte O'Meara with great gallantry and utmost fearlessness went through the barrage and subsequently assisted to bring him down to the Regimental Aid Post.[201]

Ron Carse had served with the 16th Battalion machine gunners at Gallipoli and had transferred to the 4th Machine Gun Company in Egypt in early March 1916.[202] He had suffered a severe (and very painful) shell wound to his right leg below the knee. A later medical assessment recorded that:

he was struck on front of right shin by fragment of shell. The wound here is 5 inches by 3 inches with loss of tissue and exposure of bone. At this point tibia is fractured with great splintering and displacement of splinters.[203]

Lieutenant-Colonel Drake-Brockman also encountered Martin O'Meara late on 12 August:

On the evening of the 12th inst after my Battn had been relieved I met O'Meara near Chalk Pits going in the direction of POZIERES. He had previously been sent down as a guide to "D" Coy. When I asked him where he was going he informed me that he had just heard of 2 wounded men of the Bn who had not been brought in from No Man's Land. He was subsequently seen by Lieut [Hugh] Cook in the front trenches. The following day the attached note was received from him by my Scout Officer. During the latter stages of the relief of the Battn a very heavy German Artillery barrage was put down over the Communication trenches south of Pozieres. In order to carry

---

[201] AWM28: 2/101, Recommendation file for honours and awards, AIF, 1914-18 War 4th Australian Infantry Brigade 1916.

[202] He had probably known O'Meara when they had served together with the 4th Machine Gun Company in Egypt.

[203] NAA: B2455, Carse A Ronald M.

out his mission of mercy this man voluntarily returned through the barrage referred to after having reached a position of comparative safety.[204]

The 'attached note' that Lieutenant-Colonel Drake-Brockman refers to in his report was worded:

Lieutenant Lynas Scoutmaster

Dear Sir, - I am slightly wounded. All the wounded of the 16th Battalion are now in except two. I will get them in to-night. – Yours truly, M. O'MEARA[205]

The Pozières Chalk Pits looking towards Pozières, taken in late August 1916.
(AWM EZ0112)

It appears that Martin O'Meara sustained shrapnel wounds to his abdomen whilst moving through the heavy German barrage of the afternoon of 12 August, but that he remained on duty and reported to a dressing station later that day.[206] Martin O'Meara was to later recall:

---

[204] AWM28: 2/101, Recommendation file for honours and awards, AIF, 1914-18 War 4th Australian Infantry Brigade 1916.

[205] *Zeehan and Dundas Herald*, 2 November 1916, p.4.

[206] *West Australian*, 8 November 1918, p.7.

That was my first experience of war, and it was pretty hot, too, I can tell you. We were carrying up ammunition under heavy shell fire – a sort of fatigue party – and of course a lot of fellows were wounded. I went out to do what I could do for the poor chaps that were lying all around waiting for the stretcher bearers and helped a lot of them to get in out of danger. I went down to the cookers and got some hot tea and went out again with a stretcher and brought in more.[207]

The battalion's scouting and intelligence officer, Lieutenant Bill Lynas, reported that:

I respectfully beg to draw your attention to the conduct of Pte O'Meara during the recent operations of this Bttn. Pte O'Meara is the most fearless and gallant soldier I have ever seen; besides during the arduous duties imposed on him by reason of his being in the Scouting Section efficiently and cheerfully this man used to fill in his time bringing in wounded under all conditions. Pte O'Meara is always cheerful and optimistic will volunteer for any job and can be trusted to carry any duty through with the utmost certainty.[208]

After withdrawing from the line near Pozières, the 16th Battalion's men spent the night of 12 August at the Brickfields area near Albert and at 2.30pm on 13 August they started to withdraw from the Brickfields area and moved back to the Warloy area. A fellow 16th Battalion sleeper hewer from Collie, Private William Elverd, later wrote that the men of the battalion were 'a pitiful sight when relieved and marched to the back areas.'[209]

A number of men from Lieutenant Lynas' scouting section were recognised for their bravery at Pozières and Mouquet Farm during this period. Privates Phillip Williams and Henry Arundel were awarded the Military Medal for bravery:

These two men are members of the Scouting Section of the Battaion. They accompanied the Scout Officer (Lieut. Lynas)

---

[207] *West Australian*, 8 November 1918, p.7.

[208] AWM28: 2/101, Recommendation file for honours and awards, AIF, 1914-18 War 4th Australian Infantry Brigade 1916.

[209] AMWA: PD909 Elverd WA.

into "No Man's Land" and under his direction placed the guiding lights referred to in my report concerning [Lynas]. Working together and separately they frequently made incursions into No Man's Land, and supplied me with useful and accurate nformation concerning the enemy's disposition, and on the afternoon of the 11th August through their reconnaisance were able to give me forewarning of the counter attack which subsequently developed.[210]

Privates Frederick Drew, James Stewart, Lawrence White, Harold Gottlieb, and Harold Schmidt were all recommended for the Military Medal for reconnaissance in front of the battalion's advanced positions and as runners carrying messages under fire, but were later mentioned in dispatches rather than awarded the Military Medal.[211] On 21 August Private Harold Gottlieb wrote to some friends in South Australia advising them:

We have just come out of the trenches for a spell. To describe it in a few words, it was a living hell. We had a superhuman task in rebuilding trenches for them only to be smashed again by the enemy's artillery, and we lived in everlasting din with the boom and the roar of our own and the enemy's guns. Our battalion charged and gained a good bit of the German trenches. We did well and General Birdwood complimented us on our work. The lads were game, every one of them. The enemy gave us an awful shelling, but we held our ground. I was transferred into headquarters scouts before we went in, and had the luck to be congratulated by the general of our division for the work I did in scouting and dispatch running. I was given a card of recommendation by him, and our officer stated that I would be mentioned in dispatches.[212]

Lieutenant Bill Lynas himself was awarded Military Cross for his actions, and his recommendation (in part) reads:

---

[210] AWM28: 1/180 Part1, Recommendation file for honours and awards, AIF, 1914-18 War 4th Australian Division, 7.8.1916 to 15.8.1916.

[211] AWM28: 1/180 Part1, Recommendation file for honours and awards, AIF, 1914-18 War 4th Australian Division, 7.8.1916 to 15.8.1916.

[212] *Advertiser*, 18 October 1916, p.8.

This Officer is the Intelligence Officer of the Battalion. It is impossible to overestimate the value of the work done by him during the operation on the 9/12th August, accompanied by some of the Scouts he proceeded into "No Man's Land", and personally reconnoitred the whole of the area (about 1000 yards frontage) over which the Battalion subsequently advanced … He and his scouts were instrumental in securing on this occasion some 30 unwounded prisoners of war …[213]

Dr Charles Bean later wrote:

The 16th Battalion suffered heavily. The carriage of water, supplies, and the wounded was sustained largely by the example of one man, Private Martin O'Meara, who four times went through the barrage with supplies, on one occasion taking with him a party, and who thereafter continued to bring out the wounded until all those of his battalion had been cleared.[214]

During the period in action in and around Pozières and Mouquet Farm between 8-12 August, the 16th Battalion sustained heavy casualties: 39 were killed in action, 348 were wounded and 19 were reported missing.[215] The battalion's scouts suffered a number of casualties during this period. In addition to Martin O'Meara, several other men were wounded. Private Bertie Nock was shot and severely wounded in action on 9 August and died of his wounds on 11 August.

A number of men also suffered shell shock. Sergeant George Hough suffered shell shock on 10 August and was treated for a short period at a rest station. Private Leslie Wallis suffered shell shock on 11 August and was also treated at a rest station. Private Frederick Taft suffered shell shock on 11 August and was bad enough to require

---

[213] AWM28: 1/180 Part1, Recommendation file for honours and awards, AIF, 1914-18 War 4th Australian Division, 7.8.1916 to 15.8.1916 (Bill Lynas was awarded a bar to his Military Cross for bravery during the 16th Battalion's assault in Mouqet Farm in late August 1916, and second bar to his Military Cross for actions in a raid near Hamel in June 1918).

[214] Bean, 1941a, p.750. Bean had earlier described O'Meara as a 'very good living fine type of man' in his notebook. See AWM38: 3DRL 606/140/1,Bean papers – Notebook, August 1916.

[215] Longmore, 1929, p.116.

hospitalisation, and was evacuated to England on 14 August, and then back to Australia in 1917 where he was subsequently medically discharged from the AIF.

On 13 August 1916, after the battalion had withdrawn from the front line, Martin O'Meara was admitted to the British 18th Field Ambulance suffering shrapnel wounds to his abdomen. The 18th Field Ambulance was based at Acheux (west of Pozières) at this time but operated Advance Dressing Stations near Mesnil and Hamel.[216] He was subsequently evacuated to the British 3rd Casualty Clearing Station which was located near Puchevillers (some 23 kilometres west of Pozières). On 16 August, he was admitted to the 11th Stationary Hospital at Rouen on the French coast. On 18 August Martin O'Meara embarked on the hospital ship *St Andrew* at Rouen for England, and the next day he was admitted to the 3rd London General Hospital at Wandsworth, a district along the River Thames around eight kilometres south-west of central London.

Martin O'Meara underwent surgery after arriving at Wandsworth, and it was later reported that a piece of shrapnel remained in his abdomen following this surgery as the doctors decided against removing it. O'Meara was later reported as stating 'I have always been troubled with indigestion, but it comforts me in my old age to find I can keep a piece of shell in my stummick [sic] and not feel it'.[217] On 30 September he was reported as being in Ward 65 at Wandsworth 'where he is slightly wounded'.[218]

The 16th Battalion was in action again at Pozières and Mouquet Farm in late August 1916, and suffered more casualties with a further 30 killed, 150 wounded and 51 missing. Lance-Corporal Marshall Way was amongst those reported as missing, and was later confirmed as having been killed in action on 31 August. Mouquet Farm was eventually taken by Allied forces in early September.

The campaign to take Pozières and Mouquet Farm during July and August 1916 had cost the Australians some 23,000 casualties. Dr

[216] TNA: WO 95/1603/1, 18th Field Ambulance War Diary, August 1914 – September 1919.
[217] *Border Watch*, 25 November 1916, p.3.
[218] *Nenagh Guardian*, 30 September 1916, p.5.

Charles Bean later wrote that the ridge just north of Pozieres, where an old windmill was located pre-war was 'more densely sown with Australian sacrifice than any other place on earth.'[219]

[219] Bean, 2014, p.264.

8   A Victoria Cross

Lieutenant-Colonel Drake-Brockman, in a report dated 16 August 1916, recommended Martin O'Meara for the award of the Victoria Cross, Britain's highest award for valour. Drake-Brockman's recommendation was supported by statements from other 16th Battalion officers Lieutenant Bill Lynas, Second Lieutenant Frank Wadge, Captain Albert McLeod, Major Percy Black, and Captain Ross Harwood. [220]

The Victoria Cross had been established by Queen Victoria in 1856 to recognise specific acts of bravery in the face of the enemy during the Crimean campaign. A handful of Victoria Crosses had previously been awarded to Australians during the First World War, but only one previously to a West Australian: to Lieutenant Hugo Throssell of the 10th Light Horse Regiment for actions at Gallipoli during 1915.

On 8 September, whilst he was recovering in hospital at Wandsworth in London, the announcement was made that Martin O'Meara had been awarded the Victoria Cross for his actions at Pozières and Mouquet Farm the previous month. The announcement was made in the official *London Gazette*:

HIS MAJESTY THE King has been graciously pleased to award the Victoria Cross to the undermentioned soldier:-

No. 3970 Private MARTIN O'MEARA

For most conspicuous bravery. During four days of very heavy fighting he repeatedly went out and brought in wounded officers and men from "No Man's Land" under intense artillery and machine gun fire. He also volunteered and carried up ammunition and bombs through a heavy barrage to a portion of the trenches, which was being shelled at this time. He

---

[220] Albert McLeod noted in his diary on 16 August 1916 that 'O'Meara for V.C.' (see AWM: 1DRL/0455, Albert McLeod).

showed throughout an utter contempt of danger, and undoubtedly saved many lives.[221]

Martin O'Meara being congratulated by other patients at Wandsworth following the announcement of his VC. The photograph appears to be staged for the camera, and was probably taken between 9-10 September 1916. (Noreen O'Meara & AWM P11930.001)

Four other Australian Victoria Crosses were announced at the same time: to Lieutenant Arthur Blackburn (of the 10th Battalion for action at Pozières), Private Bill Jackson (of the 17th Battalion for action near Armentières), Private John Leak (of the 9th Battalion for action at Pozières), and Private Thomas Cooke (of the 8th Battalion, posthumously, for action at Pozières).[222]

Martin O'Meara was probably quite fortunate in that he was one of the last infantrymen to be awarded the Victoria Cross during the First World War for predominately saving the lives of others. In late August 1916, the British command in France issued an order that Victoria Crosses would not be considered for cases of gallantry unless the act was materially conductive to a victory. This order was clarified by a further order in September 1916 which stated:

---

[221] *London Gazette*, Supplement No. 29740, 8 September 1916, p. 8871.
[222] The first was awarded to Second Lieutenant Hugo Throssell of the 10th Light Horse Regiment for actions at Gallipoli.

In future, the Victoria Cross or other immediate regard will not be given for the rescue of wounded, excepting for those whose duty it is to care for such cases, Such attempts, more often than not, result in the death of the would-be rescuer and rescued. Moreover, it depletes the fighting strength of units perhaps at most critical moments.[223]

News of Martin O'Meara's Victoria Cross spread quickly in his native country of Ireland and his adopted country of Australia. The first press coverage in Western Australia was on 9 September 1916 when an article appeared in the *Daily News*,[224] and within a few days the story had been covered by Australian metropolitan and regional newspapers. O'Meara was suddenly transformed from an average Australian soldier to international hero.

The first mention in the Irish press seems to be on 11 September when several Irish newspapers published the list of Victoria Cross recipients; this included the *Irish Independent* that naturally identified Martin O'Meara as being of Irish birth.[225] The lag in reporting by the Irish press is probably explained by the weekend (the Victoria Crosses had been announced on a Friday) and by O'Meara being identified as an Australian soldier rather than being of Irish birth. It is most likely that his sister Alice O'Meara, as his nominated next of kin, would have been advised by telegraph on or very shortly after 9 September. In an interview reported in one of these regional papers, the *Warrnambool Standard*, O'Meara is reported to have said:

> Shoulder to shoulder, without water, so splendid and cheery, and always ready to do anything to help each other, who could do otherwise than help them? I am lucky, while others have gone unrewarded, because either their deeds were not seen, or their officers had fallen before they could make a recommendation.[226]

---

[223] Butler, 1943, p.1045.
[224] *Daily News*, 9 September 1916, p.12
[225] *Irish Independent*, 11 September 1916, p.2.
[226] *Warrnambool Standard*, 14 September 1916, p.3.

This interview occurred sometime between 8 September when Martin O'Meara's Victoria Cross was announced and 14 September when the article was published.

Martin O'Meara's Victoria Cross was formally recognised by a number of people and groups in the days and weeks following the announcement. On 14 September 1916 the North Tipperary County Committee on Agriculture held its regular monthly meeting, and passed a motion of congratulation which was moved by James Willington, a Rathcabbin (near Lorrha) landowner:

> That we, the members of the County Committee on Agriculture, wish to express to Martin O'Meara V.C., our great admiration of his bravery and to congratulate him on gaining the V.C., the highest honour that can be offered to any soldier. We, as Tipperarymen, are proud of him, and hope soon to give him a suitable welcome, and show the appreciation he has won. We hope that he will be recovered enough to return to his native county.[227]

The battalion's Routine Order No. 295 of 17 September noted that the Commander of the 4th Division, Major-General Sir Herbert Cox, had cabled the AIF Headquarters in London congratulating O'Meara on the award of the Victoria Cross and querying his condition. The response from the AIF Headquarters noted that 'Private O'MEARA, V.C., now quite convalescent. Congratulations will be conveyed to him.'[228]

On 13 September a poorly-attended public meeting was held in Collie to discuss the matter of returned servicemen and, and Martin O'Meara was mentioned at the meeting's conclusion with the Acting Mayor promising to send him a congratulatory telegram on behalf of the people of Collie.[229] On 15 September the district board of the Hibernian Australasian Catholic Benefit Society in Perth passed a resolution:

---

[227] *Nenagh Guardian*, 16 September 1916, p.2.
[228] AWM25: 707/9 Part 242, 16th Battalion Routine Orders.
[229] *Southern Times*, 16 September 1916, p.3.

That the district board of the H.A.C.B. Society heartily congratulates Bro. Martin O'Meara, of the St. Canice's branch, Cottesloe, on the much coveted honour conferred on him in being presented with the Victoria Cross.[230]

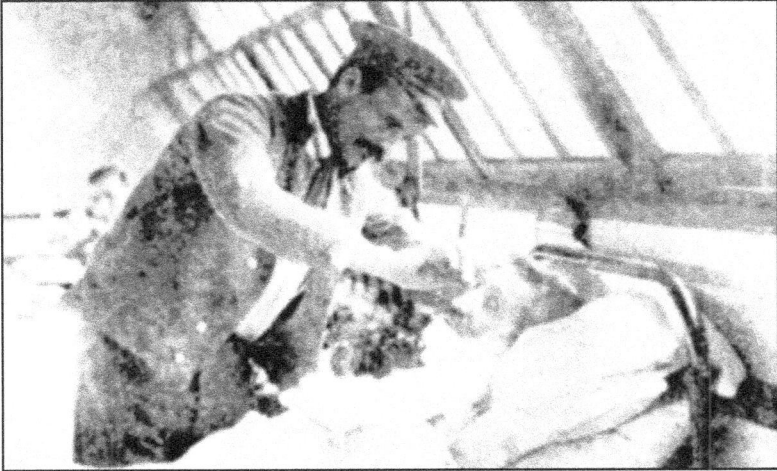

Martin O'Meara shaving other patients at Wandsworth between 9-11 September 1916. (Sunday Mirror, 19 November 1916, p.5s)

On 15 September the *Westralian Worker* published an article congratulating O'Meara and noting that:

Martin O'Meara, V.C., who is the second West Australian to get this great recognition, was a sleepercutter in the South-West, and her meritorious work has sent a thrill of pride from Jarrahdale to Karridale. We take off our collective hat to O'Meara, V.C.[231]

On 16 September the *Collie Mail*, reported from O'Meara's home town (and presumably with first-hand knowledge of him) that:

O'Meara is well-known among the timber workers he having been a sleeper cutter prior to his departure to the front … He is

[230] *West Australian*, 18 September 1916, p.8.
[231] *Westralian Worker*, 15 September 1916, p.4.

known as a man of sterling qualities although of a quiet and retiring disposition and is a staunch teetotaller ... The news of this honour being conferred upon one of our boys comes as a bright speck in an otherwise black week, for numerous relatives have received cables notifying them of death or injury ...[232]

Western Australia's weekly Roman Catholic newspaper, the *W.A. Record*, also praised O'Meara. On 16 September, the first edition published since his Victoria Cross was announced, it noted:

Already Lieutenant Hugo Throssell, a West Australian with plenty of Irish blood in his veins, brought the Victoria Cross to the Golden West, and now comes a real Celt from County Tipperary, where it fronts King's County, bringing the great honour to the land whence he went to fight.[233]

Emphasising the fact that Martin O'Meara was an Irishman, the *W.A. Record* went on to report that:

Private O'Meara's triumph comes to us not as a surprise. It is just what we should expect from a quiet, God-fearing Celt, who goes into the fray, not with bluster or brag, but with a determination to do his duty, and a confidence that the Hand or Providence directs him. Let us hope that his brave deeds will be an incentive to those other Irishmen of the Commonwealth [of Australia] who have undertaken to fight for our clean five-starred flag to study his virtues ...[234]

The Parliament of Western Australia also recognised his achievements when, on 26 September, the Legislative Assembly noted that 'this House desires to express its pleasure on learning that Private Martin O'Meara has been awarded the high distinction of the Victoria Cross.'[235] The motion was moved by the Premier, the Hon Frank Wilson MLA, and supported by the Australian Labor Party's Arthur Wilson MLA, representing the District of Collie, who noted:

---

[232] *Collie Mail*, 16 September 1916, p.2.
[233] *W.A. Record*, 16 September 1917, p.7.
[234] *W.A. Record*, 16 September 1916, p.10.
[235] Legislative Assembly of Western Australia, Hansard, 26 September 1916, pp.213-14.

I know Private O'Meara well, and I can say that a more manly and courageous fellow could not be found. Collie is peculiarly situated in having sent to the Front, in proportion to population, more than any other centre in the Commonwealth. Moreover the men of Collie who have gone to the Front are all good trades unionists. Private O'Meara was an excellent example of this.[236]

Writing to a friend in Perth whilst recovering in hospital in London (probably during September 1916), Martin O'Meara noted that he was looking forward to visiting Ireland. He also reflected on the fate of his friends from the sleeper hewers' camps and from the 16th Battalion:

I wonder where are the fine lads that used to share their last crust with me, when often we were confronted with thirst and hunger on the salt bush track in W.A.? They are gone, but we must all go the same road some day. They were all heroes of the first water. No men could be braver – none more honourable than the boys of the 16th Battalion.[237]

Martin O'Meara shakes hands with Lieutenant Albert Jacka VC at the 3rd London General Hospital, at Wandsworth, probably in late September 1916 when Lieutenant Jacka was presented with his Victoria Cross medal by King George V at Windsor Castle. (Daily Mail/Associated Newspapers)

---

[236] Legislative Assembly of Western Australia, Hansard, 26 September 1916, pp.213-14.
[237] *Freeman's Journal*, 18 January 1917, p.10. As with other contemporary reports of correspdponence from O'Meara, this account appears to have had its spelling and grammar corrected.

He was also photographed shaking hands with Lieutenant Albert Jacka VC of the 14th Battalion at Wandsworth, and later with Private Bill Jackson VC of the 17th Battalion at the ANZAC Club and Buffet in London in September 1916.[238] Jackson had lost his right arm as a result of a wound received earlier in 1916, and the photograph seems staged to hide his right side. The ANZAC Club and Buffet was originally located at 130 Horseferry Road (where the AIF Administrative Headquarters was located), but relocated to 94 Victoria Road during September 1916 and was reopened there on 20 September by Andrew Fisher, Australia's High Commissioner to the United Kingdom, and a former Australian Prime Minister. It was subsequently recorded that:

> There was a large attendance, including two V.C.'s – Private Jackson and Private O'Meara – who had a rapturous reception.[239]

Martin O'Meara (left) and Bill Jackson (right) at the ANZAC Club and Buffet. (Birmingham Gazette 22 September 1916, p.1)

---

[238] *Birmingham Gazette,* 22 September 1916, p.1.
[239] *Australasian,* 4 November 1916, p.48.

News of Martin O'Meara's Victoria Cross had spread quickly in Western Australian newspapers in the days following its announcement. The latest Victoria Cross announcements were also covered extensively in British newspapers on 11 September, and it is likely that newspaper reports of Martin O'Meara's Victoria Cross were read by his old acquaintance from Kilmacow in County Kilkenny, Mary Murphy. Mary had left Ireland in 1915 to work as a nurse at the Caterham Lunatic Asylum for Safe Lunatics and Imbeciles (later St Lawrence's Hospital) in Surrey, some 25 kilometres south of central London, on 30 November 1915.[240] The salary of a nurse, £22 per annum increasing by £1 each year, would probably have been attractive when compared with life in rural Ireland.

Mary Murphy whilst nursing at Caterham near London, probably taken in 1915 or 1916. (Margaret Clews)

It seems likely that Mary Murphy travelled to Wandsworth to visit O'Meara, probably in mid-September, after reading one of the newspaper reports. Her family later recalled an account from her that she had pushed Martin O'Meara in a wheelchair when she visited him in hospital during the war;[241] based on his periods of hospitalisation in England during the war it is most likely that this occurred at Wandsworth in September 1916.

---

[240] LMA: H23/SL/C/01/003, Caterham Hospitals Staff Records: Registers of Staff, and Roy Clews pers. comm., 4 March 2014.
[241] Margaret Clews pers. comm. 8 March 2014, and Roy Clews pers comm., 4 March 2014.

An article in the *Nenagh Guardian* on 30 September noted that Martin O'Meara was in Ward 65 at Wandsworth 'where he lies slightly wounded, but is expected back in his native place shortly.'[242] He had been discharged from the 3rd London General Hospital and posted, probably for administrative reasons, to the AIF Headquarters. On 20 October it was reported that Martin O'Meara (along with other Victoria Cross recipients Lieutenant Albert Jacka and Private Bill Jackson) had left hospital in London, and that O'Meara would be returning to the 16th Battalion. He was reported as saying 'I would sooner be back with the boys in the trenches than anywhere else.'[243]

Prior to returning to his battalion, however, Martin O'Meara visited his family in Ireland. On 16 September several Irish newspapers had reported that Martin O'Meara would be returning to Ireland after his treatment in hospital and that a presentation would be made to him.[244] Several days later, on 23 September, it was reported that Martin O'Meara was still in hospital in London, but that 'he will shortly visit his home'[245] and on 30 September it was again reported that an 'influential Committee' had been formed to organise a presentation to O'Meara when he returned to Tipperary.[246] On the evening of 26 September a concert was held at Oxmantown Hall in Birr to raise money for the planned presentation to be made to O'Meara. Featuring a military band and other musicians, the concert was reported as being a success, with the *King's County Chronicle* reporting that 'Oxmantown Hall was too small on Tuesday evening to contain the crowds of both civilians and military.'[247] A later newspaper report indicates that the concert raised £18 17s 5d.[248]

On 9 October Martin O'Meara was taken on the strength of the No. 1 Command Depot at Perham Downs near Andover, south-east of London in the county of Hampshire. O'Meara was one of many; records show that 170 Australians were taken on the strength of the No. 1 Command Depot from various hospitals on 9 October.[249]

---

[242] *Nenagh Guardian*, 30 September 1916, p.5.
[243] *Ballarat Courier*, 20 October 1916, p.3.
[244] *Irish Independent*, 16 September 1916, p.6, and *Nenagh News*, 16 September 1916, p.2
[245] *Nenagh Guardian*, 23 September 1916, p.3
[246] *Nenagh Guardian*, 30 September 1916, p.5
[247] *King's County Chronicle*, 28 September 1916, p.3
[248] *Midland Tribune*, 28 October 1916, p.5
[249] AWM4: 33/16/1, War Diary, No. 1 Australian Command Depot, October 1916

Martin O'Meara visited his homeland, as best as can be established, during the second half of October 1916, very soon after joining the No. 1 Command Depot. The trip home would have involved a railway journey from southeastern England to a Welsh port (Holyhead, Fishguard or Milford Haven), then a ferry crossing of the Irish Sea, and then several more rail journeys to Birr, the nearest railway station to Lorrha. A contemporary account of his visit noted that he arrived in the evening by train at nearby Birr and then walked to the family farm at Lissernane (around eight kilometres) along the course of the abandoned Birr to Portumna railway line. This account also records that he surprised his brother and sister when he arrived at Lissernane.[250] It was reported on 28 October that Martin O'Meara had 'arrived home quietly last week. He came without giving notice to any one, walked from the station along the disused railway to his home, and it was only when he made his personal appearance that the news spread like wild fire of his return.'[251] He was certainly in Ireland on 24 October, when he was reported as having attended a meeting that afternoon at the National School at Borrisokane near Lorrha. The meeting had been arranged to organise:

> a suitable presentation as a token of esteem and gratitude from the people of North Tipperary for the great honour he has conferred upon the historic county by winning the Victoria Cross on the western front.[252]

According to the *Nenagh News*, the meeting was chaired by Lord Dunalley,[253] with a John O'Meara (a 'near relative' of Martin O'Meara[254]) being appointed vice chairman. Two general secretaries were appointed: Mary Hickie of Oldcourt (the wife of Captain Manuel Hickie, and Lucila Hickie (Captain Manuel Hickie's sister). James Willington was appointed treasurer.[255] The rival *Nenagh Guardian*

[250] MacDonagh, 1917, pp.180-181.
[251] *Nenagh News*, 28 October 1916, p.3
[252] *Nenagh News*, 28 October 1916, p.3
[253] Henry O'Callaghan Prittie, 4th Baron Dunalley, Lord Lieutenant of County Tipperary.
[254] The *Midland Tribune* of 28 October 1916, p.5, notes that John O'Meara was Martin O'Meara's uncle.
[255] *Nenagh News*, 28 October 1916, p.3.

reported that Martin O'Meara 'was present and occupied a seat next to his relative, Mr John O'Meara, D.C, Curragha. Well knit and with a strong determined face he looked the man who would perform any act of bravery. He was the recipient of hearty congratulations from those present.'[256] The meeting did not resolve the time or place that the presentation would be made.

It is interesting to note that a similar ceremony had been arranged for Sergeant James Somers, another Victoria Cross winner from County Tipperary, in August 1915. That particular ceremony involved a similar group of dignitaries, including the same Lord Dunnalley and Captain Lefroy, the same band of the Royal Irish Regiment, and the presentation of a monetary subscription (in Somers' case, £240).[257] As we saw earlier, Sergeant Michael O'Leary of County Cork, Ireland's first Victoria Cross winner of the First World War, had previously been feted at Clonmel in County Tipperary in July 1915.[258]

The ceremony and presentation took place without Martin O'Meara who had left Lorrha by this time. A newspaper later reported that:

> At Lorrha, about twelve miles from Birr, the other evening, in the absence of Private Martin O'Meara, V.C., his sister, Miss O'Meara, was presented by General Hickie, commanding the Irish (18th) Division, with a gold watch. Mr. B.B. Trench, Laughton House [a local landowner], presided and apologised for the absence of Private O'Meara, V.C., who he said had volunteered for active service on his return from home after having been wounded, and it was only through the good offices of General Hickie that they were able to get into communication with him at all. A telegram was read from him from Waterford stating that he would be with them next day, but they were unable to postpone the presentation.[259]

---

[256] *Nenagh Guardian*, 28 October 1916, p.4.

[257] Dennehy, 2013, pp.58-59.

[258] Dennehy, 2013, pp.60-62. O'Leary had won his Vicoria Cross for actions near Cuinchy in northern France on 1 February 1915.

[259] *Freeman's Journal*, 1 February 1917, p.6.

We do not know exactly why Martin O'Meara did not attend the ceremony. It is possible that he did not want all the attention, or perhaps he was uncomfortable with being involved in what was, more or less, a recruitment rally for the British Army. He was a devout Roman Catholic and nationalist political views, even if he was not a Sinn Féin supporter. These factors in tandem suggest a tendency towards uneasiness about being publicly identified with the British Army. Previous Irish Victoria Cross winners had been regarded with contempt by some of the more radical nationalists; Michael O'Leary VC, of County Cork, had addressed several meetings in Ireland during 1915 and received a mixed reception:

> They brought Michael O'Leary, who had won the Victoria Cross, to one of their recruiting meetings but we gave them a bad reception by continuously booing, shouting and singing rebel songs.[260]

Other nationalist accounts of O'Leary noted that he 'was promoted Sergeant and, wearing his Victoria Cross, was made a willing actor in their propaganda campaign' and that 'He was licnized and feted wherever he went, or was led …'[261]

Alternatively, O'Meara's absence may have been due simply to practicalities, and that the timing of the presentation did not fit with his travel plans. He would have only had a limited period of leave, probably no more than two weeks. Martin O'Meara was not the only notable absence at the presentation; Chairman Benjamin Trench apologised for the absence of some invited guests, including Lord Dunalley and the Rev John Gleeson, the Lorrha Parish Priest.[262] Despite the absences, the event on 24 November was well attended. The *Kings County Chronicle* reported that:

> The little village of Lorrha in North Tipperary was en fete last Friday on the occasion of the presentation to Martin O'Meara, V.C., who hails from the district. By motor car, by brake, by side car, by cycle, and by foot came hundreds of people to testify their pride in the bravery displayed by the gallant North

---

[260] BMH: WS1017, Gordon Cassidy.
[261] BMH: WS1606, Patrick Hegarty, and BMH: WS1605, Rev Eugene Nevin.
[262] *Irish Independent*, 25 November 1916, p.2.

Tipperary man. A platform was erected in a ball alley by the side of a venerable old abbey. Gaily decorated poles with the Union Jack and the Shamrock added a bright appearance to the scene. Fortunately the weather was sunny and bright if a trifle windy.[263]

The ceremony started at 1.00pm. The list of attendees included a broad cross section of the notable personalities from King's County and County Tipperary, as well as Meara's brothers (presumably Thomas, Hugh and John), his sister Alice, and his cousin John O'Meara ('better known as Doctor', according to the *Kings County Chronicle*) who made a brief speech).[264] Another newspaper account noted that 'a very large gathering' saw Alice O'Meara presented with a 'valuable gold watch.' Speakers at the event, which was attended by a large crowd, included Major-General Hickie, Benjamin B. Trench who chaired the event), Captain H. Lefroy (the recruiting officer from the army barracks at Nenagh), and Martin's uncle Daniel O'Meara.[265] Benjamin Trench's speech was followed by speeches from Captain H. Lefroy and Daniel O'Meara.[266]

Back in England, on 3 November 1916, Martin O'Meara transferred from the No. 1 Command Depot to the 4th Training Battalion, also at Perham Downs, as part of a transition back to service with the 16th Battalion. A little over a week later Martin O'Meara penned a letter to the Mayor of Collie, Henry Doyle, written in response to a letter written to him by Doyle after his Victoria Cross was announced. O'Meara wrote:

Received yours on the 8th inst., for which I return my sincere thanks to you and all Collie people. I expect to return to France soon, but with God's grace I also will return to Collie some day. However, should death prevent my return, it is a consolation to know that I have the respect of you and the people of Collie - that Sou' West town which has done so much towards the freedom which we have enjoyed and hope to enjoy in our own

[263] *Kings County Chronicle*, 30 November 1916, p.1.
[264] *Kings County Chronicle*, 30 November 1916, p.1.
[265] *Nenagh Guardian*, 25 November 1916, p.2.
[266] *Nenagh Guardian*, 25 November 1916, p.2.

Australia. I will conclude by wishing you and the people of your town a very happy Xmas and may glorious Faith, Hope and Charity reign supreme in the coming New Year – Remaining yours, No. 3970, Pte. M. O'Meara.[267]

On 4 December 1916 Martin O'Meara left Folkestone on the *Princess Victoria* and sailed across the English Channel back to France. On 5 December he joined the 4th Australian Division Base Depot at Etaples where he remained until 20 December, when he started his journey back to the 16th Battalion.

---

[267] *West Australian*, 30 December 1916, p.7 and *Collie Mail*, 6 January 1917, p.2.

9   Back to the Front

Martin O'Meara rejoined the 16th Battalion on 22 December 1916, one of eleven battalion men to return that day.[268] At this time the 16th Battalion was located at Cardonnette, around eight kilometres north-east of Amiens, where it was reorganising and training having spent the first half of the month in the trenches in the Flers area north-east of Albert. The battalion remained at Cardonnette until the end of December.

On 24 December, the *Sunday Times* reported that Martin O'Meara had recently written to his friends, John and Anne Foley at West Coolup near Pinjarra, 'asking them to remember him to all his old friends, particularly those in Pinjarra. He states he is doing well, and expects to see them all again soon.'[269]

The 16th Battalion spent Christmas Day in billets at Cardonnette. Private James Cutmore of the 16th Battalion's B Company later wrote that 'We spent Christmas in billets. They are only old French farmhouses, but we manage to make them fairly comfortable.'[270] At 10.00am on 31 December a 4th Brigade church parade was held, after which Lieutenant-General Sir William Birdwood presented medals and ribbons to some of the 4th Brigade's officers and men, including presenting Martin O'Meara with his Victoria Cross ribbon.[271] A brigade sports carnival was the next day.

On 2 January 1917 the 16th Battalion marched from Cardonnette to Ribemont-sur-Ancre, some 15 kilometres to the east, and the following day Martin O'Meara was evacuated to the 4th Field Ambulance with a sprained ankle. This was presumably the result of the march. He was sent to the I ANZAC Corps Rest Station on 4 January where he remained for a short period. On 7 January the 16th Battalion marched from Ribemont-sur-Ancre to Mametz where it was

---

[268] AWM25: 707/9 Part 242, 16th Battalion Routine Orders.
[269] *Sunday Times*, 24 December 1916, p.9.
[270] *Petersburg Times*, 30 March 1917, p.3.
[271] AWM4: 23/4/15-16, 4th Brigade War Diaries, December 1916 and January 1917.

involved in fatigue work (such as building and maintaining drainage works, duckboards and buildings) until 23 January. On 13 January, a small piece appeared in the *W.A. Record* making reference to one of O'Meara's friends, Private Charles Martin.[272] The piece noted:

> He was a shipmate of the famous Martin O'Meara V.C., with whom he enjoys the closest friendship, and in letters to his parents frequently spoke in warm terms of praise for that great Irishman, not only for his deeds on the battlefield, but for his untiring energy in tending to the wants of sick and wounded comrades in hospital.[273]

In late January the battalion marched to Townsville Camp near Bernafay, about ten kilometres east of Albert, as the 4th Brigade's reserve battalion where it was involved in more fatigue work until 2 February. It then moved into forward positions with two of its companies in the front line and two of its companies further back.

Australian soldiers taking over snow-covered dugouts near Bernafay in January 1917. (AWM E00144)

---

[272] Private Charles Martin was with the 16th Battalion's 12th Reinforcements and had sailed with O'Meara from Fremantle on 22 December 1915.
[273] *W.A. Record*, 13 January 1917, p.11.

The battalion's war diary for this period notes that severe frosts made the ground hard and this made trench work difficult. Private James Cutmore, writing in late January, noted that 'This last week has been snowing heavily, and a sharp frost has set in these last few days, until the ground is quite hard. It is bitterly cold.'[274] Snow also made the work of patrolling more difficult, so the men donned white camouflage suits and were able to undertake nightly patrols well forward of their front line own positions. As a battalion scout, it is very likely that Martin O'Meara participated in these patrols.

About fifty of the battalion's men (from D Company) were detached on the night of 4 February to support a 13th Battalion operation on Stormy Trench near Gueudecourt to the east of the Albert-Bapaume Road which saw Captain Harry Murray (commanding the 13th Battalion's A Company, but formerly of the 16th Battalion) awarded the Victoria Cross. This group of 16th Battalion men sustained heavy casualties.[275]

The 16th Battalion withdrew from the front line on the night of 9 February and was relieved by the 47th Battalion. It then moved into billets near Mametz. The battalion remained near Mametz until 11 February when it moved to Albury Camp (in the Bazentin area) where it conducted fatigue duties.[276] Between 28 February and 16 March the battalion was working in the Bazentin area in repairing road, as well as conducting training of its specialist troops. On 16 March, an advance party from the 16th Battalion moved to Ribemont-sur-Ancre with the rest of the battalion following the next day. Private Bert Demasson, another 16th Battalion man wrote to his family in Western Australia on 19 March advising that:

> All of our Battalion are in a village now having a rest … we drill in the morning & mostly play football in the afternoons it is to get the men fit & well to be able to stand the strain when we have to start fighting again …[277]

Between 18 March and 21 March, the 16th Battalion was involved in training and, on 22 March, marched to Crucifix Camp near Fricourt.

---

[274] *Petersburg Times*, 30 March 1917, p.3.
[275] AWM4: 23/33/15, 16th Battalion War Diary, February 1917.
[276] AWM4: 23/33/15, 16th Battalion War Diary, February 1917.
[277] Christenson, 1988, p.141.

Private Bert Demasson wrote to his family, again, on 23 March advising them that:

> we shifted Camp yesterday & are now a bit nearer the business we expect to shift again in a day or two, but don't know whether we are going into the front line or not ...[278]

The 16th Battalion remained at Crucifix Camp until 25 March where further training was conducted.

In March 1917, the Germans had started withdrawing from their front-line positions and moving back to the Hindenburg Line, a heavily fortified line further to the east. They were pursued by Allied forces towards the Hindenburg Line where they had dug themselves in at a line of heavily fortified positions. On 25 March, the battalion marched to Bazentin-le-Petit, and then marched on to Biefvillers-lès-Bapaume (a small village two kilometres north-west of Bapaume) on 27 March. From 27 March to 31 March, the battalion was involved in digging through the ruins of the Town Hall at Bapaume that had been destroyed by an explosion; it had been booby-trapped by the retreating Germans. Battalion historian Cyril Longmore later noted that:

> The Germans were carrying out a systematic retirement. All churches were blown up to prevent the towers being used as observation points. Houses were destroyed so that they could not be used as billets. Farmhouses were burnt, fruit trees cut down and even the trees had been sawn off close to the ground and felled across the roads ...[279]

The battalion's men were looking for survivors and retrieving the bodies of those killed in the blast. In a letter to his family dated 28 March Private Bert Demasson advised, omitting any specific details relating to Bapaume that the censor would have deleted, that 'Have been using Pick & Shovel all day, & am tired. Can hear the big guns going & expect to be nearer to them in a few days.'[280]

---

[278] Christenson, 1988, p.143.

[279] Longmore, 1929, p.132.

[280] Christenson, 1988, p147. This was his last letter home. He was taken prisoner on 11 April 1917 and later died in a German prisoner of war camp.

On 31 March preparations were made for the planned move to Beugnâtre, a village around 3.5 kilometres north-east of Bapaume. On 1 April the 16th Battalion marched from Biefvillers-lès-Bapaume to Beugnâtre and relieved the 49th Battalion. The next day the battalion's A and C Companies moved up to the front to be able to support the 13th Brigade, but were not required. The weather during this period was not favourable, and battalion historian Cyril Longmore noted that it altered between sleet, snow and rain.[281] Despite the weather, the Australian scouts were still able to patrol No Man's Land. The 4th Brigade war diary noted that on 6 April:

For the last couple of nights our patrols have established superiority over hostile patrols in NO MANS LAND.[282]

On the evening of 7 April, the 16th Battalion moved into sunken roads to the north and east of Noreuil, only a few kilometres from the Hindenburg Line, with A Company moving into outpost lines to relieve other units in the railway cutting area just south of the Hindenburg Line. The Allied forces were pursuing the German forces towards the Hindenburg Line, and the next moves would be a series of attacks on the Hindenburg Line itself.

On 8 April, the 4th Division headquarters ordered that 'strong patrols suitably supported' would be sent out on 9 April to determine the strength of German forces on the Hindenburg Line.'[283] The 4th Brigade war diary later recorded that 'Strong patrols are being sent out by the 4th and 12th Aust. Infantry Brigades tonight to ascertain if the HINDENBURG Line is held.'[284]

These patrols set off from the forward positions held by 4th Division units; the 16th Battalion was located along the railway line to the southeast of Bullecourt at this time. At 9.00pm that night, a special patrol was mounted to reconnoitre the German lines. It consisted of Captain Albert Jacka VC of the 14th Battalion, and Lieutenants Frank Wadge and Henry Bradley of the 16th Battalion. The 16th Battalion's war diary records that:

---

[281] Longmore, 1929, p.133

[282] AWM4: 23/4/19, 4th Brigade War Diary, April 1917

[283] AWM4: 1/48/13 Part 2, General Staff, HQ 4th Australian Division War Diary, April 1917.

[284] AWM4: 23/4/19, 4th Brigade War Diary, April 1917.

They got as far as the enemy's wire and found that it was badly smashed in some places but in others it was still intact. They also reported that the garrison of the Hindenburg Line was very strong and that there were no signs of probable evacuation. They reported that there was considerable enemy movement in front of his own lines in the shape of strong patrols.[285]

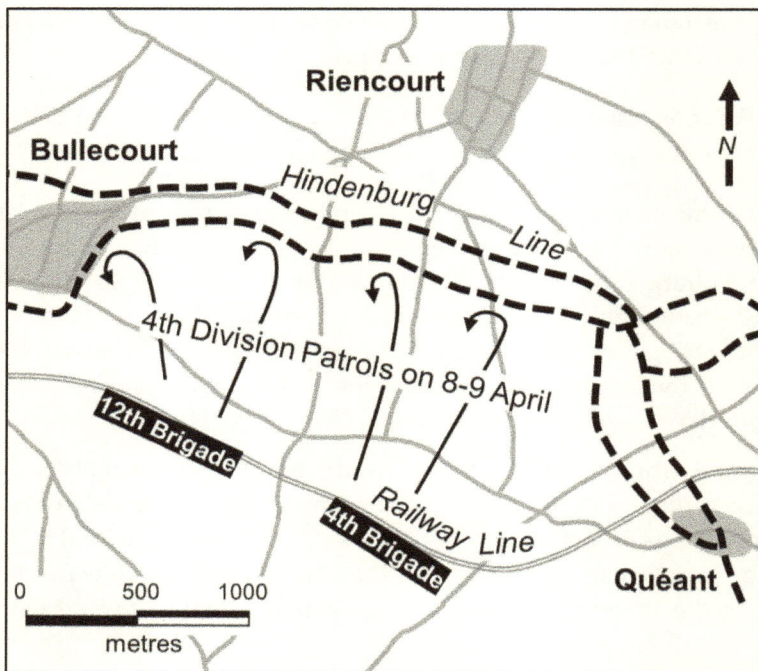

Bullecourt area on 8-9 April 1917, prior to the First Battle of Bullecourt that took place on 11 April 1917. It is likely that Martin O'Meara was involved in patrols in No-Man's Land between the Australian positions near the railway line and the German-held Hindenburg Line.

Although that particular patrol was described as an 'officers' patrol', several 'other ranks' participated. As a battalion scout, it is possible that Martin O'Meara participated in this patrol, or one of the other similar patrols described earlier. He was certainly involved in some action on 9 April, as he wounded in action (for the second time)

[285] AWM4: 23/33/17, 16th Battalion War Diary, April 1917.

that day, with wounds to his face. He was evacuated to the Australian 4th Field Ambulance which had been operating just west of Bapaume but had recently moved and established a dressing station some three kilometres north-east, near the village of Favreuil, at 9.00am on 8 April. Favreuil was located some nine kilometres from the village of Bullecourt. Interestingly, the medical staff of the 4th Field Ambulance at this time included Major James Bentley, who Martin O'Meara would later encounter after his return to Western Australia in 1918 and who had treated Western Australia's first Victoria Cross winner, Hugo Throssell, at Gallipoli earlier in the war whilst Medical Officer with the 10th Light Horse Regiment. O'Meara was then transferred to the 9th Casualty Clearing Station, and then to the 3rd Stationary Hospital at Rouen.

Some sources indicate that Martin O'Meara may have been wounded and evacuated on 11 April, during the actual Bullecourt attack,[286] but the nature of the records and absence of any recorded casualties on 9-10 April suggests that these casualties have been grouped together in the battalion's war diary as having occurred on 11 April. The 4th Brigade war diary records that the brigade as a whole suffered ten men wounded on 9 April. Martin O'Meara's wounds cannot have been very serious, as he was discharged from the 3rd Stationary Hospital three days later, on 12 April, to the No. 2 Convalescent Depot at Rouen. On 16 April he was transferred to the 4th Australian Division Base Depot at Etaples.

Whilst Martin O'Meara was being evacuated and treated, the 16th Battalion (together with the other units of the 4th Brigade and the 12th Brigade, both part of the Australian 4th Division) mounted an assault on the Hindenburg Line to the east of the village of Bullecourt, starting at 4.30am on 11 April. They were supported on the left (eastern) flank by the British 62nd Division and on the right (western) flank by the 1st Division. They were also supported by a small number of British tanks. This attack came to be later known as the First Battle of Bullecourt.[287] Although a small number of Australians were able to reach and occupy parts of the Hindenburg Line trenches (their objectives) for part of that day, a lack of artillery support and the

---

[286] AWM25: 861/9 Part 147, 16th Battalion Field Returns.
[287] A subsequent attack at the same location from 3-17 May 1917 was known as the Second Battle of Bullecourt.

failure of the British tanks to make any meaningful contribution resulted in these men being cut off from the Australian lines with many being forced to retreat. Some 1,170 Australians were eventually taken prisoner by the Germans and many were killed and wounded. Australian casualties were significant, although the number of losses various between sources. The 16th Battalion war diary records that:

> The Battalion went into the attack with a fighting strength of 20 Officers and 797 other ranks About 17 Officers and 700 other ranks actually went into the attack and only 3 officers and 87 Other ranks got back again.[288]

The 4th Brigade war diary recorded that the 16th Battalion suffered 13 officer casualties and 623 other ranks casualties whilst the 4th Division's Administrative Staff records show that the 16th Battalion's actual strength dropped from 1,130 on 7 April to 515 on 14 April.[289]

On 24 April Martin O'Meara left the 4th Australian Division Base Depot at Etaples and on 25 April he rejoined the 16th Battalion at Ribemont-sur-Ancre, where it had been located since 20 April in the aftermath of the disastrous attack at Bullecourt. The 4th Brigade commemorated ANZAC Day and held a brigade sports day on 25 April.

The battalion remained at Ribemont-sur-Ancre, training and resting, until 16 May when the men moved by train northwards to Bailleul in French Flanders, and then marched to billets near Le Doulieu, about six kilometres south of Bailleul. The 16th Battalion remained at Le Doulieu, and continued training there until 31 May when it moved over the border into Belgium and to Mahutonga Camp near Neuve Eglise. The battalion remained there until 6 June, and on 7 June moved up to the vicinity of La Douve farm (around two kilometres from the front line), as a reserve ahead of the attack on the Messines Ridge that was launched the next day. The battalion's time at Mahutonga Camp and near La Douve farm coincided with a heavy Allied artillery barrage on Messines Ridge which preceded the attack.

---

[288] AWM4: 23/33/17, 16th Battalion War Diary, April 1917.
[289] AWM4: 23/4/19, 4th Brigade War Diary, April 1917, and AWM4: 1/49/13, Administrative Staff, HQ 4th Australian Division War Diary, April 1917.

View across the Douve Valley showing a bombardment in progress in June 1917. (AWM H12264)

At 3.10am on 7 June the British Royal Engineers detonated nineteen mines placed in tunnels beneath Messines Ridge under the German lines, and the devastating effect of these mines allowed the Allies to attack and make important gains. This action later became known as the Battle of Messines, and was launched in order to capture the crescent-shaped ridge that extended south of Ypres between Messines and Wytschaete in southern Belgium.

Australia's role in the Battle of Messines focussed on II ANZAC Corps under Lieutenant-General Sir Alexander Godley. II ANZAC Corps consisted of an Australian division; the 3rd (under Major-General John Monash) together with the New Zealand Division and the 25th British Division. The Australian 4th Division (which included the 4th Brigade and, therefore, the 16th Battalion) was commanded by Major-General William Holmes[290] and was sent to reinforce II ANZAC Corps. The II ANZAC Corps was one of three corps involved in the Battle of Messines, and its front extended from east of Ploegsteert Woods in the south to the front line to the west of Messines. The 4th Division's role on 7 June was to move forward

---

[290] Major-General Holmes was killed by German artillery on 2 July 1917 and was succeeded by Major-General Ewen Sinclair-McLagan.

during the afternoon and to 'capture and consolidate the Green Line in front of the New Zealand and 25th Divisions.'[291] The 4th Division's 12th and 13th Brigades were to advance that day with the 4th Brigade (including the 16th Battalion) being held in reserve.

The 16th Battalion moved back to Mahutonga Camp near Neuve Eglise on 8 June and then on 9 June moved up to the support lines behind Messines where it relieved a New Zealand battalion in fatigue work. On 11 June the 16th Battalion moved up to the front line and relieved 3rd Division units in a sector north of the Douve River and south of Bethlehem Farm, less than one kilometre from Messines village where it was involved in actively patrolling No Man's Land:

> On completion of relief the 4th Aus. Infantry Brigade will at once commence a system of vigorous patrolling with a view to establishing posts[292]

This patrolling saw the Allied front line pushed further eastward as advanced posts were established further into No Man's Land. Dr Charles Bean later recorded that:

> It was not intended to push deeply at Messines, but during the next six weeks the front line was gradually advanced, from farm to farm, towards the Warneton Line ...[293]

The 16th Battalion scouts were actively involved in patrolling No Man's Land between 7-12 June, and Martin O'Meara's colleague Corporal Norman Terry was awarded the Military Medal for his actions during this period:

> During the whole period he was employed as a Scout. Prior to the commencement of the operations he was in charge of a section of Scouts, who made themselves thoroughly acquainted with the whole of the Corps front and all the approaches thereto. Immediately after the advance on to the MESSINES ridge was made he again reconnoitred ... on the night of the 11/12th June 1917, when we advanced our line some five

---

291 AWM4: 1/48/15, General Staff, HQ 4th Australian Division War Diary, June 1917.
292 AWM4: 1/48/15, General Staff, HQ 4th Australian Division War Diary, June 1917.
293 Bean, 2014, p.356.

hundred yards on the left bank of the river DOUVE he was in charge of the leading patrol.[294]

Another scout, Lance-Corporal Alma Bloom was also awarded the Military Medal for action at Messines. His recommendation notes that:

He is a Battalion Scout and prior to the commencement of the operation made himself thoroughly acquainted with the whole of the Corps front. His work as a guide and Runner throughout was invaluable. He was in charge of one of the patrols sent out some six hundred yards in front of the most advanced line taken over by the Battalion.[295]

The references to 'the whole of the Corps front' suggests that the 16th Battalion's scouts were active on the entire II ANZAC front line during the entire Messines operation, even though their battalion was held in reserve well behind the front line. It is quite likely that the 16th Battalion scouts were involved in marking out the jumping off positions for the 4th Brigade's attacking battalions for the second phase of the 7 June operation.

Dr Charles Bean later recorded that unspecified 4th Division 'intelligence officers and scouts had long since gone over the ridge to tape out the actual jumping off lines.'[296] One of these officers, Lieutenant Robert Murray MC, Intelligence Officer of the 45th Battalion (which was part of 12th Brigade in the 4th Division), was killed in action on 7 June at Messines:

after certain trenches had been taken, he had to go out with the battalion scouts into what was practically "no-man's land," and lay tapes so that when the battalion moved out to attack it would not lose direction. He knew he had a very difficult and dangerous job.[297]

---

[294] AWM28, Recommendation files for honours and awards, AIF, 1914-18 War.
[295] AWM28, Recommendation files for honours and awards, AIF, 1914-18 War.
[296] Bean, 1941b, pp.609-610.
[297] *Sydney Morning Herald*, 21 September 1917, p.7.

Alma Bloom's Military Medal recommendation also suggests that the scouts were operating well into No Man's Land during the Messines operation, presumably during the period between 7-11 June.

On 12 June the 16th Battalion was relieved by a British unit, the 2nd Battalion of the Lancashire Regiment, and moved back to billets at Red Lodge west of the Ploegsteert Woods. It was operating forward in the line east of Messines, again, between 16 and 27 June, and on 28 June it moved back to Red Lodge.

On 26 June 1917 HRH Prince Arthur, the Duke of Connaught and Strathearn (and uncle of King George V), visited the II ANZAC Corps Headquarters at Bailleul and inspected a contingent of Australian and New Zealand soldiers at the town's market place at 2.30pm. The Australian contingent included four representatives of the 16th Battalion: Captain Frank Wadge, Sergeant Charles Garratt, Corporal Norman Terry and Private Martin O'Meara.[298]

These men had travelled by bus from the 16th Battalion's camp at Red Lodge for the event. Other Australians present at the parade included Captain Albert Jacka VC of the 14th Battalion and Captain Harry Murray VC of the 13th Battalion. The orders given by the 4th Division noted that 'Preference is to be given to Officers, W.O.'s, N.C.O's. and Men who have specially distinguished themselves in the Messines Battle, and whom it is desired that H.R.H. should meet.'[299] Martin O'Meara's inclusion in this group, along with other scouts, suggests that he was involved in the Messines operation. Captain Frank Wadge was the battalion's intelligence officer during the Messines operation was later mentioned in dispatches for his work at Bullecourt and Messines. He had been one of the 16th Battalion's 12th Reinforcements and would have known Martin O'Meara well. Of the ceremony at Bailleul, a later newspaper report noted that:

> The square was bright with bunting, in which the flag of England, the Tri-color, and the Belgian flag were prominent. From every window of the shops and houses around the square soldiers and civilians watched the ceremony.[300]

---

[298] Longmore, 1929, p.145 and AWM4: 23/4/21, 4th Brigade War Diary, June 1917.
[299] AWM4: 23/4/21, 4th Brigade War Diary, June 1917.
[300] *Oamaru Mail*, 22 September 1917, p.8.

On 29-30 June, the 16th Battalion again moved up to the front line around La Truie Farm and the Warnave River to the south-east of the Ploegsteert Woods. The 16th Battalion remained in the front line in this area until it was relieved in early July and moved back to a support role further west, south of the Ploegsteert Woods. The battalion manned trenches and several forward outposts during this time, and it is likely that Martin O'Meara and his fellow scouts were involved in patrolling No Man's Line as far as the River Lys (to the east) during this period.

Observation post in the Ploegsteert sector in 1917. Pictured is an 18th Battalion observer watching No Man's Land. (AWM E01834)

The battalion was then relieved and moved back into a support role until 13 July, with its headquarters at Lawrence Farm south of Ploegsteert Woods. The battalion's companies were located in the southern part of the woods and in positions between Lawrence Farm and Ploegsteert village. Throughout this time the battalion had working parties engaged in fatigue work, improving the front line and support trenches. The battalion withdrew on 13 July.

The battalion positions were shelled a number of times during this period, and Martin O'Meara was involved in helping the wounded on several occasions. On 11 July another 16th Battalion man, Private John Aarons (the brother of Captain Daniel Aarons, also of the 16th Battalion) was in a dug-out (possible a YMCA dug-out) near the Lancashire Support Farm, just east of Lawrence Farm, when the dug-out was struck by a German shell. Aarons was seriously wounded by shrapnel and was taken to the 2nd Casualty Clearing Station at nearby Steenwerck, but died there later that day without regaining consciousness. He was subsequently buried at the adjacent Trois Arbres cemetery.[301] Private Charles Dyer later reported that Martin O'Meara had buried John Aarons at Trois Arbres,[302] so it is likely that O'Meara travelled to Steenwerck with, and then helped bury, his comrade.

The grave of Private John Aarons at Trois Arbres Cemetery, near Steenwerck.

Martin O'Meara is reported to have helped bury John Aarons. (AWM P11028.001.001)

Martin O'Meara was involved in similar activity on 13 July whilst the 16th Battalion was withdrawing from the line. Another Australia soldier later wrote to a friend in Collie recalling an encounter with Martin O'Meara that day:

Well, I was coming from the line with some of my mates when Fritz started to shell the road. We were lobbing them about 30 yards away. Well, some of our Infantry boys from W.A. were coming down the road whole we were crossing the field. That is how we missed, but two of the Infantry were caught by the first shell, one being killed outright, and the other being seriously wounded. Martin and another lad were coming behind a few yards when the shell burst and picked up the wounded lad and carried him to the dressing station. In the meantime my mate and I went down the road to what had been

---

[301] AWM: 1DRL/0428, 2868 Private John Fullarton Aarons and AWM: B2455, John Aarons.

[302] AWM: 1DRL/0428, 2868 Private John Fullarton Aarons.

a farmhouse, but was now only ruins and waited for our teams to take us back to camp. Mind, Fritz was shelling all the time we were waiting in shelter of the building about 50 yards down the road. About five minutes passed and Martin came up with a shell. Of course when I got close to him I recognised instantly and I started yarning to him. I also asked him where he was off to. Well, he said 'I'm off to bring one of our boys that has just been killed down the road, it's hard luck getting killed coming out of the line when you have been in a fortnight.' I told him it was useless to go while the shelling was so heavy. He said he must go through because the quicker we buried him the better.[303]

The man killed outright was Private John Claude Sermon, a signaller with the 16th Battalion's C Company. C Company had been located along the Bunhill Row breastworks in the Ploegsteert Woods and was probably withdrawing to the south, in the vicinity of the current Route de Ploegsteert when Sermon was killed. Several witnesses noted that Martin O'Meara and another man (possibly Private George Newby, another signaller with the battalion) had buried him. Private Edmund Spencer, also of the 16th Battalion, later recalled:

I saw his [Sermon's] body at Lancashire Farm near the Y.M.C.A Hut. Pte. Martin O'Meara, V.C., 16th Battalion, B Co., Scouts, helped to bury Sermon.[304]

Another 16th Battalion man noted that Sermon had been killed instantly and buried where he fell, which makes sense as his grave seems to have been later lost as the was occupied by the Germans for a period during early 1918. Private Sermon is commemorated at the Menin Gate memorial in Ypres.

After withdrawing from the line and being replaced by the 50th Battalion, the 16th Battalion was stationed at a camp near Canteen Corner, around two kilometres east of Steenwerck to the south-west of Ploegsteert Woods where it was re-equipping and re-organising from 13-18 July. It then moved to the Viex-Berquin area where it was

---

[303] *Collie Mail*, 20 October 1917, p.3.
[304] AWM: 1DRL/0428, 6202 Private John Claude Sermon.

billeted at Bleu Tour Farm. From 20 July until the end of July the battalion was located at Bleu Tour Farm and was engaged in various training activities, including outpost work, drill, bayonet fighting, and gas helmet drill. The men also conducted ten-mile route marches three times each week.

10   Meeting the King

Martin O'Meara missed some of the training with his battalion in the Bleu Tour Farm area in Flanders as he went to London to be presented with his Victoria Cross by King George V in the forecourt outside Buckingham Palace on 21 July 1917.[305] O'Meara probably left France on 19 or 20 July as the trip to London would have involved at least one train journey to one of the Channel ports, a trip across the English Channel, and then a further train journey to London.

Martin O'Meara being presented with his Victoria Cross by King George V at Buckingham Palace. (British Pathé)

The King presented 24 Victoria Crosses that day, including six to Australians: to Captain James Newland, Sergeant John Whittle (who was also presented with the Distinguished Conduct Medal, Corporal George Howell (who was also presented with the Military Medal), Private Jorgen Jensen, Private Bede Kenny, as well as Martin O'Meara. The King also presented a further eight Victoria Crosses to the families of posthumous awardees, all British. The presentation

---

[305] *West Australian*, 23 July 1917, p.5.

ceremony started at 11.00am and lasted nearly one and a half hours, with the *Times* newspaper reporting that:

> Each man's name was called singly, and Colonel Clive Wigram read a summary of the record of services for which the V.C. was awarded. Perfect silence was maintained until the King had actually pinned on each decoration, shaken hands with the recipient, and said a few congratulatory words.[306]

Grainy newsreel footage shows Martin O'Meara speaking briefly with the King, before saluting him and then marching away. He did not remain long in London, and was later quoted as saying 'Then after I had a look around the place I went back to France.'[307]

Martin O'Meara at Buckingham Palace on 21 July 1917, prior to receiving his VC medal from King George V.

He is wearing his VC ribbon on his chest above his pocket, suggesting that the photograph was taken before he received the medal. (Faithe Jones)

It was reported some years later, after his death, that O'Meara 'required great diplomacy and persuasion before he could be induced to go to Buckingham Palace to receive the distinguished decoration.'[308] He may have been more enthusiastic about visiting Mary Murphy in London; a story recalled by her family tells that he visited her during the war and pinned his Victoria Cross medal on her tunic, and that she wore the medal for the day.[309] If this story is accurate, then the most likely time that Mary could have worn

---

306 *Times*, 23 July 1917, p.7.
307 *West Australian*, 8 November 1918, p.7.
308 *Geraldton Guardian and Express*, 21 December 1935, p.1.
309 Margaret Clews, pers. comm., 8 March 2014.

Martin's medal would have been very shortly after he was presented with it in July, and that she would have worn it whilst working at Caterham where she was still nursing.[310] Martin O'Meara returned to the 16th Battalion at Bleu Tour Farm after the Victoria Cross presentation in London.

On 3 August 1917 the 16th Battalion left its billets at Bleu Tour Farm and travelled by truck back to the town of Neuve Eglise, and then marched some seven and a half kilometres to the front line (which then lay several kilometres to the east of the town of Messines) in the where it relieved the 44th Battalion. The 16th Battalion occupied locations in the vicinity of the current north-south Rijselstraat to the south of the Blauwepoortbeek River and to the north of the east-west Komenstraat near Gapaard Farm.

The 44th Battalion had been occupying and strengthening defences along this stretch of the front line, and its war diary noted that they were subject to heavy artillery fire, but that patrols sent out into No Man's Land were not encountering enemy patrols. This ground had been taken from the Germans in the massive attack that had been launched on 7 June.

The 16th Battalion occupied this sector of the line under the command of the 11th Brigade until 9 August when it was relieved by the 14th Battalion and returned to its billets at Neuve Eglise. According to the 16th Battalion historian, during this period at the front the battalion 'suffered severe casualties from several heavy bombardments' and that, despite it being summer, it:

> rained heavily most of the time and the trenches were drains full of water in which the men had to eat, sleep and live. It was impossible to build or dig dry positions. Imagine days and nights of these conditions.[311]

The 4th Brigade's war diary recorded that the 16th Battalion suffered four men killed and thirteen on the 7-8 August, out of a total

---

[310] Mary Murphy left Caterham on 19 April 1918 and then worked at the Forest Gate Sick Home in West Ham, east of London (see LMA: H23/SL/C/01/003). It is unclear whether the story about the medal originated with Mary Murphy herself or with one of her children.

[311] Longmore, 1929, p.146.

of 26 officers and men killed and 87 wounded during the period in the line from 3 August to 9 August. These casualties included Martin O'Meara, who was wounded on 8 August.

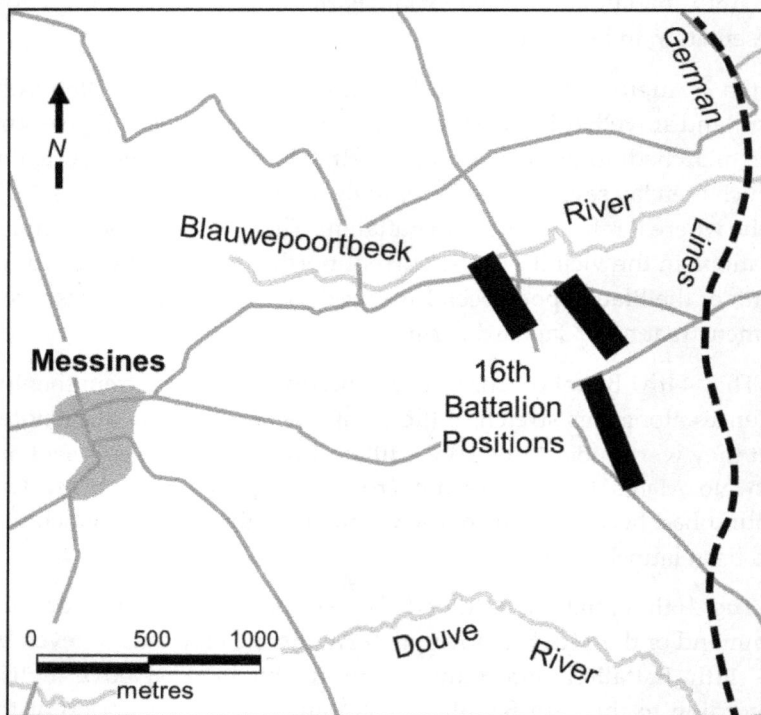

The area held by the 16th Battalion during the period 3-9 August 1917. The area had been taken from the Germans on 17 June 1917. O'Meara was in the area occupied by the 16th Battalion when it was shelled.

The 16th suffered five men killed in action that day, seven men wounded and evacuated, and one officer and two men wounded but remaining on duty.[312] The 16th Battalion war diary records that the battalion was in the front line that day, with A, C and D Companies in the forward trenches and B Company in reserve positions. The battalion's war diary noted that its positions were shelled by the Germans several times, and the 4th Brigade war diary noted that enemy artillery fire was 'very consistent throughout the day.'[313]

---

[312] AWM25: 861/9 Part 146, 16th Battalion Field Returns.
[313] AWM4: 23/4/23, 4th Brigade War Diary, August 1917.

This was the third time that Martin O'Meara had been wounded in action, this time with shrapnel wounds to his buttocks, back and right thigh. He later noted that he 'went out' to a wound on his hip and was sent back to England 'to be patched up.'[314] He was initially treated at the 16th Battalion's Regimental Aid Post, and then evacuated to the 4th Field Ambulance (which had a dressing station at nearby Westhof Farm) and then to the 2nd Casualty Clearing Station, based at Trois Arbres north of Steenwerck, located between Bailleul and Armentières. On 11 August O'Meara was transferred to the 2nd Canadian General Hospital at Le Tréport on the English Channel coast.

A week later, on 18 August, he was transferred to England and then transferred on 20 August to the Bath War Hospital. The Bath War Hospital (also known as the Royal United Hospital) was located at Combe Park north-west of Bath (in the County of Somerset) and, with around 1,300 beds, was one of the largest military hospitals in Britain at that time. Whilst in hospital at Bath, sometime between 20 August and 18 October, Martin O'Meara wrote an interesting letter to the Rev John O'Rourke, a Roman Catholic priest at All Saints' Cathedral at Port Augusta in South Australia:

> I suppose you will be surprised to hear from me after years, but when you know one never forgets it's all right. How are you getting on? Are you as thin as ever? Well, I wish I could have a talk with you now. I could tell you some grand and glorious tales about the Faith. On the other hand, as in the world over, there are plenty of Catholics who do not take advantage of it. Well, they cannot blame the priests who are with us. Every priest with the Australian forces is a man that any Government should be proud of. Go where you will you hear great accounts of them. Every battalion seems to think they have the best. The 16th regretted the loss of Father Tighe. All the boys often ask where he is, and many a yarn does be told about him. The lot are brave, anyhow. But would they be worthy some of St. Patrick (who faced the Irish kings with only a staff) if they were not brave! However, it was a good thing that the great saint did not make the same mistake that England made and faced

314 *West Australian*, 8 November 1918, p.7.

Ireland with a sword. He would never have conquered it. Well, I am just about all right again, and expect to return to France any day now. I will say good-bye, hoping this will find you in the best of health and spirits.[315]

The tone of the letter provides a clear insight into the strength of Martin O'Meara's Roman Catholic faith, as well as hinting at a commitment to Irish nationalism. O'Meara also wrote to others in Australia around this time; an article published in the *Bunbury Herald* in October 1917 reported that Martin O'Meara remained a Private and was refusing promotion, and that he said 'a spare part in the Battalion will always do me.'[316]

Martin O'Meara left the Bath War Hospital on 18 October 1917 and went on leave with orders to report to the No. 1 Command Depot at Sutton Veny in Wiltshire on 1 November. He took the opportunity to visit his family in Ireland during this period.

It is likely that Martin O'Meara's reception in Ireland in October 1917 was quite different to that of October 1916. The evolving political situation meant that returning soldiers were not feted in the same way, and he no longer had the celebrity status that he had when he visited the previous year. An article in the *King's County Chronicle* on 29 November noted simply that:

Martin O'Meara, V.C., who was wounded rather more severely than was at first thought, is, we are glad to learn, progressing favourably.[317]

As Martin O'Meara had left Ireland (and travelled via Birr, a major town where he would have boarded a train) by the end of November, we can be reasonably confident that his presence was known to the journalists at the *Chronicle* and presumably more widely in the district. It is very likely that his visit to Ireland was played down by the *Chronicle*, by the O'Meara family, or perhaps by Martin O'Meara himself. Not an attention-seeker, the changed political situation in Ireland since his last visit would have given him reason to keep his

---

[315] *Southern Cross*, 4 January 1918, p.11.
[316] *Bunbury Herald*, 24 October 1917, p.3.
[317] *King's County Chronicle*, 29 November 1917, p.3

visit as low-key as possible. The same edition of the *Chronicle* also reported something that would have been virtually impossible when Martin O'Meara had visited Ireland twelve months earlier, with a Sinn Féin demonstration being held in Birr on 24 November.[318]

Although Martin O'Meara's family members were nationalists who supported home rule for Ireland, we do not know the extent to which they might have support the more radical nationalist groups such as Sinn Féin.[319] The Lorrha area had many supporters of home rule (probably most of the local Roman Catholic population) and these would undoubtedly have included a number of Sinn Féin supporters and members. The town had its own Sinn Féin hall by 1917. A company of the Irish Volunteers had been formed at Lorrha in 1914 but most men seemed to have been moderates and had supported moderate leader John Redmond. Some of these early Volunteers may have enlisted in the British Army during late 1914 and in 1915 and later fought at Gallipoli and on the Western Front. Because of dwindling membership, the Lorrha company was subsequently disbanded. It was reformed in July or August 1917 by a local man, Felix Cronin,[320] and by the end of 1917 and the beginning of 1918 had grown to over a hundred men.[321] It would seem inevitable that a number of Martin O'Meara's friends and relatives were members of the Volunteers, making his position difficult. Some Irish soldiers, facing the same predicament, deserted from the British Army and remained in Ireland.

Support for Sinn Féin had grown since the failed Easter uprising of 1916, and Sinn Féin policy treated Irishmen in the British Army as traitors:

---

[318] *King's County Chronicle*, 29 November 1917, p.3.

[319] Useful accounts of the politics of the First World War in Ireland can be found in Kildea, J. (2007): *Anzacs and Ireland*, University of NSW Press, Sydney, and in Dennehy, J. (2013): *In a Time of War: Tipperary 1914-1918*, Merrion, Co. Kildare.

[320] Felix Cronin was the son of a teacher at Lorrha's National School, and may have known Martin O'Meara personally. Cronin later married Kitty Kiernan, fiancée of General Michael Collins, Commander-in-Chief of the Irish Free State Army who was assassinated in August 1922.

[321] BMH: WS1323, Martin Needham.

The Irishman who joins the British army, the British navy, the British 'Royal' Irish Constabulary, necessarily becomes the active enemy of his country. He has taken up arms against Ireland.[322]

Fighting with the AIF alongside the British, and receiving the Victoria Cross from the King, would have resulted in O'Meara being closely associated with the British Army. The families of soldiers were being targeted by Irish nationalists at this time. For example, the *Nenagh Guardian* reported in October 1917 the case of the wife of a British soldier living in Nenagh who had been victimised. She reported several examples of her house windows being broken and offensive graffiti ('To hell with the King; to hell with the soldiers') and the Sinn Féin flag being painted on her house.[323]

Accounts suggest that O'Meara's welcome in 1917 was not as friendly as in 1916, and that he was made to feel as if he was no longer part of the community.[324] Despite varied local attitudes to the British, it seems likely that Martin O'Meara visited the family farm at Lissernane and probably stayed there with his sister Alice and other family members. As Martin O'Meara had his gold watch (presented to his sister Alice in November 1916) with him when he returned to Australia in 1918 it is quite possible that she gave it to him when he visited Ireland at this time, and that he carried it with him when he returned to the Western Front.

It is also likely that Martin visited his brother John O'Meara and John's wife Sadie, who were farming at Sharragh near Lissernane. Martin O'Meara also visited a childhood friend (and Sadie O'Meara's sister), Margaret ('Gretta') Leavey,[325] and her daughter Myra who lived at Crinkill south of Birr. Crinkill was a garrison town and Gretta's husband, Private James Leavey, was serving with the 2nd Battalion of the Prince of Wales' Leinster Regiment (usually referred to as 'the Leinsters'), which had its depot at Crinkill's barracks. He had been captured by the Germans in the opening months of the war

---

[322] *Age*, 1 December 1917, p.12.
[323] *Nenagh Guardian*, 6 October 1917, p.3.
[324] King, 2012, p.41.
[325] The surname 'Leavey' is sometimes spelled 'Leavy'.

and spent most of the war in a prisoner of war camp. O'Meara's visit was later recalled by a very young Myra Leavey, who remembered him wearing his Australian uniform.[326]

Martin O'Meara passed through London after returning from Ireland, and he may have visited Mary Murphy, who was still nursing at Caterham.[327] Martin O'Meara had returned to England by 16 November 1917, when he made a new will at the Australian Administrative Headquarters in London after his period of leave in Ireland.[328] He was probably in London for most of the period from 15-19 November.

The new will was very different to the will that he had made in late 1915 before leaving Australia. His sister Alice was no longer O'Meara's sole beneficiary, and his estate was to comprise several separate bequests, with his Irish estate (being the money raised as a testimonial to him in 1916) being bequeathed to the Rev Gleeson, Lorrha's Parish Priest, for the restoration of the Lorrha Abbey, and his Australian estate (being his AIF back-pay) being bequeathed to the three children of his brother John O'Meara (Martin, Maureen and John) and the daughter of John O'Meara's wife's sister (Myra Leavey). He also made specific provision for his Victoria Cross medal in the new will, leaving it to Mary Murphy.[329]

The stark differences between his 1915 and 1917 wills suggest that some fracturing of relationship between Martin O'Meara and other members of his family took place during his visit to Ireland in October-November 1917.

Martin O'Meara left the Australian Administrative Headquarters after making the new will, and joined the No. 1 Command Depot at Sutton Veny in Wiltshire on 19 November. He had a medical

---

[326] Noreen O'Meara, pers. comm., 12 December 2013. The O'Meara family recalls a story that Gretta Leavey worked as a cook at Crinkill barracks during the Irish War of Independence and that she refused to spy for the Irish republicans. (Noreen O'Meara, pers. comm., 29 March 2016).

[327] Mary Murphy had left Caterham in April 1918.

[328] One of the witnesses to this will was Corporal Claude Hore who was serving on the staff of the Australian Administrative Headquarters in London.

[329] This suggests that O'Meara regarded Mary Murphy as more than simply an acquaintance.

classification of B1A3, meaning that he was regarded as being fit for overseas training camp in two to three weeks.

Horseferry Road in September 1918, looking towards Victoria Street, showing on the right AIF Administrative Headquarters, and on the left the buildings occupied by the Australian War Records Section. (AWM D00077)

On 13 December he was transferred from the No. 1 Command Depot to the nearby Overseas Training Brigade at Sandhill Camp near the village of Long Bridge Deverill, around four kilometres south of Warminster in Wiltshire. Martin O'Meara spent Christmas with the Overseas Training Brigade, and on 10 January 1918 he travelled to Southampton where he boarded a ship and sailed to Le Havre in France. He was one of 481 men who left the Overseas Training Brigade and sailed to France that day.

On 11 January Martin O'Meara joined the Australian Infantry Base Depot at Rouelles, six kilometres from Le Havre. The Australian Infantry Base Depot was a busy unit processing men in transit between the United Kingdom and the front, and the unit's war diary records that he was one of 293 4th Division men that joined and one of 236 4th Division men that left the unit during the month.[330] On 18 January he left the Australian Infantry Base Depot in Rouelles and

---

[330] AWM4: 33/10/2, Australian Infantry Base Depot War Diary, January 1918.

rejoined the 16th Battalion at La Clytte in Belgium, one of seven men who returned to the battalion from Rouelles that day [331]

The 16th Battalion had travelled from the Somme region in France back to Belgium on 10 January 1918, and was billeted at De Zon Camp near La Clytte, a village located around eight kilometres south-west of Ypres. The men had spent their first week or so at the camp cleaning and training, and were still doing so when Martin O'Meara returned on 18 January. On 20 January the 16th Battalion marched to the Kilmarnock light rail siding near La Clytte and then moved by rail to the Spoil Bank area between villages of Hollebeke and Lankhof, around five kilometres south-east of Ypres and some nine kilometres east of La Clytte.[332] It remained there until 29 January. During this time the battalion was accommodated in the tunnel system near The Bluff on the northern bank of the Ypres-Comines Canal, with the battalion war diary noting that 'Accommodation in Tunnel dug-outs good and quite sufficient for every man to have a built bunk.'[333] The battalion's role at this time was manning the front line in an area that had been taken from the Germans earlier in 1917.

During this period O'Meara continued to remain in contact with other soldiers from Collie; Labor Party Member for Collie in the Western Australian Legislative Assembly, Arthur Wilson MLA (who was serving with the AIF Tunnellers), wrote a letter in France on 20 January 1918 in which he recounted a meeting with Martin O'Meara:

> I had a long talk with Martin O'Meara V.C. What a fine chap he is, and so unassuming in spite of his high distinction. He has been through many of the bitter stunts here, and has been wounded three times – at Pozieres, Bullecourt and Messines. He won the Victoria Cross in August, 1916, and it was presented to him at Buckingham Palace on July 21, 1917. He desired to be remembered to Collie's good people, and said he was looking forward to the day when he would be able to

---

[331] AWM25: 861/9 Part 147, 16th Battalion Field Returns.

[332] This area is now a provincial nature reserve and picnic area known as the 'Provinciaal Domein Palingbeek' and the remains old fortifications and trenches are still visible.

[333] AWM4: 23/33/26, 16th Battalion War Diary, January 1918.

return to the coal town and again sit in the shade of a big jarrah tree.[334]

The battalion's men, apart from the specialists such as Martin O'Meara and his fellow scouts, spent the next few days engaged in fatigue work[335] and on 29 January 1918 the battalion then moved east to the front line closer to Hollebeke and relieved the 13th Battalion. The battalion's historian noted that 'During the next week nothing happened excepting shells and the inter-company relief – giving each a turn in the various positions.'[336] The 16th Battalion remained in the front line until 5 February when it was relieved by the 47th Battalion and moved back to De Zon Camp via rail.

The battalion remained at De Zon Camp until 20 February when it moved by truck to the Voormezeele-St Eloi area. It then marched to the Crater Dugouts and Canal Dugouts area near the Ypres-Comines Canal near The Bluff, where it had been located several weeks earlier, arriving in the early afternoon where it relieved the 47th Battalion which returned to De Zon Camp.

Members of the 4th Division standing around dugouts on the site of White Chateau near the Ypres-Comines Canal on 22 February 1918. (AWM E04569)

---

[334] *Sunday Times*, 24 March 1918, p.20.
[335] AWM4: 23/33/26, 16th Battalion War Diary, January 1918.
[336] Longmore, 1929, p.163.

The 47th Battalion, which had been at the Crater Dugouts immediately prior to the 16th Battalion arriving, described the Crater Dugouts as being driven:

> into the spoilbanks of the YPRES-COMINES CANAL and fitted with bunks & electric light and provide accommodation for 400 all ranks. The ventilation is fair, but the tunnels are damp & the sanitation is not all that could be desired.[337]

Battalion historian Cyril Longmore later wrote that 'An enemy attack was expected on this front and the digging and wiring of strong points were energetically proceeded with.'[338]

On 28 February the 16th Battalion was relieved by the 9th Battalion and withdrew to Aldershot Camp near Neuve Eglise by bus, west of the Ploegsteert Woods. The battalion then spent around eight weeks in the Neuve Eglise area training and re-equipping. On 10 March a 4th Brigade church parade was held, after which General Sir William Birdwood presented medals and ribbons to 24 of the battalion's men including Lieutenant-Colonel Drake-Brockman who was presented with the ribbon of the Distinguished Service Order (DSO).

The 16th Battalion held a number of training courses whilst in the Neuve Eglise area, and these included an intelligence course which was held from 11-23 March and attended by the battalion's scouts. The course syllabus included sessions on mapping. scouting, aerial photography, observation, intelligence reports, night marching, messages, army intelligence generally, and included visits to formation headquarters and the Australian Flying Corps' No. 2 Squadron.[339]

Whilst at Aldershot Camp, on 13 March, Martin O'Meara was promoted to Corporal in the place of Corporal Leonard Rzeszkowski who had been promoted to sergeant on 16 January. The appointment was notified in the Battalion Orders and indicated that O'Meara was still serving with the battalion scouts.

---

[337] AWM4: 23/64/21, 47th Battalion War Diary, February 1918.
[338] Longmore, 1929, p.164.
[339] AWM4: 23/33/28, 16th Battalion War Diary, March 1918.

The promotion also brought O'Meara a pay increase from six shillings per day to ten shillings per day.[340] The 16th Battalion remained at Aldershot Camp near Neuve Eglise until 25 March when it was moved south.

---

[340] NAA K1143: O'Meara Martin.

11   The Final Battles

On 21 March 1918 the German Army launched a massive offensive, the Kaiserschlacht (the Kaiser's Battle), along the Western Front. This offensive was also known as the Spring Offensive and saw the German lines pushed back westward over much of the ground that the allied forces had fought hard to retake during 1916 and 1917. Operation Michael was the part of the German offensive that focused on the Somme region, and saw them advance to within 16 kilometres of the town of Amiens. The 16th Battalion was still at Aldershot Camp near Neuve Eglise in southern Belgium when the German offensive was launched.

On 22 March 1918 Martin O'Meara was appointed from his substantive rank of corporal to acting sergeant, to complete the establishment of the scouting section, and on 23 March he was detached to the 2nd Army Musketry School to undertake a training course. As most musketry training was conducted within the actual infantry battalions, it is most likely that Martin O'Meara attended as he was being trained as a musketry instructor. As a sergeant he would have been second in command of the scouting section, assisting the battalion's scouting officer. Whilst he was away the rest of the 16th Battalion was involved in fighting at Hébuterne after it had been sent there late on 26 March to relieve British units.

On 15 April he rejoined the 16th Battalion at Rossignol Farm (near Hébuterne) and reverted to the rank of corporal at his own request. No evidence has been found to indicate why he opted to revert to the rank of corporal; it is possible that he did not want the responsibility of being a sergeant and was happy to be one of the scouting section's corporals.

The 16th Battalion was in the front line between 16 April and 19 April 1918 with the scouts involved in patrolling No Man's Land. It then moved back to Rossignol Farm and remained there until 24 April when it moved by bus to Rainneville and then marched to billets at Cardonnette. The 16th Battalion moved to Querrieu on 27 April and then moved forward as a support battalion within the 4th Brigade's sector on 28 April. Here the 16th Battalion was engaged in improvements to dugouts and digging a defensive trench line that was known as the Villiers Switch. On 4 May the battalion relieved the 13th Battalion in the front line near Villers-Bretonneux where it was recorded in the battalion's history that 'There was much movement behind the enemy lines, but otherwise the situation was quiet … [and] … As usual the 16th patrols were active in No Man's Land during the nights.'[341] As a scout, it is likely that Martin O'Meara participated in these patrols.

The 16th Battalion was relieved in the line by the 48th Battalion on 9 May. It then moved to the Blangy area and rested until 12 May when it moved to positions east of Villers-Bretonneux. On 17 May the 16th Battalion relieved the 14th Battalion in the front line near Villers-Bretonneux and remained there until 20 May when it was relieved by the 44th Battalion. It then moved back to the Blangy area, and on 22 May moved to the Cardonnette area where it remained until 31 May. It then moved forward to the 4th Brigade reserve positions and then forward again where it relieved the 56th Battalion. It was in the line until 26 June when it withdrew to the Aubigny area along the Somme west of Corbie after being relieved by the 49th Battalion.

The work of the battalion scouts remained hazardous during this period. Private Bill Skinner was wounded with a gunshot to the head whilst patrolling on 25 June, and was carried back to the battalion's lines by his brother, Private Clarence Skinner (a fellow scout) and later evacuated.[342] Bill Skinner was likely to have been wounded on a general reconnaissance patrol conducted by two officers and three other ranks just before midnight, with the 4th Brigade war diary recording that 'Patrol was sighted and fired on by strong enemy patrol concealed in crop. 1 member of the patrol was wounded.'[343]

The 16th Battalion remained in the Aubigny trench system until 3 July 1918 when the battalion had moved forward and relieved parts of the 49th and 50th Battalions along the front line in readiness for the attack near the village of Hamel that was launched the following day.

The Battle of Hamel was launched behind a creeping artillery barrage at 3.10am on 4 July, and involved the 4th, 6th and 11th

---

[341] Longmore, 1929, p.172.
[342] Greg Payne, pers. comm., 23 February 2016.
[343] AWM4: 23/4/33, 4th Brigade War Diary, June 1918.

Brigades (with American assistance) operating under the command of Lieutenant-General Sir John Monash and Major-General Ewen Sinclair-McLagan. In order to mitigate the risk of casualties badly affecting any particular division, Sinclair-McLagan commanded a 'composite division' with one brigade (the 6th) from the 2nd Division, one brigade (the 11th) from the 3th Division and one brigade (the 4th) from the 4th Division. Coordinated and comprehensively planned, Hamel was an 'all arms' battle combining infantry, armour, artillery and air support from the Royal Air Force. The object was to straighten a stretch of the Allied lines by pushing the German front back some two kilometres in the vicinity of the village of Hamel some twenty kilometres east of Amiens.

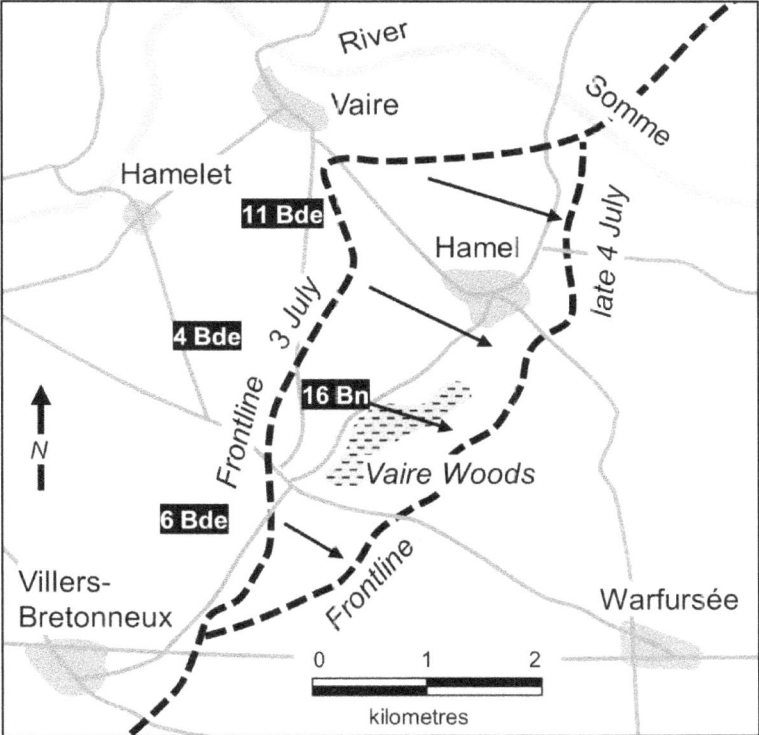

The 16th Battalion's area of operations in the Battle of Hamel on 4 July 1918.

The 16th Battalion's role was to attack the Vaire Woods and Hamel Woods to the south-west of the village, and it did so with the 15th Battalion on its left (northern) flank and the 13th Battalion on its right (southern) flank. The 4th Brigade, in turn, had the 11th Brigade on its left flank and the 8th Brigade on its right flank. The infantry advanced behind a creeping barrage support by British tanks and aerial bombing and resupply by the Royal Air Force.

The 16th Battalion's war diary noted that the intelligence officer, Lieutenant John Howell and his scouting section, which included Martin O'Meara, were involved in both laying out the jumping-off positions in No Man's Land and guiding the tanks into position late on 3 July. Jumping off tapes were laid around 300 metres in front of the battalion's positions, as well as tapes marking the battalion and company flanks and tapes marking the approach routes for the supporting tanks, by 1.00am and the infantry companies were in position by 2.00am. The men laying out the jumping off tapes in No Man's Land were protected by 'standing patrols',[344] which probably consisted of men from the scouting section. The battle was a success and the objectives had been achieved in about 90 minutes. It resulted in 1,062 Australian and 176 United States casualties, and resulted in around 2,000 German casualties with a further 1,600 Germans taken prisoner. The 16th Battalion won its second Victoria Cross near Hamel on 4 July when Lance-Corporal Thomas Axford single-handedly captured a German machine gun position, killing ten of the enemy and taking six prisoners.

Lance-Corporal Thomas Axford, the 16th Battalion's second Victoria Cross recipient.

Axford also received the Military Medal, and is pictured wearing both medals. (AWM P02939.030)

---

[344] AWM4: 23/33/32 Part 1, 16th Battalion War Diary, July 1918.

Two men of the scouting section and the intelligence officer were decorated for actions at Hamel. Private Yul Knudson was awarded the Military Medal:

> This man is a personal Runner to the Intelligence Officer, and during the preparatory stages of the attack against VAIRE and HAMEL Woods, East of CORBIE, on the morning of the 4th July 1918, accompanied him whilst laying the tapes for the Infantry jumping-off place, and on several patrols into "No Man's Land", At one stage, when it was discovered that an enemy patrol had penetrated into "No Man's Land", he volunteered to locate it and follow it with a view to preventing the enemy discovering anything unusual.[345]

Private Arthur Morgan of the scouting section was awarded the Military Medal for action in No Man's Land:

> During the laying down of the infantry jumping-off tapes he carried out a very daring patrol' well up to the enemy wire. An attempt made by the enemy to send a patrol into "No Man's Land" at the time was so quickly and effectively dealt with by him that the enemy personnel returned to their lines. During the progress of the attack he personally collected and brought in between fifty and sixty Germans ...[346]

Lieutenant John Howell, was awarded the Military Cross for his actions at Hamel as Intelligence Officer:

> During the advance he closely followed up the barrage, directing the line of advance and moving from point to point, correcting errors in direction, and maintained liaison between Companies. On the final objective being reached he went forward guiding into "No Man's Land" some tanks which patrolled for quite a considerable time ...[347]

The 16th Battalion suffered thirteen killed and 73 wounded in the battle. Martin O'Meara was active during the battle, and was involved

---

[345] AWM4: 23/33/32 Part 1, 16th Battalion War Diary, July 1918.

[346] AWM4: 23/33/32 Part 1, 16th Battalion War Diary, July 1918.

[347] AWM28: 1/254, Recommendation files for honours and awards, 1914-18 war, AIF, 4th Australian Division, 12.11.1918-28.2.1919.

in searching the battlefield afterwards; in a later report to the Red Cross O'Meara stated:

> I saw Lt. Blee's body lying on the ground beyond, and in front of Hamel Wood, we were advancing. He was dead then, killed by a shell or bomb I think. I did not notice his wounds. He was a new officer to us and some of the chaps told me who he was. I saw him after the stunt was over, and when I was looking round to see if any of the boys were wounded or killed. They carried him back for burial, but I cannot say where he was buried.[348]

American and Australian dead on the battlefield at Hamel on 4 July 1918, in front of Vaire Woods and Hamel Woods. (AWM B02620)

By 6.00am on 4 July 1918, the 16th Battalion had withdrawn to the old front line and support trenches and was being held in reserve. On 5 July it remained there as a reserve battalion, and the battalion's war diary noted 'Quiet day; few working parties supplied, and Companies did a little salvaging of the battlefield.'[349] Late on 6 July the battalion moved forward again and relieved the 13th Battalion in the front line where it remained until 10 July. It was then relieved by

[348] AWM 1DRL/0428 2nd Lieutenant Horace Edgar Blee.
[349] AWM4: 23/33/32 Part 1, 16th Battalion War Diary, July 1918.

the 39th Battalion and moved back to the Bussy-les-Daours area and then on to the Querrieu area the following day.

On 12 July 1918, whilst the 16th Battalion was at Querrieu, Martin O'Meara was detached to the 4th Army School of Scouting, Observation and Sniping (located at Bouchon some 20 kilometres north-west of Amiens), returning to the battalion's scouting section on 2 August. A training manual issued by the British Army's General Staff in 1917 noted that courses at the Schools of Scouting, Observation and Sniping involved sixty students (20 officers and 40 other ranks) and ran for 14 days.[350]

Australian soldiers at a British Army School of Scouting, Observation and Sniping in France. (Australian Army History Unit)

The syllabus for all ranks included scouting and patrolling by day and night, using cover, navigating by day and night using a prismatic compass, constructing posts for snipers and observers, observation in trenches and in the open, musketry at ranges of up to 500 metres and sniping using telescopic sights.[351] The training manual specifically noted that the purpose of the school was 'for the training of Instructors';[352] Martin O'Meara was at the School in order to equip

---

[350] General Staff, 1917, p.29.
[351] Also see AWM25: 741/1, Precis of a Lecture on Organisation and System of Training and Scouts and Patrols for Trench Warfare.
[352] General Staff, 1917, p.5.

him to train other men to be scouts, observers and snipers for the 16th Battalion. As the manual also stressed that 'musketry is a test rather than instruction because the N.C.O.s and men who attend the Course are expected to be good shots before they are sent there',[353] we must assume that Martin O'Meara was 'a good shot.'

On 2 August 1918, when Martin O'Meara returned from training, the 16th Battalion was in trenches (probably uncomfortably) behind Hangard Woods, several kilometres south of Villers-Bretonneux. The battalion's war diary noted that 'Heavy rain fell during the night AUGUST 1/2nd, and the trenches, which were otherwise good, became flooded and very muddy. Owing to the irregular depth of the trenches a great quantity of the water remained imprisoned for a long time.' By 3 August 'the trenches had considerably improved [but] they were still in a very sloppy condition'.[354] The battalion remained there until 4 August when it was relieved by Canadian units and then moved back to billets south of the Somme River between Vaire-sous-Corbie and Hamelet.

At dusk on 7 August 1918 the 16th Battalion moved from its billets and assembled for a major allied offensive. The Battle of Amiens (also known as the Third Battle of the Somme) started in thick fog at 4.20am on 8 August and was the start of the Allies' Hundred Days Offensive which was mounted against the Germans and ultimately saw them forced to capitulate in November 1918. The attack was mounted by British, Australian and Canadian forces over a front of approximately 32 kilometres, and the day was later described by German General Erich Ludendorff as 'their blackest day.'

The attacks reflected, on a far larger scale, some of the themes of the Hamel battle of the previous month; for example, the coordination of infantry, machine guns, artillery, armour and air support. The 4th Army (commanded by General Sir Henry Rawlinson) attacked with three corps, including the Australian Corps under Lieutenant-General Monash. The Australian Corps occupied the middle sector of the attack with the Canadians on the right (southern) flank and the British on their left (northern) flank. Monash had all five Australian divisions involved, with the 1st Division in reserve. The Australian Corps

---

[353] General Staff, 1917, p.29.
[354] AWM4: 23/33/33 Part 1, 16th Battalion War Diary, August 1918.

attacked along an eight kilometre front, with the 2nd and 3rd Divisions advanced to the first objective (the 'green line') with the 4th and 5th Divisions then passing through that line and advanced to the 'red line' (the second objective). Some battalions of the 4th and 5th Divisions (including the 16th Battalion) then pushed further to the 'blue line' (the third objective).

In the 4th Division sector the first phase involved the 9th Brigade and 11th Brigade attacking German positions with tank support and under the cover of an artillery barrage. The second phase followed this, with the 12th Brigade and 4th Brigade passing through the 9th and 11th Brigade lines and then attacking and holding a further series of German positions. The third phase involved a battalion each from the 4th Brigade and 12th Brigade passing through the first two sets of lines and attaching further German positions. The 16th Battalion was the 4th Brigade unit chosen to remain in reserve and participate in the third phase. The 16th Battalion's role was described by the new Intelligence Officer, Lieutenant Harry Bradley (who had replaced the injured John Howell), in a report after the battle. Lieutenant Bradley wrote that the men:

> moved up on to the first forming up position after dark on 7th August. Companies were all in allotted positions before 11 p.m., and men were instructed to get as much rest as possible before going forward nest morning. At zero plus 1 ½ hours [5.50am] the Battalion moved forward under cover of dense fog … At zero plus 3 hours [7.20am] the battalion moved forward in good formation.[355]

The 16th Battalion's war diary further described the day's activities:

> The Battalion advanced steadily during the early stages of the battle in lines of platoons in fours, passing to the left of the village of HAMEL, through RECORD WOOD and adjacent to the swamps in the low-lying country running down to the banks of the SOMME RIVER, and on to FORBES WOOD, passing immediatley to the left of KATE WOOD … The third and final stage of the battle on the left of the AUSTRALIAN

---

[355] AWM4: 23/33/33 Part 1, 16th Battalion War Diary, August 1918.

front was allotted to the 16th Battalion, and consisted of swinging round to the left from … the South bank of the Somme River … to the South side of MORGAN WOOD … and advancing approximately 2500 yards … and clear away the enemy from the outskirts of MERICOURT.[356]

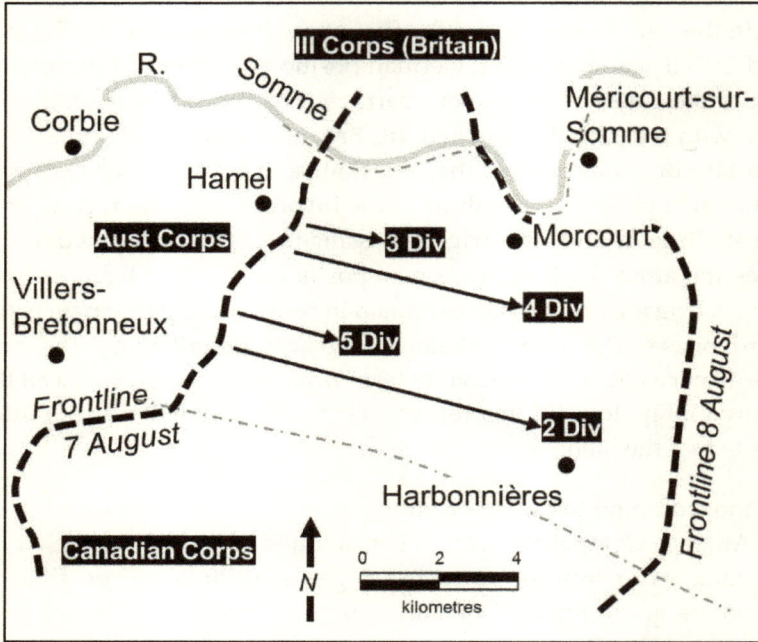

III Corps (Britain)
R. Somme
Corbie
Méricourt-sur-Somme
Hamel
Aust Corps
3 Div
Morcourt
Villers-Bretonneux
4 Div
5 Div
Frontline 8 August
Frontline 7 August
2 Div
Harbonnières
Canadian Corps
N
0 2 4
kilometres

The extent of the Allied advance on 8 August 1918. The 4th Division 'leapfrogged' the 3rd Division during the second part of the operation.

On 17 August Captain Daniel Aarons of the 16th Battalion wrote to his sister in Perth, and reported that, in relation to the 8 August offensive:

We took our objective, rushing across open and dangerous country but I must say that the boys exercised considerable craft and commonsense in their movement. Altogether I think

---

356 AWM4: 23/33/33 Part 1, 16th Battalion War Diary, August 1918.

we captured about 200 Huns and many machine guns, whilst we killed a good many.[357]

As in earlier operations, the battalion scouts played an important role in guiding the infantry companies into position as well as reconnaissance ahead of the battalion lines into the parts of No Man's Land where the battalion would be operating. This work was risky, and there were casualties. O'Meara's fellow scout, Private Arthur Morgan, was killed in action at around 2.30pm on 8 August around a mile south of Méricourt-sur-Somme, with a later report recording that '[the] objective had been gained and the Scouts were on duty having a look round' when he was shot near Madame Wood.[358]

On 9 August the 16th Battalion was headquartered in Morcourt, with troops remaining in lines south of Méricourt-sur-Somme until late on 10 August. Méricourt-sur-Somme itself remained in German hands and was not captured until 12 August. The battalion was then relieved by the 43rd Battalion, and crossed the Somme River and moved to the 4th Brigade reserve area near Sailly-Laurette on the northern side of the Somme.

On 13 August the 16th Battalion moved forward yet again, crossing the Somme and moving south where it bivouacked for the night within a triangle formed by Bayonville, Harbonnières and Guillaucort (located around ten to fifteen kilometres east of Villers-Bretonneaux) and rested there during the next day. On the evening of 15 August the 16th Battalion relieved the 12th Battalion in the 4th Brigade's reserve line where, as the 16th Battalion's war diary noted, 'the enemy shelled the position and also threw over gas. The trenches were too wide and of insufficient depth to provide adequate protection, and several casualties occurred.'[359]

Allied forces were pushing eastwards at this time continuing the offensive launched on 8 August. The battalion scouts continued to be involved in patrolling forward of the front lines during this time. The 4th Brigade war diary recorded that on 15 August 'All units reconnoitred the forward area' and on 16 August that 'Our patrols

[357] AWM: 2DRL/0166, Aarons Daniel Sydney.
[358] AWM: 1DRL/0428, 1776 Private Arthur Morgan.
[359] AWM4: 23/33/33 Part 1, 16th Battalion War Diary, August 1918

were very active along the whole front but saw very little sign of the enemy.'[360] On 16 August a German shell hit the 16th Battalion's rear headquarters orderly room, which was located in the cellar of a building at Guillaucort, killing three men.[361]

On the evening of 20 August the battalion moved forward from the reserve line and relieved the 14th Battalion in the front line. It remained in the front line area until 23 August when it moved forward on a fierce day of fighting towards the Somme River south of the town of Péronne. On 23 August the 4th Brigade mounted an attack on German trenches which saw the 16th Battalion advance some 700 metres across No Man's Land and take a line known as Courtine Trench. Zero hour was 4.45am and the troops move forward under a supporting artillery barrage.

Despite the battalion's war diary recording that its 'numerical strength had dwindled considerably owing to casualties in recent operations', the attack was successful and 'The Battalion objective was attained practically without resistance.'[362] The battalion's war diary recorded that:

> On this occasion the Boche departed from his customary tactics of surrendering when close fighting became imminent and for a long time a section of the Battalion fought a close and lively engagement with a stoutly resisting foe. The men revelled in this hand to hand encounter.[363]

A fellow West Australian, Lieutenant Lawrence 'Fats' McCarthy, won the 16th Battalion's third Victoria Cross on 23 August, near Madame Wood, west of the village of Vermandovillers.

McCarthy near-single handedly captured some 500 metres of Courtine Trench, killing some 20 Germans and capturing some 50 more in the process. His Victoria Cross was later described as the 'Super VC'. After Lawrence McCarthy's assault of Courtine Trench, the battalion's scouts (which probably included Martin O'Meara)

---

[360] AWM4: 23/4/35 Part 1, 4th Brigade War Diary, August 1918.
[361] AWM4: 23/33/33 Part 1, 16th Battalion War Diary, August 1918.
[362] AWM4: 23/33/33 Part 1, 16th Battalion War Diary, August 1918.
[363] AWM4: 23/33/33 Part 1, 16th Battalion War Diary, August 1918.

were deployed along the saps linking Courtine Trench and Wurtemburg Trench to the rear to prevent the Germans from attempting to retake the trench. The battalion sent out patrols later that day, but they failed to observe any 'unwanted activity on the part of the enemy.'[364]

Lieutenant Lawrence 'Fats' McCarthy, the 16th Battalion's third Victoria Cross recipient.

McCarthy also received the French Croix de Guerre. (AWM P02939.036)

An interesting letter from a former 16th Battalion machine gunner (writing under the pseudonym 'Pannier') published a decade after the war noted that, on 23 August:

> I was a member of a Lewis gun section advancing to the support of McCarthy's attacking company. O'Meara had been on the job since the first bang. Near the van of the disturbance I observed the gallant sergeant [actually still a Corporal on that date] on bended knees, with bared head, hands shading his eyes, praying for the rapidly departing soul of a German soldier, a victim of an awful head wound. The sublime coolness of O'Meara in the midst of the battle, his comprehensive, charity to find time to salve a soul, formed an amazing contrast to us troops rushing by him, giving vent to ejaculations neither holy nor reverent.[365]

The 16th Battalion was relieved by the 15th Battalion of the Lancashire Fusiliers late on 23 August and then travelled by bus

---

[364] AWM4: 23/33/33 Part 1, 16th Battalion War Diary, August 1918.

[365] *Smith's Weekly*, 2 October 1926, p.2 (the letter was reproduced in the Roman Catholic *Freeman's Journal* on 21 October 1926).

through Amiens to the village of Coisy, around eight kilometres north of Amiens, where the men were billeted. They rested on 24 August and remained in the Coisy area until early September 1918.

12   'Furlough' for the VCs

Despite later newspaper reports that he was looking forward to returning to Western Australia, the available evidence shows that Martin O'Meara did not want to return to Australia when he did, and probably did so reluctantly and out of a sense of obedience and duty, and possibly through financial incentive resulting from a promotion. It seems likely that his preference was to remain on the Western Front with his colleagues from the 16th Battalion, and perhaps to live in England or return to Ireland after the war. It is also possible that he thought a future marriage to Mary Murphy may have still been an option.

On 27 June 1918, whilst the 16th Battalion was resting in the Aubigny area along the Somme River west of Corbie, Defence Minister Senator George Pearce had cabled General Sir William Birdwood, Commander of the AIF (and also commander of the British 5th Army), and noted:

> It is desirous to give all V.C. winners in A.I.F. now abroad a furlough enabling them spend few months in Australia (stop) Their presence here would give great fillip to recruiting and receive popular support (stop) Please let me know your views as early as possible indicating number concerned.[366]

This cable was reported in newspapers in Australia on the same (and subsequent) days.[367] The AIF needed to maintain ongoing recruitment of new volunteers in the wake of the two unsuccessful conscription referendums, and the Victoria Cross recipients represented symbols to inspire more volunteers to enlist. As was probably the case with Martin O'Meara in Lorrha in late 1916, the presence of an Irish Roman Catholic recipient of Britain's highest award for gallantry could provide 'trophy value' in the face of the very vocal anti-conscription movement that was supported by the Roman Catholic Church in Australia. O'Meara was, on appearances,

---

[366] NAA: MP357/1: 556/33/51, Victoria Cross winners - Furlough to Australia.
[367] *Advertiser*, 27 June 1918, p.5 (and other Australian newspapers published that day).

a good example of a high achieving, patriotic, Roman Catholic Irishman.

It seems that Birdwood and the AIF staff were diligent in assessing which particular Victoria Cross winners might be suitable for return to Australia, with Martin O'Meara's name appearing on a list dated 28 June as being 'effective' and suitable for return.[368]

Most, but not all, Victoria Cross recipients seemed happy enough to return to Australia. Albert Jacka and Martin O'Meara did not want return to Australia and made this clear to the AIF commanders. The refusal of some Victoria Cross recipients to return posed a problem for the Australian Government, and much pressure was placed on those men who did not want to return. On 15 July the Commander of the 4th Division, Major-General Ewen Sinclair-Maclagan, wrote to the commander of the Australian Corps, Lieutenant-General Sir John Monash, advising that Martin O'Meara had been recommended for return to Australia on furlough, but that it was not known whether he actually wanted to return.[369] On 17 July Senator Pearce sent General Birdwood another cable following up on his 27 June cable, requesting 'Please expedite reply to my telegram 27th June WS117 Victoria Cross winners.'[370]

On 22 July Lieutenant-General Monash wrote to AIF Headquarters advising that 'Steps are being taken to ascertain whether ... No. 3970, Cpl. M. O'MEARA V.C., 16th Battalion [is] agreeable to return to Australia.'[371] These steps would probably have seen the request passed down through the chain of command with the Commanding Officer ultimately being responsible for implementation. It is likely that he would have met with Martin O'Meara around this time to test his appetite for returning to Australia.

On 25 July the Deputy Adjutant-General of the AIF, Brigadier-General Thomas Dodds, wrote to the commanders of the Australian divisions advising that 'V.C. winners in your Division who are willing to accept this furlough to report to Admin. Headqrs., A.I.F., London

---

[368] AWM25: 449/3, VC Winners Furlough to Australia.
[369] AWM25: 449/3, VC Winners Furlough to Australia.
[370] NAA: MP367/1, 556/33/51, Victoria Cross winners - Furlough to Australia.
[371] AWM25: 449/3, VC Winners Furlough to Australia.

for passage.'[372] At 9.20pm that night General Birdwood cabled Senator Pearce with a response to his 27 June cable. In it, he advised that:

> General Monash and Divisional Commanders agree that Victoria Cross winners who are willing to take it should be granted furlough and I concur (stop) approximate number who care to accept is 12 (stop) I am making arrangements at an early stage and will notify you later.[373]

On 27 July Senator Pearce announced that 'approximately 12' of Australia's Victoria Cross recipients would be returning to Australia on furlough as a recognition of them having been awarded the Victoria Cross, and also with the idea of stimulating recruitment by their presence.'[374] On 16 August the AIF Administrative Headquarters advised the Secretary of the Defence Department that ten men would be returning, but that 'no advice [had yet been] received' in relation to Martin O'Meara's willingness to return.[375]

These men assembled in London during the second half of August ahead of their return to Australia. A photograph taken on 21 August shows Sergeant John Whittle, Lance-Corporal John Carroll, Corporal Bede Kenny, Corporal Jorgen Jensen, Sergeant Walter Peeler, Lieutenant William Ruthven, Lieutenant Clifford Sadlier, Captain Percy Storkey, Lieutenant Leonard Keysor, Sergeant Robert McDougall and Corporal Reg Inwood at the Australian Administrative Headquarters at 130 Horseferry Road in London. Most of these men sailed for Australia on the *Medic*, arriving in Melbourne on 11 October.

On 23 August Senator Pearce cabled the AIF Headquarters in London asking for details of those Victoria Cross winners who were returning. The reply cabled back to Pearce from London on 25 August did not include Martin O'Meara's name,[376] although the 16th Battalion was in action east of Amiens until midnight on 23 August and making contact with the Commanding Officer may have been difficult. The battalion was resting at Coisy (just north of Amiens) from 24 August

---

[372] AWM25: 449/3, VC Winners Furlough to Australia.
[373] NAA: MP367/1, 556/33/51, Victoria Cross winners - Furlough to Australia
[374] *Evening News*, 27 July 1918, p.5.
[375] AWM25: 449/3, VC Winners Furlough to Australia.
[376] NAA: MP367/1, 556/33/51, Victoria Cross winners - Furlough to Australia.

onwards so it is possible that the Commanding Officer was not able to personally discuss the request with O'Meara and respond via the chain of command until 24 or 25 August. It now seems that Martin O'Meara made it clear to his Commanding Officer that he did not wish to return to Australia.

On 26 August Brigadier-General Dodds, wrote to Brigadier-General Thomas Griffiths at the Australian Administrative Headquarters in relation to Martin O'Meara advising:

> I am to inform you that the G.O.C. A.I.F. admires the fine spirit shown by 3970, Cpl. M. O'MEARA, V.C., 16th Battalion, in electing to remain on duty overseas in lieu of accepting the furlough to Australia which has been offered to him. In view, however, of Cpl. O'MEARA'S long service in the A.I.F., the G.O.C. directs that he should be returned to Australia on leave. This will meet the wishes of the Australian Government, and the trip to Australia will ensure for Cpl. O'MEARA a well-earned rest. Will you please arrange for Cpl. O'MEARA to report at an early date to A.I.F Administrative Headquarters, who have been instructed to arrange his passage to Australia.[377]

It is not known precisely why Martin O'Meara did not want to return home at this time. There is a range of possible reasons, and these include the possibility that he was happy to remain with his battalion (and his fellow soldiers) in Europe, that wanted to return to Ireland after the war, that he wanted to go to England because of Mary Murphy, and that he did not have anything to return to in Western Australia. There is, however, a suggestion that Martin O'Meara intended to return to Ireland after the war; his great-niece Noreen O'Meara recalls:

> I was also told that in September 1918 when he was told that he was being sent back to Australia, he said he wanted to go to back to Ireland (whether permanently or just for a visit I am not sure). He was told that was not possible.[378]

---

[377] AWM25: 449/3, VC Winners Furlough to Australia.
[378] Email from Noreen O'Meara to Dr Philippa Martyr, 31 October 2014.

It may be possible that he intended to use his deferred AIF pay and the money held in trust for him in Ireland to purchase a farm of his own so he did not have to be, as his parents (and grandparents) had been, tenant farmers. Or the reason may have been as simple as an aversion to publicity, and that he was nervous at the prospect of being a celebrity. The newspapers of the time mentioned the hesitation of some Victoria Cross winners to make public appearances:

"While preparing to do their best, the V.C. winners who have been returned to assist recruiting are very much afraid of the public platform. The mere thought of delivering speeches from the platform brings a cold sweat to their brow," said the Minister for Recruiting, Mr Orchard, to-day.[379]

Some of the Victoria Cross recipients, however, seemed happy to return home and the speaking engagements were probably seen as the price they had to pay for the privilege of an early return to Australia.

Events moved quickly after that, and on 30 August 1918 Martin O'Meara was promoted to sergeant in the place of Charles Russell who had been evacuated sick earlier that year. Given Martin O'Meara's imminent return to Australia for an extended period of leave, it is possible that the promotion was made by the battalion's Commanding Officer as a financial incentive (or perhaps a consolation) for O'Meara to return to Australia. It would seem unusual to promote a man into a position and then have him on extended leave. The promotion resulted in O'Meara's pay increasing from 10s per day to 10s 6d sixpence per day.[380]

The lure of additional financial reward for Victoria Cross recipients returning to Australia becomes obvious when the special arrangements are considered. Senator Pearce had agreed to very generous financial arrangements for these Victoria Cross winners, including being paid in advance for a period of up to sixty days' leave in Australia, a subsistence allowance of three shillings per day for up to sixty days (increasing to a travel allowance of fifteen shillings per

---

[379] *Kalgoorlie Miner*, 18 October 1918, p.5.
[380] NAA: K1143, O'Meara Martin.

day when actually on recruiting duties), and payment of up to 25% of the troops' accumulated deferred pay if desired.[381]

On 31 August the newly-promoted Sergeant Martin O'Meara left the 16th Battalion for the last time and on 1 September he sailed across the English Channel and disembarked at Folkestone from where he travelled by train to London and probably reported to the Australian Administrative Headquarters in Horseferry Road. Brigadier-General Dodds wrote to Brigadier-General Griffiths at the Australian Administrative Headquarters, on 7 September, noting that 'the [Defence] Minister has definitely expressed his wish that all V.C. winners be returned to Australia.'[382] Captain Albert Jacka was somehow fortunate enough to get approval to remain in England until late 1919, when he eventually returned to Australia. Martin O'Meara, however, remained in London until 12 September.

It is likely that O'Meara visited Mary Murphy at the Forest Gate Sick Home whilst in England in early September. Mary had left Caterham in April 1918, and had taken up nursing duties at Forest Gate east of London. It is possible that she was looking after his Victoria Cross medal, and that he wanted to take it with him to Australia. It is also likely that Mary Murphy had met another man, Walter Clews (a British soldier), by this time. O'Meara was interviewed by a representative of the Red Cross before he left England (probably between 1 and 12 September), and his address was given as West Ham, which suggests that he was staying near the Forest Gate Sick Home for some period between leaving France and leaving England.[383]

On 12 September he travelled to Weymouth on England's southern coast, where he joined the No. 2 Command Depot. He remained at Weymouth until around 5.45am on 15 September when he boarded a special train at Weymouth railway station and travelled northward to the port city of Liverpool, arriving at Riverside railway station at around 5.30pm the same day. He boarded the troopship *Arawa* that evening.[384] The group that left the No. 2 Command Depot

---

[381] NAA: MP367/1, 556/33/51, Victoria Cross winners - Furlough to Australia.
[382] NAA: B2455, Albert Jacka.
[383] AWM 1DRL/0428 2nd Lieutenant Horace Edgar Blee.
[384] AWM7: Arawa2.

and boarded the *Arawa* included around 500 invalids, 98 submarine guards, 36 'other reasons' and fourteen 'underage' passengers. Martin O'Meara was one of the 'other reasons' men who was returning on furlough and, despite his very recent promotion to sergeant, was listed as a corporal on the ship's nominal roll.[385] His name appears at the end of an alphabetical list of other ranks passengers, suggesting that he was possibly a relatively late inclusion as a passenger on the *Arawa*.

The Arawa at Port Melbourne on 18 November 1918. (AWM PB0114)

The *Arawa* remained at anchor on Liverpool's Mersey River on 16 September, and sailed at 8.30am on 17 September. The ship initially sailed with a Royal Navy escort, including the armed merchant cruiser *Orotava*, but this was no longer required after 26 September as the ship sailed further south through the Atlantic Ocean.

On 26 September 1918, aboard the *Arawa*, O'Meara signed a registration form for the Australian Government's Repatriation Department. He indicated a desire to be a sleeper cutter after his eventual discharge from the AIF; alternatively, he expressed an interest in being a farmer and a desire for financial assistance from the Repatriation Department to establish himself as a farmer. His intended address in Australia was care of the Drill Hall in Francis

---

[385] AWM7: Arawa2.

Street, Perth, which was the 5th Military District headquarters at the time. Importantly, the form did not indicate that O'Meara had any health problems.[386]

The *Arawa* sailed around the west coast of Africa and arrived at Cape Town on 12 October 1918, but the men were not allowed ashore due to 'pneumonic influenza raging in the city and suburbs'.[387] Coal, water and provisions were taken aboard at Cape Town. Departing Cape Town on 15 October, the *Arawa* arrived at Durban on 19 October where additional coal, water and provisions were taken aboard. Again, the men were unable to disembark and 'Everyone on board greatly disappointed', although one man, Private James Farley of the 28th Battalion, managed to swim to shore, where he was later arrested by local police.[388] The *Arawa* departed Durban on 22 October and sailed for Fremantle.

Martin O'Meara arrived at Fremantle on the *Arawa on* the morning of 6 November, but the possibility of influenza infection amongst the passengers resulted in Western Australia-bound passengers being transferred by boat the next day to the Woodman's Point Quarantine Station, nine kilometres south of Perth, for a seven-day quarantine period.[389] The admission registers for the quarantine station record that eight officers and 117 soldiers were admitted for 'suspected influenza.'[390] There had been an outbreak of influenza on board the *Arawa* during the voyage:

An epidemic of influenza broke out amongst the crew immediately after leaving England. Precautions were taken to prevent spread of disease, and although influenza broke out amongst the troops, it was quickly stamped out.[391]

---

[386] The registration form signed by O'Meara is held by the Army Museum of WA, and appears to have been removed from a Repatriation Department file.

[387] AWM7: Arawa2.

[388] AWM7: Arawa2. James Farley was returned to Australia on another vessel after his apprehension and subsequent court-martial.

[389] *Kalgoorlie Miner*, 7 November 1918, p.4.

[390] NAA: PT1675/1, NN, Woodman Point Quarantine Station Admissions.

[391] AWM7: Arawa2.

The men were quarantined despite the AIF Medical Officers on board the *Arawa* advising that there were no longer any cases of influenza aboard.[392] A contemporary newspaper report noted that five of the men were admitted to the quarantine station's hospital, one with a suspected case of influenza and four with 'other complaints' on 7 November, but that some of the men had already been discharged by 9 November.[393]

The men were undoubtedly disappointed about this delay, but the time at Woodman's Point was not uncomfortable, with a local newspaper carrying a report that the men were 'grateful for the care and attention which has been shown them by the doctors and the quarantine staff, and by the Red Cross Society, which has left them wanting nothing in the way of comforts.'[394] The quarantining of the men on the *Arawa* did, however, upset local plans to welcome them back to Australia:

> The returned wounded soldiers and Anzacs on furlough, listed to arrive to-day, will not be quarantined unless anyone on the vessel landed at any infected port, or unless there are any cases of influenza on the ship. If they are permitted to land, the disembarkation flag will be flown from the Fremantle Town Hall at least an hour before. The V.C. winner and the Anzacs will land in a separate party and will progress up High-street to the Town Hall where they will be tendered a civic reception.[395]

On 8 November the *West Australian* newspaper reported on a telephone interview conducted with Martin O'Meara from the quarantine station. It is likely that the interview took place on 7 November. The report recorded (and some parts have been reproduced elsewhere in this biography) that O'Meara stated:

> "I was born in Tipperary 34 years ago this month," he said, "and I came out here in 1911 like a lot of other young Irishmen had done before me, to try my luck in Australia. I spent a couple

[392] AWM7: Arawa2.
[393] *West Australian*, 9 November 1918, p.6.
[394] *Daily News*, 11 November 1918, p.4.
[395] *West Australian*, 6 November 1918, p.8.

of years in South Australia, but in 1914 I came to the West and settled in the bush about 34 miles out from Collie. Yes, I was sleeper cutting. In August 1915 I got into khaki and in December of the same year I left with the 12th reinforcements of the 16th Battalion, and in the following August went into action at Mouquet Farm. That was my first experience of war, and it was pretty hot, too, I can tell you. We were carrying up ammunition under heavy shell fire – a sort of fatigue party – and of course a lot of fellows were wounded. I went out to do what I could do for the poor chaps that were lying all around waiting for the stretcher bearers and helped a lot of them to get in out of danger. I went down to the cookers and got some hot tea and went out again with a stretcher and brought in more. Then I got a slight stomach wound, and they told me I was recommended for the Victoria Cross for something that had happened during the time from the 8th of August until the 12th, I suppose it was for fetching those wounded officers and diggers. You see, after the first day's fighting and while I was out on my own, the battalion was relieved, so I just stayed there by myself doing this little job. After I got hit I walked back to the dressing station and, to cut things short, soon got over to Blighty. I had about four months in hospital and then went out to France again and had put in about seven months when I was sent to London on special duty, and then the King gave me the Cross. That was on July 21, 1917. Then after I had a look round the place I went back to France and was only there a couple of days when in the fight at Messines I 'went out' to a wound on the hip and was sent back to England to be patched up and – here I am in quarantine. Where is my home? Why, I haven't one. Under any old gum tree I suppose is the best way to describe it. No, I'm not married and this place'll do me 'for the duration'. We are quite comfortable and happy, and I don't care when the doctor sees me.[396]

It seems possible that at least one other newspaper reporter had contact with Martin O'Meara whilst he was at Woodman's Point, perhaps through one of the staff there or one of the other returned soldiers. The *Midlands Advertiser* (published each Friday in the small

[396] *West Australian,* 8 November 1918, p.7.

town of Moora some 200 kilometres north of Perth), published a small article on the men of the *Arawa* who were in quarantine:

> Amongst these heroes is the Irish-man, who is still wondering why he, more than any other soldier, should have been decorated with a V.C.[397]

This could only have been a reference to Martin O'Meara, as he was the only Victoria Cross recipient on the *Arawa*. The *Advertiser* added that 'These "boys of the Empire" were to have a fine reception both in Perth and Fremantle.'[398]

---

[397] *Midlands Advertiser*, 15 November 1918, p.1.
[398] *Midlands Advertiser*, 15 November 1918, p.1.

13 'Delusional Insanity'

Perth's newspapers carried extensive coverage (and speculation) about armistice negotiations whilst Martin O'Meara and his fellow servicemen were in quarantine at Woodman's Point during November 1918. Speculation about a possible German surrender spread quickly around Western Australia; the *Kalgoorlie Miner* reported on 9 November 1918 that:

> Unwanted scenes of excitement were witnessed in the several centres of goldfields activities yesterday morning, following upon the announcement of unofficial news that Germany had yielded to the allies' terms for granting an armistice to her.[399]

Speculation increased over the following days and by the morning of 11 November arrangements were already being made for formal celebrations of the end of the war. The *Daily News* reported that a massed gathering ('in the nature of a thanksgiving service') would be held at Fremantle oval[400] and the *West Australian* reported that the 'military authorities wish it made known that in the event of an armistice being signed licensees of hotels will be requested to close their premises on the day notification is received.'[401]

Following the quarantine period, the men would be transported by boat from Woodman's Point to Victoria Quay at Fremantle, arriving there at 11.30am on 14 November 1918,[402] although a group of them was released a day early (on 13 November) to make way for new arrivals.[403] The Western Australia Government had declared 13 November as a public holiday in celebration of the end of the war and major commemorations were planned, including a march by returned servicemen through the streets of central Perth commencing at 2pm. The parade was proposed to include both Lieutenant Clifford Sadlier

---

[399] *Kalgoorlie Miner*, 9 November 1918, p.4.
[400] *Daily News*, 11 November 1918, p.7.
[401] *West Australian*, 11 November 1918, p.5.
[402] *West Australian*, 12 November 1918, p.4.
[403] *West Australian*, 13 November 1918, p.4.

and Martin O'Meara, both Victoria Cross recipients,[404] but O'Meara was still in quarantine and obviously unable to attend.

The end of the war was greeted with great excitement by most of those men in quarantine who were returning home to friends and family, but things were not as straightforward for Martin O'Meara. He did not have a home ('under any old gum tree I suppose', he had told the reporter from the *West Australian*) and no family in Australia. He did not have a job, and was faced with the prospect of a hero status that he did not seem to want.

He was also a very long way from his former home in Ireland, where his status as a Victoria Cross hero is unlikely to have made him popular, even with his own family. A return to Ireland would have been difficult. His relationship with Mary Murphy also seems to have ended, as she become interested in another man, a British soldier, by this time. In short, there seemed to be little for him in Australia, Ireland or Britain.

Martin O'Meara had some sort of serious mental breakdown at Woodman's Point between 8-13 November 1918. A lack of surviving records and a broad media 'silence' on mental health issues at the time make it difficult to accurately determine what actually happened. The *Call and WA Sportsman* reported that, without being specific about the nature of his illness:

> After being released from quarantine at Woodman's Point Martin O'Meara, V.C., was so unwell that he was detained for treatment at another hospital. We understand his case will require careful attention from specialists for some considerable time.[405]

His hospitalisation meant that he was not amongst the returned servicemen who landed at Fremantle on 13 and 14 November. On 13 November he was transferred to the 24th Australian Auxiliary Hospital ('Stromness'), a thirty-bed army facility for the mentally ill that had been opened in April 1918,[406] and that was located on the corner of St Leonard's Street and Monument Street at Mosman Park

---

404 *West Australian*, 13 November 1918, p.6.
405 *Call and WA Sportsman*, 15 November 1918, p.6.
406 Butler, 1943 ,p.752.

in suburban Perth. Stromness had been established by the Australian Government to accommodate returned soldiers with mental problems who were being accommodated (unsatisfactorily) in the Western Australian Government's mental health system. It had earlier been described as 'a well built stone house with nine good lofty rooms … It is an ideal place for mentally afflicted cases.'[407] Stromness was under the command of Captain (later Major) J. Theo Anderson, who was also the Western Australian Government's Inspector-General of the Insane under the *Lunacy Act 1903*. Anderson travelled to Stromness from the nearby Claremont Hospital for the Insane on a regular basis to attend to the patients.[408]

On 17 November 1918 the *Sunday Times* reported that Martin O'Meara had returned to Perth 'but is unfortunately ill', but did not elaborate on the nature of his illness. [409] A civic reception for Martin O'Meara and the other returning soldiers had been planned for Fremantle on 14 November to coincide with their expected release from quarantine, but had to be postponed. The *West Australian* reported on 14 November that 'arrangements which were made to tender a civic reception to Sergeant O'Meara V.C. and other returned Anzacs unfortunately have to be postponed owing to the serious indisposition of the V.C. winner'.[410] A separate formal reception by the Hibernian Society was planned for 26 November but, 'for obvious reasons, was postponed.'[411]

Martin O'Meara's mental condition whilst at Stromness does not appear to have been good. In December 1918 Dr Anderson reported that:

this patient is suffering from Delusional Insanity, with hallucinations of hearing and sight, is extremely homicidal and suicidal, and requires to be kept in restraint.[412]

---

[407] NAA: MP367/1, 500/1/349, Purchase of Stromness Mental Cases Treatment 5MD.
[408] The Claremont Hospital for the Insane was known as the Claremont Mental Hospital after 1933.
[409] *Sunday Times*, 17 November 1918, p 8.
[410] *West Australian*, 14 November 1918, p.4.
[411] *W.A. Record*, 30 November 1918, p.7.
[412] NAA: B2455, Martin O'Meara.

His behaviour was so poor that several special attendants were sent from Claremont Hospital for the Insane to look after him whilst at Stromness, and he was kept in a straight jacket at times whilst there.[413] His condition, however, was too severe for Stromness to manage. At 4.45pm on 3 January 1919 Martin O'Meara was transferred from Stromness to the Claremont Hospital for the Insane where he was admitted 'on account of his suicidal and violent tendencies';[414] he was admitted to Ward M3, the male infirmary ward which was also used for new admissions. This account is consistent with another account, given by Claremont's Dr James Bentley[415] in October 1919, that 'O'Meara got so troublesome that he had to be shifted to Claremont.'[416]

The main building of the former Claremont Hospital in 2014. The other buildings in this complex have been demolished and the land redeveloped as suburban housing. The main building will be used as an aged care facility.
(Author)

O'Meara's transfer to Claremont was facilitated by the *Mental Treatment Act 1917*, which allowed serving and former military and naval personnel 'suffering from mental disorder of recent origin

---

[413] Legislative Assembly, 1919, p.117.

[414] NAA: PP13/1, C5474, O'Meara Martin VC.

[415] Dr Bentley had returned from the Western Front (he had served with the 4th Field Ambulance) in 1918. He had then resumed his pre-war employment at Claremont. In 1926 he became Inspector-General of the Insane for Western Australia and medical superintendent at Claremont.

[416] Legislative Assembly, 1919, p.117

arising from wounds, shock, disease, stress, exhaustion, or any other cause' to be admitted to institutions like Stromness for treatment without being certified insane. Importantly, the *Mental Treatment Act 1917* removed the normal admission requirements, and Regulations made under that Act provided that the request for admission could be made by the military's Principal Medical Officer in Western Australia or the Officer in Charge of the base hospital at Fremantle (being the 8th Australian General Hospital). The Regulations also provided that a patient could be admitted for a period not exceeding six months, but that this could be extended by the Inspector-General of the Insane.[417]

Martin O'Meara's brief admission records indicate that his admission to Claremont was requested by Colonel Arthur White of the Australian Army Medical Corps, the Principal Medical Officer with the 5th Military District (the state of Western Australian), that he was suicidal, and that the cause of his insanity was 'religion'.[418] Amongst Martin O'Meara's property at the time of admission to Claremont was some cash (£2 14s 3d), his old Army pay book, several Victoria Cross pension notices, his Victoria Cross medal, a gold watch (probably the one presented by the people of Lorrha in November 1916), a crucifix, a jewellery box, four prayer books, a pack of cards, and his army uniform.[419] The Victoria Cross medal and the watch were subsequently locked in the hospital's safe.

Although Martin O'Meara's mental illness is commonly attributed to his wartime service, and some records indicate that his illness was due to his war service, no comprehensive diagnosis exists that proves this conclusively. Owing to the passage of time and the paucity of primary sources, we are unlikely to find evidence of such a diagnosis.

---

[417] The *Mental Treatment Act 1917* was assented by the Governor on 28 March 1917 and the Regulations were approved by the Governor on 27 April 1917 and gazetted that day See Western Australia, *Government Gazette*, No.19, 27 April 1917, pp.619-620.

[418] SROWA: Series 4500, Consignment 1120, Item 27: Patient Admissions Register (Claremont Mental Hospital, Military Personnel Only). This information is consistent with that required under the Regulations made under the *Mental Treatment Act 1917*.

[419] SROWA: Series 4500, Consignment 1120, Item 27, Patient Admissions Register (Claremont Mental Hospital, Military Personnel Only).

Based on the material that does survive in archival and newspaper accounts, however, it is not possible to conclude that he was suffering what is now known as Post Traumatic Stress Disorder (PTSD), or alternatively a condition that was often known as 'shell shock' at the time. There is no doubt that the conditions experienced by Martin O'Meara during the war were traumatic, and that they were most likely a contributing factor to his breakdown. His wartime service as a scout would have been stressful; a British Army officer noted that the tasks of scouts were demanding: 'Psychologically, going out into No Man's Land in the dark, especially if you are alone, is a distinctly eerie business.'[420]

Generally, it is accepted that many Australian soldiers did suffer poor mental health as a result of their wartime service and a whole chapter appears on the subject in one of Australia's First World War official histories.[421] From the evidence available, however, it appears unlikely that Martin O'Meara's wartime service was the sole cause of his mental illness. It is very likely (and almost certain) that a range of other factors also played a role. The possibility that Martin O'Meara had a pre-existing condition or predisposition to mental health problems cannot be excluded. The official Australian war histories note that there was no real screening of men for mental illness at the point of enlistment:

Nothing in the nature of a systematic and deliberate elimination of recruits "morally and mentally" unfit took place in Australian recruiting.[422]

Upon enlistment, a man's mental condition seems to have been taken very much at 'face value' without any further investigation. The official war histories identified this matter as a problem during the war:

But one of the most definite "lessons" of this war is the importance of the family and personal history in determining moral and mental breakdown in war. Here by far the chief

---

420 Hesketh-Pritchard, 1920, p.199.
421 Butler, 1943, pp.56-147.
422 Butler, 1943, p.76.

difficulty lay in mis-statement or suppression by the recruits in the matter of personal and family history.[423]

The discipline of psychiatry was poorly developed in the early part of the twentieth century, and the study of the relationship between combat and mental illness was relatively new. Nearly a century later, psychiatry still recognises that pre-existing factors are important contributors to mental illness. The World Health Organisation has identified three broad determinants of mental health.[424]

Firstly, a person's individual attributes and behaviours are a factor, in that innate and learned strengths (or weaknesses) combined with genetic and biological factors are important. In Martin O'Meara's case, this would have consisted in his own personality, social interaction, and behaviours (some of which we can identify through primary and secondary sources) and genetic factors.

Secondly, social and economic circumstances are important, and these include issues of family, community, education, economic status. In Martin O'Meara's life, his position as the youngest son in a relatively large but relatively poor farming family with limited social mobility is relevant. Being unmarried may also be important, as it is quite possible that a change in his relationship with Mary Murphy played a part in his breakdown in November 1918. The likely change in his relationship with his family in Ireland from late 1917 onwards may also be relevant.

Thirdly, the World Health Organisation identifies environmental factors as also being important. In Martin O'Meara's life, some of the key external factors are likely to have included his Roman Catholic faith (particularly as it impacted on his social and ethnic identity), the impact of emigration from Ireland to Australia, his dependence on short-term labouring work, and his wartime service. His friendship with Mary Murphy may have been a source of ongoing disappointment.

Possibly linked to this are the circumstances surrounding his return to Australia in 1918, where he was reluctantly brought to Australia for a period of leave, only to have this arrangement radically

---

[423] Butler, 1943, p.77.
[424] World Health Organisation, 2012, p.3.

altered as a result of the Armistice on 11 November 1918. This meant that his plans to return to Europe could not continue. Political circumstances in Ireland following the uprising in April 1916 are likely to have made a return to Ireland difficult. The matter of religion may also be a factor, as his admission record to Claremont in early 1919 refers to 'religion'[425] but is hardly ever raised elsewhere. Numerous other sources reveal Martin O'Meara's devout Roman Catholic faith, but no evidence exists to conclusively link this to his mental condition.

Rather than PTSD, a more likely diagnosis for his condition seems to be a schizoaffective disorder such as a long term trauma-induced psychosis triggered by the factors identified above.[426]

Martin O'Meara's early days at Claremont were unpleasant: he spent up to 24 hours a day in a straight jacket during the first week or so. A later medical report on Martin O'Meara recorded that:

On observation at Claremont Asylum attacked attendants without provocation, but apparently instigated by voices – Depressed and restless – Strikes attendants without cause – Sullen and morose – will not speak at times – Suicidal.[427]

He was a difficult patient. At around 2.15am on the night of 3-4 January 1919, his first night at Claremont, he escaped from his straight jacket and had to be restrained by attendants with the help of another patient. He was then medicated and slept for several hours. He escaped from his restraint again the following night and was 'abusive and violent' and was again medicated. He continued to break out of his straight jacket on the nights of 7 January, 9 January, 11 January, 12 January and 15 January.[428]

Records show that O'Meara did manage to sleep through some nights without problems. His overall behaviour improved over the months, but tended to be characterised by unpredictable violent

[425] SROWA: Series 4500, Consignment 1120, Item 27, Patient Admissions Register (Claremont Mental Hospital, Military Personnel Only).

[426] Martyr & Davison, 2015, pp.537-8.

[427] NAA: PP13/1, C5474, O'Meara Martin VC.

[428] SROWA: Series 1771, Consignment 1120, Item 116.

outbursts. A letter from the Mental Hospitals Department to the Repatriation Department, written some years later, recorded that:

At first the patient was very restless and subject to very acute hallucinations of hearing, in response to which he was frequently violent and attacked the Attendants. He was very obstinate and difficult to manage. Occasionally he shouted out and beat the air with his hands. He saw various visions. Later he got into frenzied states at times. He thought he was attacked by mobs of people and that he had to fight his way out. He was subject to visual and auditory hallucinations and was frequently noisy during the night.[429]

On 6 January he was 'taken out of Restraint for 2 ½ hours he was very quiet and had his bath and [did] everything he was told and gave us no trouble' but the next day he was taken out of his straight jacket for around one hour and 'became very violent' and had to be restrained again.[430]

The attendants' diaries for 16 January notes that '[he was let] out of restraint for one hour when he tried to rush windows and door. Struggling very violent against the [attendants] …'[431] A week later, on 26 January, the attendants noted that he 'got out of restraint and was very violent. Struggling … He bit off a piece of his clay pipe.'[432] The attendants' day registers record that Martin O'Meara 'bit the top off his tongue' on 12 February.[433] Martin O'Meara was also disruptive in non-violent ways. On 9 March he was 'restless and noisy singing at intervals' and on 15 March he was 'laughing and singing early part of morning.' Two days later he was 'trying very hard to knock his head on back of bed' and on 22 May he was 'very restless, bouncing his bed and bumping his head on bedstead.'[434] On 3 August he threw a plate of food on the floor, and on 15 September he hit one of the attendants

[429] NAA: PP645/1, M5474, Martin O'Meara VC.
[430] SROWA: Series 1771, Consignment 1120, Item 115.
[431] SROWA: Series 1771, Consignment 1120, Item 116.
[432] SROWA: Series 1771, Consignment 1120, Item 116.
[433] SROWA: Series 1771, Consignment 1120, Item 115.
[434] SROWA: Series 1771, Consignment 1120, Item 116.

and broke his tooth whilst the attendant was lighting his pipe for him.[435]

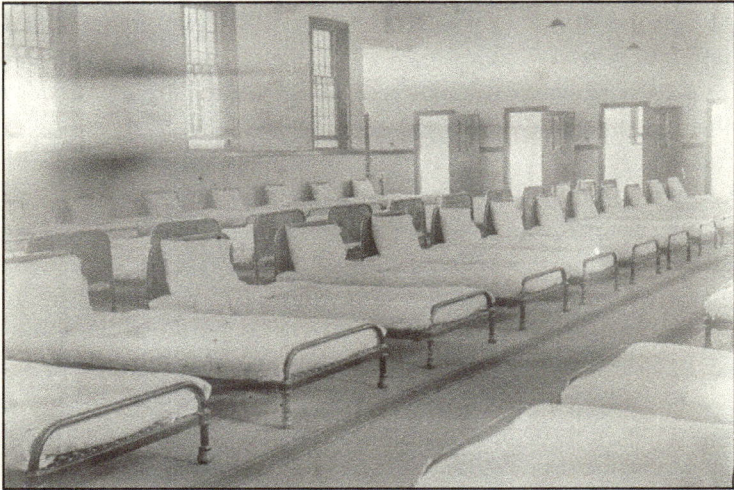

Interior of a ward at the Claremont Asylum for the Insane, 1909. (SLWA 154095PD)

Martin O'Meara largely disappeared into obscurity after his admission to Claremont, although he did appear in occasional articles in Perth newspapers. One such article appeared in the *Sunday Times* on 23 February 1919, nearly two months after his admission to Claremont, when it was reported that:

> Poor Martin O'Meara V.C. has made no appreciable progress since a serious illness struck him down on the return to the State of his adoption.[436]

No mention was made of the nature of his illness, although it was likely the subject of discussion around Perth.

Claremont Hospital remained an ongoing topic of interest during 1919. On 27 August 1919 Walter Jones MLA, the Labor member for Fremantle, moved a motion in the Legislative Assembly to establish a Royal Commission into the conditions of employment of the staff at

---

[435] SROWA: Series 1771, Consignment 1120, Item 115.
[436] *Sunday Times*, 23 February 1919, p.5.

Claremont, the methods under which the patients were admitted and detailed, and the fitness of the Inspector-General of the Insane, Dr J. Theo Anderson, to hold his position. Jones outlined a range of allegations about the treatment of both staff and patients.[437] Debate on the Jones motion resumed on 24 September with the Colonial Secretary (the Hon Frank Broun MLA) responding 'To a large extent the points raised by [Mr Jones] are founded on misrepresentation and exaggeration, and are untrue.'[438]

After some debate the Legislative Assembly amended the motion and appointed a Select Committee (rather than a Royal Commission) to inquire into the management of the Claremont Hospital for the Insane. This Committee is sometimes referred to as the 'Angwin Committee' after its chairman, the Hon William Angwin MLA, Member for North-East Fremantle. It held 22 meetings and interviewed 55 witnesses, and inspected the Claremont hospital. Those interviewed included Dr J. Theo Anderson and several of his staff, as well as a number of patients and relevant others. Dr Anderson's evidence to the Select Committee suggested that:

O'Meara is an extremely impulsive and homicidal patient, and he has many delusions, particularly of a religious nature, and it would not be safe for him to be out of a straight jacket after 9 o'clock.[439]

Similar testimony was given by Dr James Bentley, who stated that:

[in September or October 1919 O'Meara] made a violent attack on the attendants, and he was very much off again a few days ago [mid-October 1919] ... he was lying on the ground and kissing the earth and listening. His form of insanity is that the Almighty is calling upon him to attack some one.[440]

The records from Claremont indicate O'Meara's recurring tendencies to attack the attendants and, on occasions, other patients. For example, on 8 February 1919, he was injured during a struggle

---

[437] Legislative Assembly of Western Australia, Hansard, 27 August 1919, pp.359-360.
[438] Legislative Assembly of Western Australia, Hansard, 24 September 1919 p.628.
[439] Legislative Assembly of Western Australia, 1919, p.139.
[440] Legislative Assembly of Western Australia, 1919, p.117.

with an attendant that he had attacked, and on 18 November 1919 he was treated for facial injuries suffered during a fight with several other patients that he had attacked.[441] Dr Anderson also testified that 'It is not so long ago since he deliberately bit the tip of his tongue clean off.'[442]

An 'official visitor' to the Hospital, Dr William Birmingham, attested to Martin O'Meara's suicidal behaviour, reporting that 'he has been intensely suicidal.'[443] Another official visitor, Benjamin Darbyshire, testified that:

> I saw O'Meara, V.C., when he was in a straight jacket. There was an attendant with him, and O'Meara was smoking a pipe. On this occasion Dr. Anderson said to him, "O'Meara, will you give me your word that you will not knock anybody about, and I will let you out" ... O'Meara simply swore.[444]

The chief attendant at Claremont, James McKeown, testified about O'Meara in testimony before the Select Committee:

> He has not been violent since I have been there, for the last eight months. He is always in restraint at night time. There are two attendants on him during the day.[445]

James McKeown added that O'Meara was put in a straight jacket at night 'For the protection of the night officer. There is only one night officer' and that he had spent each night in a straight jacket for the 'past six or seven months.'[446] This practice was to continue into 1920.

Not all reports to the Select Committee, however, were as bad. A charge attendant, Thomas Smith, testified that:

---

[441] SROWA: Series 1771, Consignment 1120, Item 115.

[442] Legislative Assembly of Western Australia , 1919, p.139.

[443] Legislative Assembly of Western Australia, 1919, p.123. The two official visitors were appointed under the *Lunacy Act 1903* to visit public mental health facilities and provide some external scrutiny of how they were being operated.

[444] Legislative Assembly of Western Australia, 1919, p124.

[445] Legislative Assembly of Western Australia, 1919, p.85.

[446] Legislative Assembly of Western Australia, 1919, p.85.

[between 4.00 p.m. and 9 p.m. he] … has been very good. There is only one occasion on which he has been uncontrollable since I have been in charge of the hospital. That was four or four and a half months ago. It was between 5 and 6 in the morning.[447]

Thomas Smith also noted that:

The doctor's order is that O'Meara is to be put in a straight-jacket, and I carry out that instruction … He is of a very morose disposition, and a man who is likely to go off at any time. Then it would take four or five men to handle him. He is a very powerful man.[448]

Another attendant from Claremont, Alexander Watt, testified that he knew Martin O'Meara, and:

At times … [he was troublesome] … He was always in a straight-jacket at night. He has got out of the straight-jacket by himself … He hardly ever speaks; he just mumbles to himself.[449]

A former attendant, Mark Wakeford, also testified that O'Meara had escaped from the straight jacket, 'I was called out three times in one night for O'Meara, V.C., who had got out of his restraint.'[450] This probably took place within the first few weeks of O'Meara arriving at Claremont.

The Committee's report was tabled in the Legislative Assembly on 11 November 1919, and covered a range of topics including staffing, the provision of food, the influenza epidemic and the administration of croton oil (a powerful laxative) to patients. In relation to staffing, the committee found that a lack of attendants on duty overnight meant that 'patients have to be put under restraint.' In short, putting Martin O'Meara in a straight jacket seemed like an easier option than having more attendants on duty overnight. The Committee considered Martin O'Meara's case in detail, noting that:

---

[447] Legislative Assembly of Western Australia, 1919, p.89.
[448] Legislative Assembly of Western Australia, 1919, p.89.
[449] Legislative Assembly of Western Australia, 1919, p.109.
[450] Legislative Assembly of Western Australia, 1919, p.15.

The evidence discloses that Sergt. O'Meara, V.C., is kept under restraint in a straight-jacket for approximately 14 ½ out of the 24 hours every day. He is put in the straight-jacket each evening between 8.30 and 9 o'clock, when one of the attendants goes off duty, and is not released from the restraint until about 11 o'clock next morning. This patient is in the same ward between the hours of 4 p.m. and 8.30 p.m. without being under restraint, but there are additional attendants on duty.[451]

Claremont Hospital, however, did have a number of single ('seclusion') rooms with lockable doors, and these could have been offered as an alternative to physical restraint. The attendants' record books show that straight jackets were not commonly used at Claremont, and only in cases that seemed to be extreme.

The nature of Martin O'Meara's illness became public on 11 November 1919 following the tabling of the 'Angwin Committee' report in the Legislative Council. A debate took place in the Legislative Assembly on 20 November, with Labor Party opposition leader, the Hon Philip Collier MLA, noting:

> Sergeant O'Meara, the second Western Australian to win the Victoria Cross, is unfortunately an inmate in this institution. Although he is well enough to be free from about 4 o'clock in the afternoon until 8 o'clock in the evening he is then placed in a straight jacked and remains in that until 11 o'clock the next day.[452]

On Friday 21 November the *West Australian* reported on the previous night's Legislative Assembly discussion surrounding the Select Committee's report, noting that 'Trenchant criticism of the management of the Claremont Hospital for [the] Insane was made in the Legislative Assembly last night'. The report added that 'the Inspector-General [of the Insane] was wholly unfit for the position ... [and] ... there had been nothing but chaotic management.'[453]

It is quite possible that Martin O'Meara may have been selected for particularly harsh treatment by Dr Anderson and the other staff as he

---

[451] Legislative Assembly of Western Australia, 1919, p.ix.
[452] Legislative Assembly of Western Australia, Hansard, 20 November 1919, p.1585.
[453] *West Australian*, 21 November 1919, p.7.

had given them such a hard time when he was first admitted to Claremont in January 1919. Many patients were recorded as 'troublesome' in the attendants' record books but Martin O'Meara seems to be the one consistently held in restraint during 1919 and the first part of 1920. The *West Australian* noted that 'Patients had been kept in straight-jackets for extremely long periods, and among them was O'Meara V.C.' and William Angwin MLA, the Chairman of the Select Committee, was reported as saying that 'it was a disgrace and scandal to the State that Sergeant O'Meara V.C. should be confined in a straight-jacket for 14 ½ hours out of every 24.'[454]

Meanwhile, Martin O'Meara remained both a patient at Claremont and a serving member of the AIF. An Army medical report prepared by the No. 8 Australian General Hospital at Fremantle on 14 October 1919 (whilst the Select Committee was taking evidence) noted that Martin O'Meara's present condition was:

Rambling in his statements – generally suspicious – Resented being asked about voices – depressed and restless – memory uncertain – States feels well – Staring overstrung appearance.[455]

In October it was decided that he was permanently unfit for further military service, and he was discharged from the Australian Imperial Force on 30 November. His AIF wage of 10s 6d per day, with an allotment of 3s per day to Alice O'Meara as his next-of-kin, ceased on that date. The Western Australian Supreme Court's Master in Lunacy, as trustee for his financial affairs, then applied for a war veteran's pension on his behalf, and he received this pension for the rest of his life on the basis that his condition was 'a sequel to, or was … aggravated by his employment in connexion with warlike operations.'[456] He also received an additional annual payment from the British Government of £10, as the recipient of the Victoria Cross.

Martin O'Meara remained in mental institutions in Perth until his death in 1935, although references to the state of his mental health are

---

[454] *Kalgoorlie Miner*, 22 September 1919, p.5.
[455] NAA: PP13/1, C5474, O'Meara Martin VC.
[456] NAA: PP13/1, C5475, O'Meara Martin VC. Whilst it is not possible to prove conclusively that O'Meara's condition was the direct result of his war service, it would be difficult to argue that his war service did have a deleterious impact on his mental health.

inconsistent. His treatment as a patient at Claremont continued to receive sporadic media coverage during the succeeding few years. On 14 December 1919 a newspaper report noted that:

> No. 2 district council of the R.S.A. has endorsed a motion from the East Perth branch recommending the immediate transfer of all returning soldier mental cases from Claremont to convalescent home, and condemning the treatment of Martin O'Meara V.C.[457]

However, the year did not finish well for Martin O'Meara; on 29 December he got into a fight with another patient.[458]

The start of 1920 saw Martin O'Meara 'restrained' for 10 ½ hours each day. Interestingly, the attendants' record books for the year identify which patients were restrained and Martin O'Meara stands out as the only patient routinely restrained (for up 10 ½ hours each day). He remained in Ward M3 for all of 1920, with the Attendants' day and night record books providing a good overview of his behaviour during the year.[459]

On 1 January 1920 O'Meara turned another patient out of his bed and then broke the bed. That night he was sleepless, noisy, and troublesome, and was attacked by another patient, suffering cuts around his left eye. He was also abusive towards the attendants 'inviting them to fight & urging other patients to put [one of the attendants] out of the ward.' He was given a dose of paraldehyde at midnight but it did not take effect until 2am. His disruptive behaviour continued through January and he was frequently noisy and troublesome and frequently required a sedative (usually paraldehyde, but sometimes bromide) to sleep at night. On 5 January 1920 he was reported as being 'very abusive and threatening to [the medical superintendent, Dr James Bentley].'[460]

---

[457] *Sunday Times*, 14 December 1919, p.5.
[458] SROWA: Series 1771, Consignment 1120, Item 115.
[459] SROWA: Series 1771, Consignment 1120, Items 120 and 122.
[460] Paraldehyde was a hypnotic, commonly used in psychiatry in the first half of the twentieth century. 'Bromides' (usually sodium bromide) were mild sedatives developed and sold over the counter in the first half of the twentieth century, and were also used in psychiatry as a sedative. They were also believed to dampen

His troublesome behaviour on 7 January saw him restrained on a straight jacket for three and a half hours during the day (he was in a straight jacket each night but rarely during the day at this stage). On 16 January he was recorded as being troublesome and received a 'slight cut on nose and forehead struck with spittoon' during a fight with another patient; O'Meara had managed to hit the other patient on the head with a spittoon during the same fight. On 20 January he got himself into a fight with another patient, and ended up with a cut on his forehead. The attendants had recorded that O'Meara was 'Troublesome fighting says he is King of England'. Ironically, Martin O'Meara was probably the only person in Claremont who had actually met the King of England.

Late in the evening of 28 January he was noted as being' restless, and noisy invites [another patient] … to let him out of the jacket and assist him to knock out the attendant and clear the establishment.' Such behaviour suggest the attendants continued to feel threatened by O'Meara, particularly at night when fewer attendants were on duty.

O'Meara continued being threatening and abusive into the early part of February. On the evening of 10 February he was particularly troublesome, and was abusive to the attendants and other patients, and wanting to escape from his straight jacket so he could fight. The next day he had the opportunity to fight, when another patient initiated violence. O'Meara ended up with an abrasion near his eye. On 13 February the same patient, who was described by the attendants as 'dangerous in the ward using a broom may strike someone', struck him again.

On 17 February O'Meara reported a physical illness, something that he suffered rarely, when he 'complained of sore throat appears slightly swollen temp 98.' Records suggest that he spent that night unrestrained, a rarity, and that he slept well. The next day he hit, but did not injure, another patient. Attendants' records indicate that he slept unrestrained, but possibly locked in a single room, for several nights in late February.

---

sexual appetite, which would be seen as advantageous in single sex custodial care.

Although he was sedated with paraldehyde on most nights during February and through into March and April, he had several troublesome outbursts during this period. On 8 March he was recorded as being 'troublesome at tea time was placed in Restraint' and spent fifteen hours (rather than the 'usual' ten and a half hours) restrained in a straight jacket. Several days later he was reported as being 'noisy & abusive at intervals' and 'noisy & threatening towards morning'. On 15 March he was 'troublesome & threatening the Atts. & attempted to strike [another] patient'.

The attendants recorded that, overnight on 25 March, he 'became very noisy at 1.30am attempted to drag his bed along the floor when prevented he became very violent and abusive he punched [an attendant] in face, was given [paraldehyde].' Two days later he broke a mug.

On the evening of 15 April O'Meara 'objected to be put in jacket saying the Dr. had not ordered it. Force had to be used to place him in restraint'. It is possible that Dr James Bentley, the medical superintendent, was considering ceasing the practice of restraining O'Meara in a straight jacket every night, but that the attendants did not support this. The next day O'Meara was 'abusive & troublesome towards attendants.' On 27 April he was noisy and became involved in a fight with another patient, who was 'quarrelsome fighting with O'Meara the latter has a swollen eyebrow'. That night, however, O'Meara was quiet and slept well. The next day he fought with another patient. The pattern of night-time restlessness continued into May; on 6 May he was 'very noisy & threatening & wanted to fight [another] patient … who was also noisy' He was sedated after this, and slept well.

On 10 May 1920 an important breakthrough for Martin O'Meara occurred. Dr James Bentley decided that he no longer needed to be restrained in a straight jacket each night, and he was kept in a single room (presumably with the door locked) each night. He remained generally well behaved during the day and restless overnight during the remainder of May and was sedated on most nights.

He did have a brief relapse of troublesome behaviour on the evening of 30 May when he was 'very noisy shouting & banging his bed about the room was given draught good effect.' His troublesome behaviour continued into June, with his behaviour on 1 June being 'restless and abusive.' The next evening he was 'abusive & threatening to Atts. he also threw away one draught but was given a second one.' His behaviour as much calmer during the rest of June, although he did continue to have problems sleeping and was frequently restless at night.

Records suggest that some of Martin O'Meara's behaviour was linked to the behaviour of the other patients. In particular, one patient seems to have been quite a problem during this time. On 1 July another patient was 'abusive & threatening', which resulted in O'Meara hitting him on the face. During the evening of 6 July O'Meara was recorded as being 'noisy and threatening to fight [the same] patient' and ten days later [on 16 July] he was recorded as being 'very noisy caused by [the same] patient … abusing him draught no effect.' Several times during July he hammered at the door of his single room asking for a sleeping draught. He clearly wanted to sleep, but could not.

He was reasonably well behaved during August, but was usually noisy overnight as he seems to have had difficulty sleeping. He was given a sleeping draught several times during the month to help him sleep. On the evening of 18 August he was recorded as being 'destructive pulled hair out of his mattress.'[461]

He was recorded as usually well behaved, but often noisy and restless at night, during September. He seemed to have had problems sleeping on most nights and was sedated with a sleeping draught or paraldehyde on several nights during the month. Despite this, he was reported as being threatening and abusive during late September. During the evening of 18 September he was reported as:

> noisy & abusive to attendants, banging on door of [single room] was given Draught at 10pm slept till 12am when he again became very noisy and abusive banging on door and shouting for medicine he was given Paraldehyde.[462]

Several days later, on 21 September, he was reported banging his bed around his room and was given a sleeping draught. He repeated this type of behaviour later during the month. The next day he got

---

[461] SROWA: Series 1771, Consignment 1120, Item120.
[462] SROWA: Series 1771, Consignment 1120, Item 122.

into a fight with another patient and had a severe cut under his eye. This resulted in him locked in a single room during the day; he was normally only confined to a single room overnight.

During October he was frequently sleepless and noisy at night, but often given a 'sleeping draught' which helped him sleep. He was not recorded as being violent or troublesome during the month but on 19 October he was hit by another patient, suffering a cut to his face; it was dressed and treated with iodine. His condition seems to have settled during the last few months of 1920. He was recorded as being noisy and restless, but usually overnight when he seems to have had ongoing problems sleeping. He was sedated on most nights during these months. He was not recorded as being troublesome or violent during either November or December. He remained in Ward 3 at the end of 1920.

Martin O'Meara's treatment by the Western Australian mental health system remained an ongoing topic of debate during 1921, when Walter Courthope, a Perth solicitor and former Claremont Hospital patient, petitioned the Western Australian Government for a Royal Commission into the mental health system. In February 1921 he raised the treatment of returned soldiers as a cause for concern:

> I will now briefly refer to the treatment accorded to returned soldiers under the present inhumane regime, but before doing so I wish to state that only a comparatively few attendants are guilty of this incredible brutality, the majority being decent, humane men … [and of O'Meara] … I have never seen him or other patients suffering from the same complaint receive any treatment, and he is gradually getting worse.[463]

The earlier treatment of Martin O'Meara at Claremont Hospital was made an election issue by the Labor Party in March, when it advised that a vote for the existing Nationalist Party government would involve voting 'for the sort of murderous man-handling that O'Meara V.C. received at the hands of the Asylum tyrants.'[464]

References to Martin O'Meara in newspapers drop off from 1921 onwards, although the Claremont hospital attendants' record books

---

[463] *Sunday Mirror*, 13 February 1921, p.1.
[464] *Sunday Mirror*, 6 March 1921, p.3.

provide an interesting overview of changes in his condition. A pattern is evident through these records, with his condition overnight typified by difficulty in sleeping (frequently requiring sedation) and his daytime condition varying significantly. He is often recorded as being violent or disruptive, but the attendants' day record books often ignore him for periods of days or weeks suggesting peaceful and compliant behaviour.

During this time O'Meara seems to have developed a reliance on paraldehyde (and other sedatives) to help him sleep. On 31 March he asked for, and was given, paraldehyde at 10pm. He was frequently sedated at night, sometimes at his own request. On 8 April he was sleepless and 'complained at 11pm that he could not sleep & asked for a draught which was given to him' and the following night he was restless and noisy 'asked for & was given a draught at 11.20pm.'

O'Meara's mental health deteriorated during July and he was sedated overnight frequently, as he was often sleepless and noisy. He was also given daily doses of bromide during the day during the early part of the month. On 6 July he attempted to 'pick a quarrel' with another patient, and on 14 July he was 'troublesome came out of his room and challenged [another] patient … to a fight.' The following evening he was 'very restless will not keep to his bed continually coming out into dormitory & disturbing other patients.'

This pattern of nightly behaviour continued. On 21 July he was 'very restless & troublesome will not keep to his bed continually coming out to fire' and on 23 July he was 'continually leaving his room & standing by the fireplace.' On 28 July he was 'very restless & troublesome: continually coming out of his room demanding the keys of the door to the medicine chest.' This suggests that he, again, wanted to be sedated.

August was another bad month for Martin O'Meara. On 1 August he was recorded as being noisy and sleepless, and was 'very troublesome & noisy refusing to go to his room & continually demanding draughts', which he was given. During mid-August he had a particularly bad run. On the evening of 15 August he was 'noisy and abusive towards attendants' and on 17 August another patient started a fight with him. The following day he was hit by another patient and got abrasions on his face.

He remained frequently sleepless and restless at night during September, and was often noisy. He was sedated virtually every night during September to assist him with sleeping. On 2 September he suffered a minor, but unspecified, injury fighting with another patient, and on 7 September he was hit in the face by another patient, resulting in a bleeding nose. His mental health, however, did begin to improve as he grew used to being at Claremont, and on 7 September the Inspector-General of the Insane wrote to the Deputy Repatriation Commissioner advising that:

> this patient is less trouble-some and he shows a slight mental improvement, but he is still talkative and at times noisy, and often his conversation is incoherent.[465]

There was an influenza outbreak in the hospital during the second and third weeks of September, and Martin O'Meara was unwell and bedridden with a high temperature from 12-26 September.

On 28 September 1921, the Hon William Angwin MLA, Mr Horace Jackson (a solicitor) and Dr William Jones (Victoria's Inspector-General of the Insane) were appointed as Royal Commissioners to inquire into and report upon a range of matters related to the treatment of the mentally ill in Western Australia. The Royal Commission's consideration of specific patient cases was to be limited; the Commission's report later noted that:

> Certain individual cases have been brought very prominently under public notice, and such cases as have not already been made the subject of Royal or other Commissions of inquiry were investigated.[466]

These 'certain individual cases' seem to have included Martin O'Meara. The Royal Commission took evidence during October, November and December 1921.

Martin O'Meara was the victim of an assault on 1 October 1921 when another patient 'attacked O'Meara without provocation striking

---

[465] NAA: PP645/1, M5474, Martin O'Meara VC.
[466] SROWA: Series 4700, Consignment 2961, Item 1, Report - Royal Commission on Lunacy, p.8.

him in the mouth & face no visible injury.'[467] A medical assessment carried out in October for the renewal of his war pension indicated that there had been no improvement in his condition and that he would remain in hospital for 'some considerable time.'[468] His condition remained similar for the rest of 1921. On 8 November he fought with another patient in the airing court of his ward, and on 13 November he was abusive to the attendants. He hit another patient on 17 November.[469] This pattern continued into December. He was sedated with paraldehyde on most nights, but the pattern of sleeplessness and restlessness seems to have abated as the attendants only recorded seven nights where he was sleepless and/or restless.

Only the attendants' day record books survive for 1922,[470] so we have an unclear picture of the state of his overnight health and behaviour for the year. During the first few months of 1922 he was frequently restless and noisy during the day, and troublesome. On 14 January he was 'very restless and noisy in airing court' and on 17 January he 'threw [another patient] to the ground. No apparent injury.' On 13 March he was 'very abusive to Dr on rounds.'

The work of the Royal Commission on Lunacy was completed in early January 1922, and its report was provided to the Government on 5 January. The Commissioners' report concluded that:

An emotionalism which has effected [sic] the judgement of many persons of ill-balanced mentality has resulted in the publication in the Press of incredible or distorted tales reflecting on the character of an institution and staff whose service presents difficulties wholly unintelligible to the average individual.[471]

This would seem to refer to the repeated comments made by former patient Walter Courthope that had largely triggered the Royal Commission.

---

[467] SROWA: Series 1771, Consignment 1120, Item 126.
[468] NAA: PP13/1, C5474, O'Meara Martin VC.
[469] SROWA: Series 1771, Consignment 1120, Item 126.
[470] SROWA: Series 1771, Consignment 1120, Item 131.
[471] SROWA: Series 4700, Consignment 2961, Item 1, Report - Royal Commission on Lunacy, p.15.

In relation to the matter of 'restraint' and 'seclusion', the report noted that 'Statements made by patients and ex-patients appear to suggest that both restraint and seclusion are too frequently used at Claremont.' The reported provided statistics that showed that restraint had been used on four male patients during 1920 (on 194 occasions totalling 2,757 hours), and on four male patients between 1 January 1921 and 12 December 1921 (on 27 occasions totally 398 hours). Seclusion (in single rooms) was not used on male patients during 1920, but was used on three male patients (21 occasions totally 188 hours) from 1 January to 12 December 1921.[472] The report added that:

> The Inspector General explains that much of this restraint is necessary for medical and surgical reasons, to prevent self-mutilation, and in one case in particular, for extremely destructive habits and self-mutilation. This explanation in all probability does not give the whole reason for such a large amount of restraint.[473]

The 'one case in particular' was Martin O'Meara, although the report did not elaborate on the nature of his 'destructive habits.' Dr Anderson had been questioned by the Chairman, Dr Jones, on 29 December 1921 and provided the following evidence relating to Martin O'Meara (although he was not mentioned specifically by name):

> [Dr Anderson] On the male side there is one patient to whom restraint was applied on 122 occasions for a total of 1295 hours.

> [Dr Jones] Is there anything special in that?

> [Dr Anderson] He was very homicidal and very suicidal, and practically the whole of the restraint was at night. When taken out of the restraint he was one of the few who would come and

---

[472] SROWA: Series 4700, Consignment 2961, Item 1, Report - Royal Commission on Lunacy, 1922, p.13. Restraint and seclusion was used at much greater levels in the female wards at Claremont..

[473] SROWA: Series 4700, Consignment 2961, Item 1, Report - Royal Commission on Lunacy, 1922, p.13.

ask to be put in restraint again as he had no confidence in himself.[474]

It seems that the Royal Commissioners were not fully convinced about Dr Anderson's explanations on the use of restraint and seclusion. No other evidence has been found to confirm that O'Meara actually wanted to be restrained overnight, although he was later reported as wanting to be sedated at night as he had problems sleeping. The only specific reference to Martin O'Meara by name in the evidence given to the Royal Commission was by patient Walter Courthope:

I never saw Martin O'Meara, V.C., actually ill-treated but I have seen him tied down and in a straight jacket for 14 of 15 hours out of 24 … I never saw O'Meara in any way treated for his complaint. He was getting worse all the time.[475]

Martin O'Meara remained intermittently noisy and restless during mid-1922, but during July it seems to have improved enough for him to leave the ward and wander around the hospital grounds, as the Claremont records for 17 July note that he was 'Out with wood party this afternoon.'[476] Presumably this group collected firewood for cooking and heating at the hospital.

His behaviour appears to have improved the second half of 1922, although with some restless periods from November onwards. On 23 November he suffered 'Abrasions on the face caused by fighting with [another] Patient … O'Meara the aggressor' and on 27 November he was 'Excited and troublesome, made an attack on [the same] patient … in the day room no apparent injury.' The next day he was similarly behaved and 'Continually challenging others to fight.'[477] He

---

[474] SROWA: Series 4701, Consignment 2962, Item 1, Transcript of Evidence - Royal Commission on Lunacy, p.761.

[475] SROWA: Series 4701, Consignment 2961,, Item 1, Transcript of Evidence - Royal Commission on Lunacy, p.155. Courthope's evidence was regarded with suspicion by the Royal Commissioners and should not be regarded as fully reliable. His comments on Martin O'Meara, however, are consistent with other accounts.

[476] SROWA: Series 1771, Consignment 1120, Item 131.

[477] SROWA: Series 1771, Consignment 1120, Item 131.

continued this pattern of aggressive behaviour through until the end of 1922.

Despite intermittent periods of improvement, Martin O'Meara's mental health did not improve significantly whilst at Claremont. The Inspector-General of the Insane noted that, in 1923, he:

> showed loss of control and failure of power of voluntary attention. His hallucinations persisted. At times he became exceedingly restless and noisy and not infrequently required sedatives.[478]

This account is generally corroborated by the Claremont hospital day and night attendants' record books for 1923.[479] His behaviour saw him noisy and restless on several occasions during the day and usually restless (and requiring sedation to sleep) each night. On 8 January he was hit without provocation by another patient and suffered abrasions on his face. That night he was recorded as being sleepless and noisy. At 8.20pm he struck one of the attendants on the head and challenged him to fight. He was ordered back to bed but struck the attendant again and then struggled violently with the attendants. He was put into a single room 'with great difficulty' and given a draught to help him sleep. The next day (9 January) O'Meara was 'Very troublesome challenging patients & Atts to fight', hitting patients.' The fighting continued on 10 January when he suffered 'Abrasions on the face caused by fighting with Patients .... O'Meara the aggressor.' This type of behaviour continued through the first half of 1923. On 4 February he was 'restless & very noisy in & out of single room, jumping & shouting loudly. Given draught 9.30pm. No effect. Continued jumping & shouting at intervals.' On 18 February he suffered slight facial abrasions while fighting with another patient and, on 18 March, he hit a fellow patient on the face. A week later he started a fight with another patient. During the evening of 29 March he was 'very troublesome, given sulphanal powder, fair result became restless & noisy at 12 M.N. demanding draught on being refused became very noisy & excited struck Att. McKenzie on head.'[480]

---

478 NAA: PP645/1, M5474, Martin O'Meara VC.
479 SROWA: Series 1771, Consignment 1120, Items 135 and 137.
480 Sulphonmethane was sold under the brand name Sulphanal, and was a hypnotic.

On 8 April he fought with another patient, the attendants' records noting 'O'Meara abrasions on face O'Meara the aggressor', and the next evening he 'became troublesome & noisy wanting to fight attendants was given draught.' On 1 May O'Meara was struck on the head with a plate by another patient, but suffered no visible injuries and, on the evening of 16 May, he was 'noisy and threatened the attendants, and the following evening he was 'troublesome wanted to fight [another] patient.' On 26 May he hit, without provocation, an attendant who suffered abrasions to his face; he was subsequently sedated. On 28 May he started another fight with a fellow patient, and on 30 May he struck another patient on the face.

His behaviour remained poor during the second half of 1923. He managed to get into several fights during the month; on 17 July he fought with another patient and got a slight cut on his nose and on 25 July he received an abrasion on his nose whilst fighting. On 3 August he was recorded as troublesome and 'continually annoying other patients & wanting to fight.' He was noisy and fought with another patient on 21 August and on the evening of 25 August he 'went into telephone room and obtained a suit of clothes. He insisted upon putting clothes on, so with assistance of Att. on rounds they were taken from him, trousers were torn.'

On 14 September he received a 'slight abrasion on head & cut on lip, fighting' and subsequently had his lip stitched by the Medical Superintendent. His behaviour during the final months of 1923 remained much the same. He seems to have been relatively good during the day and overnight he was generally sleepless and noisy and was usually sedated.

The attendants' record books for 1924[481] record that Martin O'Meara was still in Claremont's Ward M3 at the start of 1924, and the first half of January saw him generally restless and noisy, but infrequently sedated. On 4 January he was 'Excited & violent struck [another] patient ... on the forehead, also kicked [another] ... on the right leg.' He hit another patient again the next day and on 6 January he hit another patient. Several days later, on 8 January, he started a fight with another patient, with both men suffering facial scratches.

---

481 SROWA: Series 1771, Consignment 1120, Items 140 and 242.

The treatment of returned soldiers with mental health conditions had continued to simmer as a topic of discussion during the early 1920s but resurfaced again during January 1924. During that month, a former AIF officer, Lieutenant-General Sir Joseph Talbot Hobbs, had visited the Claremont Mental Hospital on behalf of the Returned Sailors and Soldiers Imperial League of Australia (RSSILA)[482] and found that returned soldiers were sharing wards with 'Chinamen and Afghans.'[483] This resulted in a series of emotive articles appearing in Perth newspapers, with the *Sunday Times* being particularly outspoken. On 27 January it published a strongly-worded editorial noting:

> It is well known that amongst the terrible legacies of the war is the mental affliction of many of our brave soldiers ... It has come to our knowledge that those poor fellows who may be in any way violent of judged hopelessly insane – frequently only a matter of opinion – have been removed from Stromness and placed in the Hospital for the Insane at Claremont, there to herd with the mentally deranged of all nations and colors. The Hospital for the Insane may be a desirable sort of residence or it may not – most people will incline to the latter opinion – but it is certainly no place to put our mentally afflicted soldiers.[484]

The *Sunday Times* was to take a leading role in advocating for better conditions for Martin O'Meara and the other returned servicemen at Claremont. A meeting between the RSL and the Colonial Secretary (who was the State Government minister responsible for mental health matters) was quickly arranged, and action was taken quickly; a number of returned soldiers in Claremont were transferred to a separate ward (X Block) on 1 February. Martin O'Meara was one of these patients. The X Block wards were physically separated from the other buildings at Claremont, and had been constructed from 1908 onwards to increase capacity in the overstretched main hospital buildings. X Block consisted of four two-

---

[482] Later known as the Returned Services League and now the Returned and Services League. The acronym RSL is used for consistency in this biography.
[483] *Daily News*, 1 February 1924, p.5.
[484] *Sunday Times*, 27 January 1924, p.1.

storey buildings, with dormitory accommodation upstairs and day room facilities downstairs.

The report of the Royal Commission in Lunacy conducted in 1921-22 had noted that 'these wards are of a simple and suitable design' but that 'one day room is in use as a dormitory and all dormitories contain rather more patients than originally provided for.'[485] However, conditions in X Block were regarded as better than those in the other wards, and patients were accorded a much greater level of freedom and independence.[486]

On 3 February the *Sunday Times* published another editorial on Claremont, reporting good progress on the matter of the returned soldiers:

It is pleasing to relate that public opinion and an agitation by the R.S.L. has forced the State Government to realise its obligations to the men fought for the Empire in the great war.[487]

On 12 February the *Daily News* reported that a representative of the Perth sub-branch of the RSL had:

reported having visited the returned soldiers at the Hospital for the Insane, Claremont. He was pleased to state that, following the recent agitation, a noticeable alteration had taken place in the treatment of the soldier inmates of the institution, who were now all in one ward in "X" block under the care of returned soldier attendants.[488]

The same article reported that 'a number of things were required for the amusement of the inmates' and that 'One of Western Australia's V.C. heroes, now an inmate of the soldiers' ward, would be grateful for the gift of a flute.'[489] This could only have referred to

<hr>

[485] SROWA: Series 4700, Consignment 2962, Item 1, Report - Royal Commission on Lunacy, p.4.

[486] The X Block buildings have since beensignifcently expanded and now form part of the mental health facility known as Fortescue House, which is part of the Graylands Hospital complex.

[487] *Sunday Times*, 3 February 1924, p.13.

[488] *Daily News*, 12 February 1924, p.8.

[489] *Daily News*, 12 February 1924, p.8.

Martin O'Meara, although it is not known whether O'Meara could play the flute.

The RSL formalised its lobbying efforts on this matter, and formed a 'visiting committee with a view to bringing about better conditions for the mentally afflicted returned men.'[490] Martin O'Meara's transfer to X Block, however, means that we have very scant information on his time at Claremont from February 1924 onwards, as the attendants' record books (which contain much useful information) focus on Wards 1 to 5 with virtually no information recorded on the X Block patients.

Former X Block buildings in 2015, now Fortescue House, part of the Graylands Hospital complex. (Author)

In March 1924 an agreement was reached between the Commonwealth and Western Australian Governments for the construction of a new mental hospital for returned soldiers. The State was to provide the land at West Subiaco (around two kilometres east of Claremont) and half the cost of actual construction (with the Commonwealth providing the other half) and the Commonwealth would fund the State Government to care for those patients, such as Martin O'Meara, who were the responsibility of the Repatriation Department.[491] Those former soldiers who were not the responsibility

---

490 *Sunday Times*, 3 February 1924, p.13.
491 *Sunday Times*, 9 March 1924, p.5.

of the Repatriation Department remained the responsibility of the State Government. Claremont housed a number of such patients who may have been hospitalised after their discharge from the AIF, or whose mental condition may not have been due to their war service. There was also a small group of former British Army soldiers at Claremont.

Conditions for the formers soldiers at Claremont Hospital started to improve after their transfer to X Block from the other wards. On 19 May, representatives of the RSL visited the men at X Block and reported that there was improvement in the men's conditions; they also made specific reference to Martin O'Meara's condition:

> We are glad to report that the improvement in certain individual cases has been excellent ... a V.C. hero, who before the R.S.L. took action to have the change brought about was deemed to be in a hopeless condition and was addicted to violent outbreaks, is now enjoying the limit of freedom, and spends most of his days in the open grounds tending a garden. It is hoped that he will soon regain the full vigour of his health and be well enough to return home.[492]

The issue of the new hospital continued during 1924, with continued agitation by the RSL and others for quicker progress. The *West Australian* described the lack of progress as being due to disagreements between governments:

> The controversy between the Federal and State Governments in regard to the care of soldier mental patients drags on, but we are apparently getting no nearer to the removal of the unfortunate men now housed at Claremont to more congenial surroundings.[493]

Negotiations continued during 1924 and agreement on the terms of an arrangement between the Federal and Western Australian Governments was ultimately reached, and construction of the new hospital at West Subiaco commenced in mid-1925.

---

[492] *Daily News*, 26 May 1924, p.2.
[493] *West Australian*, 15 September 1924. p.8.

On the afternoon of 25 December 1924 the Red Cross hosted a Christmas tea for the returned soldiers at Claremont's X Block and each patient was presented with his own Christmas parcel. This was the first Christmas function organised exclusively for the returned soldiers at Claremont.[494] Despite the improvement in conditions experienced by Martin O'Meara following his transfer to X Block, his health remained variable. During this period he was later described by staff as being:

> obstinate and difficult to manage, sometimes refusing to get out of bed. On other occasions it was difficult to put him to bed, it sometimes taking three or four Attendants to accomplish this.[495]

Martin O'Meara's family in Ireland continued to have a limited amount of interest in him, and perhaps more interest in the financial benefit they derived from him. In August 1925, his sister Alice O'Meara wrote to the Repatriation Commission seeking an allocation of £2 10s per month from his AIF pension.[496] She was, until his discharge in November 1919, receiving an allotment of 3s per day from his AIF wage. Martin O'Meara was subsequently interviewed in relation to this matter at Claremont's X Block by the Inspector-General of the Insane, still Dr J. Theo Anderson at that time. Dr Anderson noted the following comments:

> His statements are very erratic and he denies that he has a sister named Alice. He admits that he has a sister named Mary who is married in New York to a man named Rohmer. He says that he has not supported any sister, but has occasionally sent them a present when he had the money. O'Meara's mental condition is such that it would be inadvisable to place much reliance on any statements that he makes.[497]

Some of O'Meara's statements, however, *could* be relied on; his sister Mary *did* live in New York and *was* married to Bernhard

[494] *Sunday Times*, 28 December 1924, p.1.
[495] NAA: PP645/1, M5474, Martin O'Meara VC.
[496] NAA: PP13/1, C5474, O'Meara Martin VC.
[497] NAA: PP13/1, C5474, O'Meara Martin VC.

Rohmer, and it seems that Martin O'Meara *did* send money back to his family in Ireland. On 28 September 1925 Alice O'Meara's claim for a portion of her brother's pension was rejected, but she was granted an allowance of 25s per fortnight from his pension.[498] This allowance continued until his death.

Interest in the welfare of the former soldiers at Claremont started to grow further during 1926. On 24 February, the RSL wrote to the Repatriation Commission advising that the Western Australian Branch had established a committee to 'watch the interests' of the former soldiers housed in Claremont's X Block.[499] The committee consisted of Rabbi David Freedman, the Rev Eric Nye and Tom Lennon. Rabbi Freedman had served as the senior Jewish chaplain with the AIF during the war and continued to take an active interest in the welfare of former servicemen after the war. He was active in the RSL until his death in 1939. Rev Nye was a Methodist minister who had served as a chaplain with the AIF in Europe, and Tom Lennon had served with the 28th Battalion.

Being accommodated in X Block provided the opportunity for the returned serviceman at Claremont to spend time away from the hospital in recreational activities. In March 1926, Mrs Agnes Jacoby (wife of Frederick William Jacoby, proprietor of the Mundaring Weir Hotel and mother of Frederick Wilson Jacoby, a former officer in the Australian Flying Corps and a mental patient at Claremont) was reported as having finalised arrangements 'for six charabanc trips for the mental patients of X Block.'[500]

A charabanc was a large motor car with several rows of bench seats (an early type of mini-bus), typically used for outings and day trips. As a typical charabanc may have been able to seat up to fifteen passengers, it is likely that all of the X Block patients could have enjoyed a day trip away from Claremont. It is possible that these trips provided the first opportunity for Martin O'Meara to spend time away from hospital since his return to Australia in November 1918.

498 NAA: PP13/1, C5474, O'Meara Martin VC.
499 NAA: K89, G29/247, Mental Homes – HQ Correspondence [care of Repatriation Patients].
500 *Sunday Times*, 21 March 1926, p.7.

14   The Final Decade

On 12 July 1926 a new hospital for returned servicemen, the Soldiers' Mental Hospital Lemnos, was opened at West Subiaco by the State's Governor, Sir William Campion.[501] Built to accommodate around 70 men, it was a collaborative venture between the Commonwealth and Western Australian Governments and was designed to provide a more comfortable environment that that at Claremont where many of its patients were being accommodated.

Lemnos Hospital buildings under construction with the 'C' Ward building in the foreground and 'B' Ward to its right. A small portion of 'A' Ward is visible at top right. (Sunday Times, 4 July 1926, p.1)

A newspaper report of the time described the effort required to have the Lemnos facility established:

The revelation of the conditions under which these unfortunate soldiers were existing at the Claremont Hospital for the Insane, came as a shock to the community. Some alleviation of their unhappy lot followed the publicity, but it has taken more than

---

[501] The site is adjacent to Shenton Park railway station and the buildings still exist and now form part of Shenton College, a secondary school.

two years, including months of vigorous and sustained agitation by patriotically-minded citizens, to ensure their being housed and care for as befits their state, and the sacrifices which they made ...[502]

The Lemnos hospital consisted of three separate ward blocks ('A', 'B' and 'C' Wards) together with administration and kitchen/dining room blocks. The more acute cases occupied the northernmost ward ('A' Ward) which had beds for 23 patients. This ward was more secure than the other two, with the same newspaper report noting that:

Here, it will be possible to exercise all necessary Control and Supervision over refractory patients. All the windows are chocked in such a manner that the patient may be confined there in safety and yet the window may be kept open for a space of about six inches. There is a day room attached to this, and to all other wards. A billiard table, handsome upholstered chairs, bookcases, and a cosy fireplace are provided while the bay windows are magnificently draped and the walls plentifully decorated with pictures.[503]

This block was further divided into two dormitories, one with ten beds and another with twelve beds, and three single rooms 'for special cases',[504] presumably for patients such as Martin O'Meara.

On 13 August 1926, Lemnos Hospital was declared a hospital for the insane under the *Lunacy Act 1903* and an institution for the treatment of war veterans under the *Mental Treatment Act 1917*.[505] The process of moving patients from the Stromness and Claremont hospitals to Lemnos then began, with twenty of Claremont's X Block patients being transferred to Lemnos from 23 August. Martin O'Meara and twenty more X Block patients were transferred on 20 September, and five more from Wards 1 and 3 were transferred on 27

---

[502] *West Australian*, 13 July 1926, p.6.

[503] *Daily News*, 12 July 1926, p.5.

[504] *West Australian*, 13 July 1926, p.8.

[505] Western Australia, *Government Gazette*, No.37, 13 January 1926, p.1584.

September.[506] The Stromness patients had been transferred on 16 August.[507]

Lemnos Hospital 'A' Block in December 2015. (Author)

A Board of Visitors was established for Lemnos Hospital at the request of the Chief Secretary's Department under the *Lunacy Act 1903*. This board was constituted with effect from 1 October.

On 23 October, the *Daily News* reported that Dr James Bentley had been selected to replace Dr J. Theo Anderson who had retired as Inspector-General of the Insane.[508] Dr Bentley had worked at Claremont Mental Hospital prior to the war, and had served as a Medical Officer with the Australian Army Medical Corps at Gallipoli and on the Western Front during the War. He was very familiar with Martin O'Meara and his condition.

On 27 October, an RSL visiting committee reported on a recent visit to Lemnos, and was impressed with the difference between Claremont and Lemnos. They noted that the patients had more freedom, wore ordinary clothing (rather than a hospital uniform), and had better accommodation and facilities. The Committee also noted an improvement in the patients:

---

[506] SROWA: Series 1771, Consignment 1120, Item 150.
[507] NAA: K89, G29/247, Mental Homes, HQ Correspondence [care of Repatriation Patients].
[508] *Daily News*, 23 October 1926, p.1.

Your Committee was impressed by the apparent improvement in the demeanour of the patients under the new conditions. They seemed stronger physically, quieter and saner in conversation, and general mental outlook … In the acute cases block ['A' Block, where Martin O'Meara was housed], men were interviewed who, in the C.H.I. appeared wild, rowdy and troublesome, At 'Lemnos' the same men seemed to be much quieter and quite well behaved.[509]

The men at Lemnos were provided with a wide range of activities to keep them entertained, including football matches, dances, concerts, the cinema, picnics, tennis, walking parties, billiards, euchre, sports competitions, morning teas, cricket, and excursions by motor vehicle. The various ladies' auxiliaries of former AIF units, particularly the 44th Battalion Ladies' Auxiliary, and a number of RSL sub-branches from the Perth area also organised monthly concerts at Lemnos for the men.

Martin O'Meara's mental health remained variable after he arrived at Lemnos, with the Mental Hospitals Department later advising the Repatriation Department that:

In 1927 he paced the floor at times and stamped his feet. He would rush wildly to and fro cursing imaginary persecutors. He was still subject to hallucinations of sight and hearing.[510]

A Melbourne estate agent, Alex McMillan, wrote to the Repatriation Department in early 1927 seeking information on Martin O'Meara's health. McMillan had visited Ireland during the second half of 1926 and had met one of Martin's brothers (probably John O'Meara), and John O'Meara seems to have sought his assistance in getting information about his brother, of whom he had heard nothing since 1923.[511] The response provided to Mr McMillan in January 1927 noted that O'Meara 'shows no mental improvement but his health otherwise is excellent. At times he is restless and very talkative, but

---

[509] NAA: K89, G29/247, Mental Homes – HQ Correspondence [care of Repatriation Patients].

[510] NAA: PP645/1, M5474, Martin O'Meara VC.

[511] NAA: PP645/1, M5474, Martin O'Meara VC.

appeared to appreciate "Lemnos" ... and its extensive surroundings.'[512]

On 13 April 1927 Martin O'Meara was invited, as a Victoria Cross recipient, to attend ANZAC Day celebrations and a special dinner to be held in Melbourne that month. He did not attend, with the Repatriation Department telegramming in reply to the invitation stating that *'O'MEARA V C CONFINED MENTAL INSTITUTION ATTENDENCE ANZAC DAY CELEBRATIONS IMPOSSIBLE'*.[513] Those Victoria Cross recipients who did attend dined in the presence of the Prime Minister, Hon Stanley Bruce MP, and Sir John Monash on 24 April and then joined 25,000 returned servicemen who marched in Melbourne the next day. The Duke of York (later King George VI, the father of Queen Elizabeth II) took the salute and later personally greeted each Victoria Cross recipient.[514]

The Duke was in Australia with his wife, the Duchess of York (late Queen Elizabeth, and then Queen Elizabeth the Queen Mother), to open Parliament House in Canberra on 9 May. The Duke and Duchess visited Western Australia in late May and spent the morning of 25 May (the last day of their Australian tour) visiting returned servicemen at Perth Hospital. A small group of patients from Lemnos travelled to Perth Hospital to meet the Duke and Duchess,[515] but the composition of this group is not known. As a Victoria Cross recipient it would be expected that O'Meara would attend, but this seems unlikely given his condition.

The RSL's visiting committee visited Lemnos again on 17 November and noted that it was 'impressed with the improvements of the grounds, and the general demeanour of the patients, and in fact everything pertaining to the soldier's welfare at this very up-to-date institution.'[516]

A report in the *Sunday Times* on 13 May 1928 noted that a number of Lemnos patients attended the 25 April ANZAC Day

---

[512] NAA: PP643/1, M5474, Martin O'Meara VC.
[513] NAA: PP643/1, M5474, Martin O'Meara VC.
[514] *West Australian*, 26 April 1927, p.6.
[515] *Western Argus*, 31 May 1927, p.10.
[516] *Sunday Times*, 20 November 1927, p.7.

commemorations in Perth. The report described Lemnos in glowing terms:

> The striking experiments initiated at this splendid Institution by the late Dr. Anderson, Inspector General, and efficiently carried on by his successor, Dr. J. Bentley, have dissipated by actual experience all fears expressed in the early days of "Lemnos" ...[517]

Despite his confinement in a mental institution, Martin O'Meara did have some level of social engagement with the outside world, participating the various types of activities offered at Lemnos. It seems that he enjoyed himself on such occasions. The *West Australian* reported on 27 December 1929 that Martin O'Meara 'danced an Irish jig to the pleasure of all present' at a concert held at Lemnos earlier in the month,[518] and an article in the *Daily News* of 14 March 1930 reported that:

> Madame Bennett Wilkinson was assisted this week by Miss Treadgold and Miss Thornbury in entertaining the soldier patients at Lemnos. The dancing of Mr. Martin O'Meara, V.C., was a feature of the evening and songs were given by the patients.[519]

On 9 April 1930 the patients of Lemnos were entertained by the Perth sub-branch of the Ladies' Auxiliary, with Martin O'Meara reported as having danced an Irish jig.[520] The 44th Battalion Ladies' Auxiliary organised a fancy-dress Christmas function at Lemnos on 17 December 1930, and a newspaper report later noted that 'Our first V.C. temporarily forsook military service to become a Naval commander.'[521] Given that Martin O'Meara was the only Lemnos patient with a Victoria Cross, it is quite likely that this refers to him. The report also noted that the event featured dancing and music, together with a meal and the exchange of gifts. A newspaper report

---

[517] *Sunday Times*, 13 May 1928, p.3.
[518] *West Australian*, 27 December 1929, p.14.
[519] *Daily News*, 14 March 1930, p.2.
[520] *West Australian*, 11 April 1930, p.5.
[521] *Daily News*, 19 December 1930, p.8.

noted that a Mr O'Mara had performed during a visit by the Perth RSL sub-branch to the Lemnos hospital on 8 April 1931, and it is very likely that also this refers to Martin O'Meara.[522]

Martin O'Meara is known to have had infrequent contact with his family in Ireland during the years that he was in Claremont and Lemnos, but none of the letters are known to have survived. His great-niece Noreen O'Meara notes that, according to her father (another Martin O'Meara, Martin's nephew) a recurring theme in the letters was that Martin O'Meara believed that he was the only sane person in the hospital.[523] In January or February 1932, Alice O'Meara wrote to the Repatriation Commission inquiring about her brother's health, and the Inspector-General of the Insane was subsequently asked to ascertain if 'he is able to write a letter to his sister (if he still remembers her).'[524] A response, dated 27 February, noted:

He is at times very restless and delusional, as for example, when he was requested to write to his sister he replied that he would not write as there were two fellows at the Repatriation Department who could read his thoughts by telepathy, and consequently he refused to put anything on paper. His general health is good.[525]

His odd response to the request to write to his sister is interesting, and can be compared with his response in August 1925 when he denied actually having a sister called Alice, yet acknowledged having a sister called Mary whom he had probably not met or spoken with since her departure from Ireland for the United States in 1906.

The surviving records of O'Meara's mental health during 1934 are scant, and confirm his poor mental health, which seemed to be deteriorating during this time. It is possible that both his mental health and physical health were showing signs associated with ageing during this period. The Mental Hospitals Department was reporting that, at this time:

---

[522] *Sunday Times*, 12 April 1931, p.12.
[523] Noreen O'Meara, pers. comm., 8 July 2014.
[524] NAA: PP13/1, C5474, O'Meara Martin VC.
[525] NAA: PP13/1, C5474, O'Meara Martin VC.

he was abusive and impulsive, and rambling and disconnected in his conversation. At times he used abusive language and was difficult to manage. He was shameless and exposed himself at times.[526]

Martin O'Meara's health, however, did not always prevent him from continuing to engage in social activities. A newspaper report noted that he gave a 'step dance' at the 44th Battalion Ladies' Auxiliary monthly concert at Lemnos in April or May 1934,[527] and an article published in November 1934 reported that the Lemnos patients visited the Nedlands Picture Theatre on 28 October 1934 in an outing organised by the Nedlands sub-branch of the RSL.[528] As the article records that Martin O'Meara spoke on behalf of the patients in thanking the organisers, it seems that he was one of the men on the outing.

It is also possible that consideration was being given to releasing Martin O'Meara from Lemnos, but that this could not occur as he did not have any family or friends to look after him. His family recalls that the hospital wrote to them in relation to this matter, and that plans were made for his brother John O'Meara to come to Perth to collect him, but that Martin died before this could occur.[529] Later that year an article in the *Sunday Times* on 30 December 1934 reported that:

Madame Bennett Wilkinson spent Christmas Day chatting with and distributing parcels to the Lemnos soldier patients, and at the conclusion was given a rousing cheer of thanks. Martin O'Meara, V.C … on behalf of the patients, proposed a vote of thanks to Matron McDonald and the Sisters, and all who had made their Christmas a bright and happy one.[530]

Martin O'Meara was able to leave the Lemnos hospital and attend the ANZAC Day service held on the Perth Esplanade on 25 April 1935, which was the twentieth anniversary of the first Gallipoli landings by

---

[526] NAA: PP643/1, M5474, Martin O'Meara VC.
[527] *Sunday Times*, 6 May 1934, p.1S.
[528] *Daily News*, 1 November 1934, p.11.
[529] Noreen O'Meara, pers. comm., 15 August 2014.
[530] *Sunday Times*, 30 December 1934, p.1S.

the AIF. An article in the Perth *Daily News* that afternoon reported that:

> Twenty ex-service patients from Lemnos went to the Anzac Day service today through the efforts of Miss Mary Meares, who marshalled car-owners and collected patients, took them to the service and then returned them to the hospital. Among the ribbons and medals worn there was one Victoria Cross, one Military Medal, and two of the patients wore both Boer War and Great War ribbons.[531]

Given that Martin O'Meara was the only Victoria Cross recipient in Lemnos Hospital at this time, it would have been O'Meara who attended, although it is, perhaps, a sign of his fade into relative obscurity after nearly seventeen years in mental hospitals that he was not recognised and specifically named in the press as having attended.

On 19 May 1935 the patients from Lemnos had an outing, by motor vehicle and organised by the South Perth RSL sub-branch, to the Swan districts north-east of Perth, visiting Caversham House and then to South Perth's Masonic Hall where afternoon tea was served. Martin O'Meara was reported in the press as one of the patients who thanked the organisers on behalf of the patients.[532]

On 6 November 1935, three days after his fiftieth birthday, his deteriorating mental health and increasingly violent behaviour saw him transferred from Lemnos Hospital back to the Claremont Mental Hospital. As noted earlier, it is possible that he had started to develop a different form of mental illness, perhaps senility associated with ageing, and it is also possible that his physical health was starting to deteriorate by this time. The Claremont attendants' report books for the male wards during 1935 no longer exist, so we must rely on other sources to piece together Martin O'Meara's last few weeks. It seems that both his mental and physical health continued to deteriorate after he was admitted to Claremont, and he collapsed on 19 December 1935 and died there on 20 December. His death was certified by Dr Ernest

---

[531] *Daily News,* 25 April 1935, p.5.
[532] *Mirror,* 25 May 1935, p.18.

Thompson, a doctor on the staff of Claremont Hospital who had last seen O'Meara the previous day.[533] The cause of his death, as described by Dr Thompson on the death certificate, was 'pulmonary oedema' with 'chronic mania' and 'exhaustion' being factors. A letter from the Mental Hospitals Department to the Repatriation Department of 8 January 1936 noted that:

> On 19/12/35 he collapsed following a period of continued excitement and died on 20/12/35 from pulmonary oedema – 1 day, chronic mania and exhaustion – indefinite.[534]

Pulmonary oedema is a medical condition involving an abnormal buildup of fluid in the lungs. This can lead to a shortness of breath and can be caused by a range of cardiac and non-cardiac health factors. The cardiac factors include heart attack, any heart disease that weakens or stiffens the heart muscle, leaking or narrowed heart valves, and sudden, severe high blood pressure. Pulmonary oedema may also be caused by a range of non-cardiac factors such as use of certain medications, exposure to high altitude, renal impairment, lung damage, or major physical injury. The major contributing factor, chronic mania, would typically refer to the presence of manic symptoms for more than two years without remission. This would have referred to O'Meara's ongoing mental illness, although it is interesting (and perhaps disappointing) to note that his final diagnosis was no more elaborate than his initial diagnosis in November 1918, some seventeen years earlier.

Notice of Martin O'Meara's death appeared on the front page of Perth's *Daily News* that afternoon and in other newspapers in Perth and other towns and cities in the following days. Dr James Bentley advised the Defence Department in Perth of Martin O'Meara's death that day, and the Prime Minister's Department in Canberra was subsequently asked to cable the Australian High Commissioner in London asking him to advise Alice O'Meara, as next of kin, of her brother's death.

---

[533] Dr Ernest Thompson was also appointed Inspector-General of the Insane, this time succeeding Dr James Bentley, in 1940.
[534] NAA: PP643/1, M5474, Martin O'Meara VC.

Martin O'Meara was buried in the Roman Catholic section of Perth's Karrakatta Cemetery late on the morning of 21 December 1935. His funeral cortege had left the funeral home of Mead, Son and Co. undertakers at 190 Albany Road in suburban Victoria Park, at 10.30am and had made its way to Karrakatta Cemetery, arriving at around 11.10am.

Martin O'Meara's funeral procession at Karrakatta Cemetery (Mirror, 21 December 1935, p.1)

There his coffin, draped in an Australian flag and topped with his Victoria Cross medal, a hat, and side arms, was transferred to a gun carriage manned by members of the Army's Guildford Remount Depot. Headed by a firing party from the Royal Regiment of Australian Artillery, the cortege proceeded to the Roman Catholic section of the cemetery.[535]

A graveside service was conducted by the Rev John Fahey DSO (formerly a chaplain with the 11th Battalion during the war, and originally from County Tipperary in Ireland). The funeral service was attended by a number of dignitaries, including other Victoria Cross recipients (Clifford Sadlier, Tom Axford and James Woods), Senator the Hon Sir George Pearce (the former Defence Minister who had given instructions that Martin O'Meara be brought back to Australia in 1918), Walter Nairn MP, the Hon Charles Latham MLA (himself a

---

[535] *West Australian*, 21 December 1935, p.23.

16th Battalion veteran), Dr James Bentley, Lieutenant-Colonel George Wieck, and David Benson and Colonel Arthur Olden representing the RSL.[536]

A firing party from the Royal Australian Artillery fires a volley over the grave of Martin O'Meara. Rev John Fahey DSO is partly visible at the right side of the photograph. (Daily News, 21 December 1935, p.1)

The funeral was also attended by several other former 16th Battalion veterans, including Major Ross Harwood. It was impressive that such a distinguished turnout was assembled with less than twenty-four hours' notice, although O'Meara's death may have been anticipated because of his declining health.

The funeral was also attended by some of Martin O'Meara's closest friends, his fellow patients from Lemnos Hospital. *The Mirror* noted of their attendance that, 'A pathetic feature of this morning's funeral was the sight of several of his comrades in hospital uniform.'[537] At the end of the funeral service a firing party fired three volleys and a bugler sounded the last post. A number of floral tributes were given,

[536] *Daily News*, 21 December 1935, p.6.
[537] *Mirror*, 21 December 1935, p.2.

including a wreath from 'Old Comrades of the Sixteenth' bearing the blue and white colours of the 16th Battalion colours.[538]

Martin O'Meara's grave at Perth's Karrakatta Cemetery. The grave is maintained by the Office of Australian War Graves. (Author)

The funeral expenses of £16 13s were borne by the Repatriation Department, and the Defence Department subsequently contributed £15. The Office of Australian War Graves, part of the Department of Veterans' Affairs, continues to maintain his grave.

---

[538] *West Australian*, 23 December 1935, p.21.

15 A Tale of Two Wills

Martin O'Meara's financial legacy was complicated by the existence of two very different wills: the one made in November 1915 before he left Australia and the one made in London in November 1917 when he was recovering from wounds received at Messines. It was further complicated by the existence of two separate estates, one in Ireland and one in Western Australia.

On 20 January 1936, the Western Australian Curator of Intestate Estates, part of the Supreme Court, wrote to the Repatriation Commission advising that he would be administering Martin O'Meara's estate in accordance with the terms of the November 1917 will. On 29 January, the Repatriation Commission wrote to Alice O'Meara formally advising her of her brother's death and advising her of the role of the Curator of Intestate Estates in administering the estate. Shortly after receiving the letter from the Repatriation Commission, probably in early February 1936, Alice O'Meara provided a copy of her brother's 1915 will to the Repatriation Commission's representatives in London.[539] It is likely that Martin O'Meara had provided her with this will either by mail, or in person when he visited her in late 1916.

This will, made in Western Australia in November 1915, was relatively simple and in it he left everything to his sister Alice O'Meara:

THIS IS THE LAST WILL of me MARTIN O'MEARA, formerly of Lissernane, Rathcabbin, Birr, Ireland, but now a member of His Majesty's Forces engaged on active service. I REVOKE all prior testamentary dispositions and I DEVISE and BEQUEATH all my real or personal estate of whatsoever kind or description and wheresoever situate to my sister, ALICE O'MEARA, residing at Lissernane, Rathcabbin, Birr, Ireland, whom I

---

[539] This will had been provided to the Repatriation Commission in London in 1925 as part of a claim by Alice O'Meara for a portion of her brother's war pension. See NAA: PP13/1, C5474, O'Meara Martin VC.

HEREBY APPOINT as Executrix and Trustee hereof UPON TRUST, for her sole use and benefit ...[540]

In March the Curator of Intestate Estates wrote to Martin O'Meara's relatives in Ireland advising of the existence of another will, the one written by him in London in November 1917, of which his family seemed to be unaware. It is likely that the news of this later will was received with disappointment by Alice O'Meara, but possibly welcomed by John O'Meara and the other beneficiaries named in it. It seems that O'Meara did not advise his relatives in Ireland of his intention to make a new will when he visited them in Ireland in late 1917, and this may be evidence of a breakdown in his relationship with his sister, Alice O'Meara.

John and Sadie (Sarah) O'Meara taken ca. 1917, pictured with Martin O'Meara, Myra Leavey, Maureen O'Meara and John O'Meara. (Noreen O'Meara)

The second will, made on 16 November 1917 was more complicated. In it, O'Meara appointed three trustees, all of whom had connections with Lorrha and who had been involved in the

---

[540] NAA: PP13/1, C5474, O'Meara Martin VC.

presentation of the gold watch to his sister, Alice O'Meara, at Lorrha in November 1916. The trustees were Mrs Mary Hickie (the wife of Captain Manuel Hickie, a relative of Major-General William Hickie), James Willington (a prominent local landowner), and John O'Meara (a relative of Martin's, probably his brother).

Martin O'Meara's November 1917 will dealt with two separate pools of money: the money owed to him by the Australian Government for his service in the AIF, and the money raised by public subscription at Lorrha in 1916.

The money due to him for his service in the AIF was to be invested by the three trustees for the benefit of four children: Martin, John and Maureen O'Meara, and Myra Leavey. Martin, John and Maureen were the children of John (his brother) and Sadie O'Meara (formerly Lehane) of Sharragh (the townland immediately to the east of Lissernane), and Myra Leavey was the daughter of Private James Leavey and his wife Margaret ('Gretta'). Margaret was the sister of Sadie O'Meara, Martin O'Meara's brother.

As noted earlier, Private James Leavey was a member of 'the Leinsters'. He was a professional soldier (not a wartime enlistee) and had been stationed at Crinkill barracks before the war. He had married Gretta Lehane at Birr on 13 September 1911. Gretta was related by marriage to Martin O'Meara's brother John. James Leavey served with the 2nd Battalion of the Leinsters in France, and was taken prisoner by the Germans near Armentières in late October 1914. He spent the remainder of the war in prisoner of war camps.[541] James and Gretta's daughter, Myra, was born in 1912.[542] Martin's brother John O'Meara had married Sarah (Sadie) Lehane in late 1913 and by 1917 had three children: Martin, John and Maureen.

Martin O'Meara had his Victoria Cross medal with him at Claremont when he died. It may have been in the possession of his old friend Mary Murphy during 1917 and 1918; however, sometime before he sailed from Liverpool in September 1918 Mary Murphy returned the medal to him and he brought it back to Australia in November 1918. It was passed to the Department of Defence after his death. His other medals, the British War Medal and the Victory

---

[541] Noreen O'Meara, pers. comm., 12 December 2013.
[542] Myra Leavey died in London 2004 aged 92. Gretta Leavey had died in Birr in 1948.

Medal, were posted to his family in Ireland and were received by his brother, Hugh O'Meara, in June 1924. They subsequently passed into the possession of Hugh's brother John O'Meara. The Victory Medal is now in the possession of Noreen O'Meara (John's granddaughter and Martin O'Meara's great-niece), and the British War Medal was given by Noreen's father Martin O'Meara to a friend of his at some point in the past, and its current location is unknown.[543]

Martin O'Meara's 1917 will prescribed some unusual conditions relating to his Victoria Cross medal. The conditions were:

My V.C. Medal is to remain in the possession of Miss Mary Murphy Dangan Kilmacow Co. Kilkenny Ireland for the term of natural life on conditions (firstly) that she brings it to West Australia within twelve months after peace being restored (and second) that she resides thereafter for twelve months within the said State if the conditions mentioned be not fulfilled or in the event of Miss Murphy's death the Medal will be forwarded to the Public Trustee of the City of Perth Western Australia to be placed with the trophies won by the 16th Batt. A.I.F. until such time as my nephew Martin O'Meara eldest son of my brother John O'Meara Sharragh Birr Ireland arrives in Australia on which occasion the Medal will be presented to him to keep and leave to whatever institution he thinks fit. Should the conditions already stated be fulfilled by Miss Murphy and she still be alive on the occasion of my nephew Martin's arrival in Australia The Medal is not to come into his possession until Miss Murphy's death. Should the said nephew of mine die or fail to arrive in Australia after attaining the age of 25 years the medal will be presented to the next oldest nephew of mine in Australia (if there be) but only on condition that it will not be removed from the State of West Australia. Should it so happen that the Medal becomes the property of the latter nephew it will become the property of the State of Western Australia after his death.[544]

---

[543] Noreen O'Meara, pers. comm., 5 April 2014.
[544] SROWA: Series 34, Consignment 3403, Item 1938/1078, Probate Files - Martin O'Meara.

Whilst working at Caterham, Mary Murphy had met Guardsman Walter Clews of the Coldstream Guards.[545] Walter Clews had enlisted in September 1914 and served with the 3rd Battalion of the Coldstream Guards on the Western Front during the First World War. He was wounded in action on 18 September 1916 at Ginchy (about eight kilometres west of Pozières), and spent the rest of the war with the Coldstream Guards in England before being demobilised in January 1919. Mary Murphy had remained in England and kept in touch with Walter Clews after he was demobilised, marrying him on 17 September 1921 at St Francis in the Grove Roman Catholic Church in West Ham (close to the Forest Gate Sick Home).[546] She was, obviously, unable to meet the second will's conditions relating to the medal.

On 2 May 1936 the Western Australian Curator of Intestate Estates advised the Repatriation Commission that Martin O'Meara's relatives (presumably his sister, Alice O'Meara) would be contesting the validity of the 1917 will through the Irish courts, and that he would wait for an outcome from Ireland before dealing with O'Meara's Australian estate. As part of this challenge, Messrs. Adam Mitchell and Son of Birr, representing Alice O'Meara, wrote to the Repatriation Commission's London representatives in July seeking information on O'Meara's military service, his medical condition, the circumstances of his discharge, and 'the date on which your file first discloses any evidence of mental instability on the part of O'Meara, and particulars of the instability.'[547] It now seemed that the 1917 will was being challenged by Alice O'Meara on the basis that her brother may not have been of sound mind when he signed the will in November 1917, and that the 1915 will (which left all of Martin O'Meara's estate to her) should stand. The benefactors of the 1917 will (John O'Meara, Maureen O'Meara, Martin O'Meara and Myra Leavey) were represented by John J. Kennedy, a solicitor of Birr in County Offaly.

Alice O'Meara's solicitors continued working on her case during early 1937, and on 13 January they wrote to the Repatriation Commission in Perth seeking information on the YMCA

[545] Roy Clews, pers. comm., 27 February 2014, and Margaret Clews, pers. comm., 8 March 2014.

[546] Margaret Clews, pers. comm., 14 May 2014.

[547] NAA: PP13/1, C5474, O'Meara Martin VC.

representatives who had witnessed the 1915 will. Following inquiries of the YMCA in Perth, the Repatriation Commission wrote back on 15 February 1937 advising that both men had since died. On 15 March, Alice's solicitors wrote to the Repatriation Commission asking for a history of O'Meara's military service, with a particular focus on his activities between 16 October 1917 and 15 April 1918, and after 30 August 1918 when he left France to return to Australia.

Interestingly, they also asked the Repatriation Commission whether there was 'any medical report whatsoever to show how long deceased's mind was or might have been affected before his discharge?'[548] On 12 July the Repatriation Commission replied, providing a summary of O'Meara's medical history and stating that nothing on record referred to his mental state prior to 13 November 1918.

On 24 July Mr Justice Hanna of the Irish High Court admitted Martin O'Meara's 1917 will to probate, and 4 April 1938 he granted Letters of Administration to his brother, John O'Meara. Justice Hanna also set aside the caveat lodge by Alice O'Meara (the sole beneficiary of Martin O'Meara's 1915 will) as she had come to agreement with other members of her family. Justice Hanna was satisfied that the 1917 will had been made when Martin O'Meara was on active service and that he had been of sound mind at the time the will was made.

Martin O'Meara left an estate in Ireland of £350 plus interest (a total of some £370) held by James Willington in Tipperary (the only surviving trustee), being the result of the public subscription taken from Lorrha and the surrounding parishes.[549] The will specified that the money subscribed by the people of Lorrha and the surrounding parishes 'as a testimonial for me and which is now invested in the war fund' was to be given to the Rev John Gleeson (the parish priest at Lorrha) or his successors 'to be expended towards the restoration of the Old Abbey of Lorrha now in ruins'. In April 1937 St Ruadhan's Abbey at Lorrha was entrusted to the care of the Commissioners of Public works and became a national monument.[550] The Rev John Gleeson had died in 1927 and the Very Rev Canon John Moloney had

---

[548] NAA: PP13/1, C5474, O'Meara Martin VC.
[549] *Irish Press*, 24 July 1937, p.6.
[550] *Meath Chronicle*, 10 April 1937, p.3.

succeeded him as Parish Priest at Lorrha. In order to settle the matter of the £370, Martin O'Meara's brother John O'Meara petitioned the Irish High Court ('John O'Meara v the Attorney-General') during December 1938 for declarations that, primarily:

That it may be declared that the Charitable Trust contained in the Will of the above-named Testator [Martin O'Meara] is a good and valid Charitable Trust and ought to be carried into execution.[551]

Other declarations sought related to the administration of the Charitable Trust, related matters, and to costs. The petition was supported by affidavits sworn by John O'Meara and the Very Rev Canon John Moloney. John O'Meara's affidavit was sworn at Birr in neighbouring Co. Offaly on 17 December 1938; in it he notes that the old abbey at Lorrha was in such a ruinous state that 'It would be impossible to restore it in any way.'[552] John O'Meara was clearly of the view that the terms of his brother's will relating to the restoration of the abbey were impossible to implement, and that the Court's direction was needed in order to apply the £370 to another purpose. Moloney's affidavit was sworn at Borrisokane in County Tipperary on 15 December; in it he specifically asked the Court:

I respectfully pray this Honourable Court to declare the said bequest a charitable one and impossible to implement and that the moneys be applied cy-pres £60. being applied to the purchase of two Confessionals by way of memorial to the Testator and the balance to the erection of the schools at Redwood.[553]

The matter went to court on 16 January 1939. Alice O'Meara's barrister argued that the amount of money left by Martin O'Meara would be only 'a drop in a bucket' and inadequate to restore the abbey. He suggested that O'Meara's motive for the bequest was 'that

---

[551] A copy of the petition is in Noreen O'Meara's possession.

[552] A copy of the John O'Meara's affidavit is in Noreen O'Meara's possession.

[553] A copy of Rev Moloney's affidavit is in Noreen O'Meara's possession. Cy-près is a legal doctrine relating to the power to apply funds from estates, predomently in situations where a charitable trust exists but no trustees remain.

he wanted posthumous glory or fame as the restorer of Lorrha Abbey.'[554] He seems to have sought a decision by the Court that the money should go to O'Meara's next of kin.

Counsel for the Irish Attorney-General argued that O'Meara's bequest for the restoration of the abbey was a 'for the advancement of religion, and as such, it would be a valid charitable trust.'[555] It is easy to speculate that the Irish state wanted the money to subsidise the upkeep of the abbey as a recently-created national monument, or perhaps to part-fund the new National School at Redwood in a manner consistent with the Very Rev John Moloney's affidavit.

John O'Meara's petition did not succeed. Mr Justice William Johnson of the Irish High Court ruled that there was no charitable bequest and that the £370 should go to Martin O'Meara's next-of-kin, Alice, Hugh and Thomas O'Meara. The *Irish Examiner* reported the next day that:

> Mr. Justice Johnson said it was a very peculiar case, but it did not suggest any difficulty as far as he was concerned. He could not see that it was a charitable bequest at all, or that a charitable intention had been disclosed by the will. There was no Judge in the High Court more anxious to see that charities were properly dealt with than he was, but he thought the limit had been reached in that case. It was right that the summons should have been brought before him, in view of the terms of the will, but it failed, and the money must go to the next of kin. The plaintiff and the Attorney-General would be allowed their costs, and the next of kin would be allowed a measured sum for costs.[556]

Although the Court's decision was that the bequest should go to Martin O'Meara's next of kin, it seems that some funds were used improving the Roman Catholic church at Lorrha. Noreen O'Meara recalls:

> We were told that the money mentioned in the will as having been raised by the people of the neighbourhood as a testimonial, and which Martin wanted to be put towards the

---

[554] *Irish Independent*, 17 January 1939, p.8.
[555] *Irish Independent*, 17 January 1939, p.8.
[556] *Irish Examiner*, 17 January 1939, p.9.

restoration of the old abbey, was actually used to modernise the current catholic church in Lorrha. Two new confessional boxes in particular were installed with inscriptions on them. The confessional boxes are no longer in the church but the two small inscription plaques are still there.[557]

It has been suggested that some of the bequest was actually used to part-fund the construction of the new National School at Redwood during 1939,[558] and if this actually occurred then it is feasible that Martin O'Meara's next of kin chose to use the bequest for this purpose. There is no evidence that the court ordered the bequest to be used for that purpose.

Martin O'Meara's Western Australian estate now needed finalising. It consisted of the pay and pension owing to O'Meara since his return to Australia in 1918, and was held in trust. Part was held as cash and the remainder was invested in interest bearing bonds. Interestingly, the estate included an amount of £239 17s 0d which had been deducted over the years from O'Meara's pension to cover the costs of his hospitalisation, and which had been subsequently refunded by the Australian Government.

On 10 September 1938 Martin's brother John O'Meara gave power of attorney to Perth solicitor John Lavan so that he could finalise Martin O'Meara's estate in Australia. On 21 December an application for Letters of Administration with Will Annexed (meaning that O'Meara had died testate but with no valid executor) was made to the Supreme Court of Western Australia, and the application was granted by the court on 6 January 1939. John Lavan then wrote to the Repatriation Commission on 10 March advising that he was in a position to collect Martin O'Meara's estate. It remained unclear, however, as to whether Martin O'Meara's Western Australian estate should be divided on the basis of intestacy or in the terms of the 1917 will, and on 5 April the Hon Justice Wolff of the Supreme Court of

[557] Noreen O'Meara, pers. comm., 17 February 2016.
[558] King, S. (2014): 'Redwood National School Celebrates 75 Years', *The Lamp*, 2014 Edition, pp.14-19. *The Lamp* is published by the Lorrha and Dorrha Historical Society.

Western Australia ordered that the terms of the 1917 will should stand and that the estate be divided equally.[559]

Martin O'Meara's Western Australian estate amounted to £3,544 16s 5d, with an amount of £212 12s 0d being retained by John Lavan to cover the costs of administering the estate. £3,332 3s 5d was subsequently forwarded (in the second half of 1940) to solicitor John J. Kennedy in Ireland for distribution to John O'Meara, Maureen O'Meara, Martin O'Meara and Myra Leavey.[560] They should have received a little over £833 each, which was a reasonably sizeable sum for the time.

The Victoria Cross medal and the gold watch that was presented to him in 1916 were the only items that Martin O'Meara possessed that are known to have survived. Everything else that he brought with him to Claremont in 1919 has disappeared, either lost, stolen or disposed of.

As noted earlier, Mary Murphy was married to Walter Clewes and living with her family in England, and unable to fulfil the will's conditions relating to the Victoria Cross medal. None of the other conditions relating to the Victoria Cross medal were met.

The Victoria Cross medal was retained by the 16th Battalion Association in Perth, and was presented by the Association to the 16th Battalion (the Cameron Highlanders of Western Australia), a Perth-based Citizens' Military Forces (reserve) unit, in Perth on 11 August 1940.

The presentation was made by 16th Battalion veteran Thomas Axford VC to Major Frederick Warner of the Cameron Highlanders.[561] The Cameron Highlanders had been formed in Perth in 1936 as a militia unit and inherited the honours and traditions of the AIF's former 16th Battalion.

---

[559] SROWA: Series 34 Consignment 3403 Item 1938/1078, Probate Files - Martin O'Meara.

[560] SROWA: Series 34 Consignment 3403 Item 1938/1078, Probate Files - Martin O'Meara.

[561] *West Australian*, 12 August 1940, p.4.

Thomas Axford VC (right) presents O'Meara's VC medal tc major Frederick Warner. (West Australian, 10 August 1940, p.4)

In 1986 his Victoria Cross medal was donated by the 16th Battalion, the Royal Western Australian Regiment, successor to the Cameron Highlanders, to the Army Museum of Western Australian at Fremantle near Perth. It is still held by the museum, but is not on permanent public display. Martin O'Meara's watch was valued at £10 in Western Australia probate papers.[562] It was forwarded by John Lavan to John J. Kennedy in Birr during 1940, anc it was given by Kennedy to Martin's brother John O'Meara. After John O'Meara's death in 1961 the watch was passed on to his sor John ('Johnnie') O'Meara. Johnnie O'Meara died in the 1980s but the location of the watch remains unknown.[563]

---

[562] SROWA: Series 34 Consignment 3403 Item 1938/1078, Probate Files - Martin O'Meara.

[563] Noreen O'Meara, pers. comm., 29 January 2015.

16   Remembering Martin O'Meara

Martin O'Meara leaves relatively few physical reminders of his life, although he is commemorated in both Ireland and Australia. More importantly, perhaps, is the non-physical legacy of Martin O'Meara that has existed since the First World War, much of which is inaccurate and borders on folk mythology dating from the 1920s.

On 2 June 1921 the Australian War Museum (now the Australian War Memorial) wrote to Martin O'Meara care of his sister Alice O'Meara in Ireland, seeking the donation of 'Some piece of equipment, uniform, document, etc which has some close association with [his] war services, and preferably with the act for which [he was] awarded the V.C.' Alice responded on 27 July, writing 'I am enclosing herewith one badge of the tunic worn by my Brother on the occasion of his winning the V.C.' She added 'P.S. My Brother is in Perth W. Australia, but I have not heard from him since last January [1920].'[564] Presumably the badge was given to Alice O'Meara when he visited Ireland in late 1916. The badge remains part of the Australian War Memorial's collection, but is not on display.[565]

In Australia, Martin O'Meara is remembered in a number of places, mainly in Western Australia. There is a memorial plaque at King's Park in Perth and a memorial rose garden and memorial at the Soldiers' Memorial Park in Collie, as well as a plaque for Martin O'Meara amongst plaques for other Victoria Cross recipients at the memorial located at the site of the Blackboy Hill Camp east of Perth.

The 16th Battalion of the Royal Western Australian Regiment has a soldiers' club known as 'O'Meara's Canteen'[566] at Irwin Barracks in the Perth suburb of Karrakatta. The Army Museum of Western Australia, at Fremantle's historic Artillery Barracks has displays dedicated to several Western Australian Victoria Cross winners, including Martin O'Meara. An interpretive panel with information on Martin O'Meara is located adjacent to his grave at Perth's Karrakatta

---

[564] AWM93: 7/4/639, O'Meara M. Sgt VC Trophies and Relics for Exhibition.
[565] AWM Collection ID RELAWM01096
[566] This is ironic as O'Meara did not drink alcohol.

Cemetery, and the grave is included on one of two historical walking trails promoted by the Metropolitan Cemeteries Board that operates the cemetery. In addition, there is the 'O'Meara Ward' in the Palliative Care Unit of Perth's Hollywood Private Hospital,[567] which is located close to the Karrakatta Cemetery.

In Ireland, bronze plaques at Lorrha's Roman Catholic Church commemorate him; they were originally mounted on confessionals funded by a portion of the proceeds of his estate and were installed in the 1930s. Martin O'Meara's parents, and many other family members, lay buried in the adjacent cemetery. In June 2013 a memorial stone for Martin O'Meara was unveiled in Lorrha by the Lorrha Development Association.

Memorial to Martin O'Meara in Lorrha, County Tipperary. (Noreen O'Meara)

Several geographical features also commemorate Martin O'Meara. O'Meara Drive in the Perth suburb of Burekup is the only such commemoration in Western Australia; other geographical features are O'Meara Street in Wodonga in Victoria and O'Meara Place in the

---

[567] Hollywood Private Hospital was established as the 110th Military Hospital during the Second World War and became a Repatriation General Hospital in the late 1940s. It was purchased by the Ramsay Health Care Group in 1994.

Canberra suburb of Gowrie. In addition, in April 2016, the Western Australian Government announced that plaques honouring the state's Victoria Cross and George Cross recipients would be placed at rest areas on the South Western Highway and Albany Highway south of Perth. Martin O'Meara's plaque will be placed at a rest area a short distance south of Pinjarra, close to where he lived and worked in 1914.

One suggested geographical commemorative that was not taken up was published in the *Collie Mail* on 16 November 1916:

The Collie municipal councillors want to eradicate the name of Lunenberg from a railway station in their midst, and have suggested as a suitable name, Fernbrook, to the Commissioner of Railways. I though the Collie citizens appreciated the name of their great hero and Victoria Cross man O'Meara. What's wrong with O'Meara?[568]

The greatest legacy left by Martin O'Meara, however, is not physical. It is his life story, through him having the unique combination of being an AIF Victoria Cross recipient, being born in Ireland, and his lengthy time in mental hospitals. All Victoria Cross recipients attract a certain degree of popular mythology, but O'Meara's is more extensive. A popular mythology of Martin O'Meara (the 'O'Meara myth') emerged from 1916 onwards and was fed, at least in part, by the paucity of information on O'Meara and his background. This paucity relates to nearly all aspects of his life, from the circumstances of his arrival and early life in Australia through to the circumstances surrounding his hospitalisation after his return to Australia in 1918.

The mythology about his life extends back to his time in Ireland and his coming to Australia, around his wartime service (what can be described as the 'stretcher-bearer myth'), and around his mental illness. In addition, some parts of his life, such as his time living in County Kilkenny before coming to Australia, his friendship with Mary Murphy, his time as a railway construction worker in South Australia, and his service as a machine gunner, scout, observer and sniper have not previously been reported and have not formed part of the story of Martin O'Meara until now. So why did the 'O'Meara

---

[568] *Collie Mail*, 16 November 1916, p.4.

myth' actually emerge when it did, and how did it persist unchallenged for so long?

Firstly, a dearth of information on Martin O'Meara's pre-war life meant that contemporary accounts had very little upon which to base themselves. This dearth continues - for example we still do not know the name of the ship on which he travelled to Australia, or precisely when he arrived here.

Secondly, his life was effectively 'frozen' in November 1918 when he returned to Australia and was hospitalised. The circumstances and the attitudes of the day did not allow him to contribute to the telling of his own story as other Victoria Cross winners had been able to, even if reluctantly. His descent into mental illness after his return to Australia in 1918 resulted in much of his life being 'air-brushed' out of history. The information vacuum meant that other 'voices' filled the void. The other voices included the accounts of Martin O'Meara that appeared in newspapers from September 1916 onwards, some of which were seemingly based on an imperfect portrayal and a degree of embellishment.

The particular aspect of his life that has thrived on the paucity of information is the mythology of the stretcher-bearer that emerged from the 1920s onwards when a reference to Martin O'Meara 'as a stretcher bearer' appeared in Cyril Longmore's history of the 16th Battalion, *The Old Sixteenth*, that was published in 1929.[569] As O'Meara was a patient in a mental hospital, he did not play any role in contributing to his own story in Longmore's book. The story that emerged was based on the official records available at the time and limited first-hand accounts of the 16th Battalion's wartime service, particularly relating to Martin O'Meara. The citation for the award of Martin O'Meara Victoria Cross was published in the *London Gazette* on 8 September 1916 and is quite clear:

> For most conspicuous bravery. During four days of very heavy fighting he repeatedly went out and brought in wounded officers and men from "No Man's Land" under intense artillery and machine gun fire. He also volunteered and carried up

---

[569] Longmore, 1929.

ammunition and bombs through a heavy barrage to a portion of the trenches, which was being heavily shelled at the time. He showed throughout an utter contempt of danger, and undoubtedly saved many lives.[570]

This account provided the basis for subsequent newspaper reporting in Australia and elsewhere with a major focus being on his role in going out and rescuing wounded officers and men. There was no mention of him being a stretcher-bearer; merely that he saved lives. None of the testimonies of 16th Battalion officers supporting his nomination for the Victoria Cross refer to him as a stretcher-bearer.

The stretcher bearer myth seems to have been further fuelled by comments given by Martin O'Meara in an interview given by telephone from the Woodman's Point Quarantine Station and reported in the *West Australian* on 8 November 1918. In this interview he stated that 'I went out to do what I could for the poor chaps that were lying all around waiting for the stretcher bearers ... I went down to the cookers and got some hot tea and went out again with a stretcher and brought in more.'[571] O'Meara clearly indicates that he was not a stretcher-bearer, but that he did rescue men using a stretcher. This also suggests that O'Meara was assisted by other men, as it would be almost impossible for him to have rescued others using a stretcher without another man to assist him. These men could have included actual stretcher-bearers, other scouts, or regular infantrymen. Battalion stretcher-bearers were specially trained soldiers attached to infantry companies, and the term 'stretcher-bearer' is a specific function, and does not refer to a soldier who simply assists in evacuating the wounded using stretchers. [572]

Cyril Longmore history of the 16th Battalion's wartime actions contains only a brief reference to O'Meara:

For conspicuous bravery during this period Private Martin O'Meara was awarded the Victoria Cross. He carried

---

[570] *London Gazette*, Supplement No. 29740, 8 September 1916, p. 8871.

[571] *West Australian*, 8 November 1918, p.7.

[572] Stretcher bearers wore the SB armband which distinguished them from the medical platoon (the Regimental Medical Officer, and his men) who wore the familiar Red Cross armband which afforded protection under the Geneva Convention.

ammunition to the front line under a heavy barrage and, as a stretcher-bearer he brought in many wounded officers and men from No Man's Land.[573]

A comparison of Longmore's book with the 16th Battalion's official war diary maintained by the Commanding Officer[574] suggests that Longmore relied very heavily on this diary for his history and that much of the material was not corroborated by other sources, even though former members of the battalion in Western Australia could have been readily available to provide first-hand accounts of actual events. The circumstances of O'Meara's Victoria Cross seem only to have been verified against the award citation that appeared in the *London Gazette* in September 1916 and not against the recommendation made by Lieutenant-Colonel Drake-Brockman in August 1916.[575]

Longmore's history of the battalion was serialized in Perth's *Western Mail* newspaper during 1937, and the myth of the stretcher-bearer seems to become entrenched from that time onwards. A newspaper report at the time that Martin O'Meara's Victoria Cross medal was presented by the 16th Battalion Association to the 16th Battalion (Cameron Highlanders of Western Australia) in August 1940 noted that O'Meara won the medal 'as a stretcher-bearer with the 16th Battalion.'[576] This article probably relied on Longmore's battalion history as a source of information, albeit inaccurate, on Martin O'Meara. This inaccuracy persisted, and the *Western Mail* of 6 May 1943 noted that 'It was at Pozieres that the late Martin O'Meara gained his well-earned VC as a stretcher bearer with the 16th Battalion.'[577]

The stretcher-bearer myth persists to this day in a wide range of books and articles, although some references are a little more pragmatic. Many other works that touch on aspects of Martin O'Meara's life, however, perpetuate the stretcher-bearer myth without question. As a Victoria Cross recipient, references to Martin

---

[573] Longmore, 1929, p.116.
[574] AWM4: 23/33.
[575] A failure to consult sources is not entirely Longmore's fault; access to official records in the 1920s was not as easy as it is now.
[576] *West Australian*, 10 August 1940, p.8.
[577] *Western Mail*, 6 May 1943, p.9.

O'Meara abound in a wide range of books and articles relating to the AIF on the Western Front. Dr Charles Bean, quite correctly, does not describe O'Meara as a stretcher-bearer in his official history, remaining succinct and factual:

> The carriage of water, supplies, and the wounded was sustained largely by the example of one man, Private Martin O'Meara, who four times went through the barrage with supplies, on one occasion taking with him a party, and who thereafter continued to bring out the wounded until all those of his battalion had been cleared.[578]

The stretcher-bearer myth was, however, given a degree of legitimacy when Lionel Wigmore et al. included it in their information on Martin O'Meara in the reference work on Australian Victoria Crosses, *They Dared Mightily*, that was published by the Australian War Memorial in 1963.[579] It also includes another more obvious error, recording that O'Meara served with the 16th Battalion from the Gallipoli campaign in 1915 through to the fighting at Le Verguier.[580] *They Dared Mightily* was subsequently revised and condensed by Anthony Staunton and republished (with the same title) in 1986 and republished again (as *Victoria Cross: Australia's finest and the battles they fought*) in 2005.[581] O'Meara's entry in the 1988 *Australian Dictionary of Biography* indicated that he was 'acting' as a stretcher-bearer, an ambiguous reference suggesting that he was doing the duties of a stretcher bearer but that he might not have actually been one.[582] The evidence, however, clearly indicates that O'Meara was doing the duties of a scout. These two sources are generally regarded as authoritative and have been used as references by many others, thus perpetuating the myths about O'Meara. Those who have relied on

---

[578] Bean, 1941a, p.750.

[579] Wigmore, Lionel, Harding, Bruce A. & Australian War Memorial, 1963), pp.64-66.

[580] This error is hard to understand; O'Meara sailed from Australia *after* the 16th Battalion had left Gallipoli and he returned to Australia *before* the fighting at Le Verguier took place. Le Verguier was caputerd by the Australian 1st and 4th Divisions on 18 September 1918.

[581] Staunton does not repeat the two major errors in Wigmore et a..'s 1963 edition.

[582] Serle, 1988, p.86. The entry for O'Meara is available online at <http://adb.anu.edu.au/biography/omeara-martin-7908/text13755> [Accessed 4 April 2016].

these sources include journalists, museum curators, writers, historians, parliamentarians, and even a playwright.

A number of biographies of other Australian Victoria Cross recipients have perpetuated the O'Meara myths. The myth is also perpetuated in various general First World War history works, and in the 'battlefield guide' genre of literature. No slur on the quality of these works is intended; merely a suggestion that some the authors relied on imperfect source material in peripheral areas of their own works.

Martin O'Meara's life was also the subject of the play *Under Any Old Gum Tree - The Story of Martin O'Meara VC*, written and directed by Irish-born Perth playwright Noel O'Neill. The play has a single act and a cast of only two, and premiered in Perth on 1 February 2014. It was subsequently re-staged in Perth, Collie, Bunbury and Galway, in Ireland, during 2014 and 2015. Based loosely on O'Meara's time in mental hospitals, the play has a strong focus on the link between O'Meara's mental health and his wartime service, suggesting that his service resulted in his mental illness. It also has a strong focus on O'Meara as a stretcher-bearer.

In this, the centenary of Australia's first actions on the Western Front and the centenary of those actions that resulted in Martin O'Meara being awarded the Victoria Cross, it is important that his legacy as brave soldier is not diminished. The research into his life that resulted in this biography has reassessed some of the myths around his military service, and has cast a brighter light on his time in mental hospitals after the war.

Despite the unearthing of new material on his life, Martin O'Meara should be remembered primarily for his actions of early August 1916. The qualities of bravery, humanity, loyalty and diligence that typified that period remain the qualities that we remember him for; we also remember him as an Australian soldier but recognise his Irish heritage and the sacrifice that Irish soldiers and sailors made during the First World War, regardless of the badges on their uniforms. As Lieutenant Bill Lynas noted in August 1916, Martin O'Meara is 'the most fearless and gallant soldier I have ever seen …' And undoubtedly he was.

Acknowledgments

This biographical project has been a fascinating journey through both time and space, and plenty of people and organisations have helped me along this journey, and have made significant contributions in their own right. Thanks are due to the various custodians of official and personal records, such as the Australian War Memorial, the Army Museum of Western Australia, the National Archives of Australia, the British National Archives, the London Metropolitan Archives, the State Library of Western Australia, the State Records Office of Western Australia, State Records of South Australia, and the National Archives of Ireland.

Particular thanks are due to Tony Hooper at the Western Australian Department of Health, Edel Heffernan from the Tullamore Central Library in County Offaly, Dr Philippa Martyr (particularly for her knowledge of the history Western Australia's mental health system), Ian Gill and Greg Payne, and Frank Murphy and Fred Rea, diligent stalwarts of Western Australia's Irish diaspora.

I acknowledge the assistance of Seamus King from County Tipperary for his knowledge and advice on matters relating to that county, and Sarah Nolan from the Columbia County Historical Society in New York State for assistance in tracking down the O'Mearas who migrated to the United States.

I must thank the various copyright holders who granted permission for various information sources and images to be reproduced in this book; this includes Dr Roger Lee of the Australian Army History Unit for permission to reproduce certain Commonwealth records and the Fremantle Press for allowing me to reproduce excerpts from Bert Demasson's wartime letters. Thanks are also due to Dr Charles Bean's family for permission to reproduce parts of his private papers.

I must also acknowledge British Pathé for approval to reproduce imagery from old newsreel footage. I have endeavoured to acknowledge sources where copyright no longer exists, and have endeavoured to contact and seek the approval of copyright holders where it continues to exist.

Finally, I must express the deepest gratitude to Martin O'Meara's grand-niece, Noreen O'Meara, and to Mary Murphy's daughter, Margaret Clews (as well as Roy Clews, her nephew). Noreen and Margaret freely shared information on their families, recognising the importance of recording and telling Martin O'Meara's story.

Appendix – Martin O'Meara Pictured

Very few photographs of Martin O'Meara are known to have survived, and most of those that do survive were published in newspapers during the First World War.

I endeavoured to collect as many photographs of Martin O'Meara as possible whilst I researched and wrote this biography, and have reproduced them here in chronological order with a brief description of each photograph. Some of the photographs have been reproduced in earlier chapters. Most of the photographs of O'Meara are of relatively poor quality, as they survive only in newspapers or other publications. Despite extensive searches, it seems that most of the original photographs have been lost.

Only one photograph of Martin O'Meara prior to arriving in Australia is known to exist, apart from the cigarette card image described later. It shows him as a young man and was probably taken around 1910 or several years prior to that year,

Martin O'Meara as a young man, probably taken several years before he left Ireland (perhaps around 1910).

This photograph was published in at least one Irish newspaper in September 1916 following the announcement of his Victoria Cross. (Noreen O'Meara)

It was very common for AIF recruits to have a portrait taken at a photographic studio prior to embarking for overseas service, and two such portraits of Martin O'Meara are known to exist. They would most likely have been taken at one of many studios in or around Perth.

Portrait of Martin O'Meara, probably taken at a studio somewhere in Perth (perhaps near Blackboy Hill) shortly after he enlisted in August 1915.

Note the absence of badges or insignia on the uniform. His relatively youthful appearance can be compared with later photographs. (AWM H12763)

Portrait of Martin O'Meara, probably taken at a studio somewhere in Perth (perhaps near Blackboy Hill) sometime after he enlisted in August 1915.

His uniform has AIF insignia, although he wears a service cap without a badge. (AWM A02613)

It was also common for AIF members to have a portrait taken overseas, and this often occurred in places such as Egypt. One such portrait of Martin O'Meara exists, and was taken in a studio near Cairo (with a painting of the pyramids as a backdrop) sometime between January and May 1916. It is possible that the photograph was taken shortly after he arrived in Egypt as his equipment is very clean.

Portrait of Private Martin O'Meara taken in a studio in Egypt, between January and May 1916.

He is wearing the AIF tunic and breeches with leather boots and puttees, and a fur felt ('slouch') hat with the brim down.

He is also wearing 1908 pattern webbing, consisting of a belt, shoulder straps and ammunition pouches and stands with the Small Magazine Lee Enfield (SMLE) .303 rifle with bayonet fixed.

It is likely that O'Meara sent the original of this photograph to soembody in WA after it was taken. (Army Museum of WA)

Several photographs were taken of Martin O'Meara at Wandsworth near London shortly after his Victoria Cross was announced in September 1916.

Some of these photographs were reproduced in newspapers in Britain and Australia during September 1916 and in the following months. Some of the pictures were obviously 'staged' for the benefit of the photographer, and originals (rather than newspaper reproductions) exist for some of them.

Martin O'Meara at Wandsworth following the announcement of his VC. The photograph appears to be staged for the camera, and was probably taken between 9-10 September 1916. (AWM H12763)

Martin O'Meara being congratulated by other patients at Wandsworth following the announcement of his VC. The photograph appears to be staged for the camera, and was probably taken between 9-10 September 1916. (Noreen O'Meara & AWM P11930.001)

Martin O'Meara shaving other patients at Wandsworth between 9-11 September 1916. (Sunday Mirror, 19 November 1916, p.€s)

Other photographs of Martin O'Meara were taken in London in September 1916. He and fellow Victoria Cross recipient Bill Jackson were photographed at the ANZAC Club and Buffet.

Martin O'Meara (left) and Bill Jackson (right) at the ANZAC Club and Euffet. (Birmingham Gazette 22 September 1916, p.1)

Martin O'Meara was also photographed with Albert Jacka, another Victoria Cross recipient, in late September 1916.

Martin O'Meara shakes hands with Lieutenant Albert Jacka VC at the 3rd London General Hospital, at Wandsworth, probably in late September 1916 when Lieutenant Jacka was presented with his Victoria Cross medal by King George V at Windsor Castle. (Daily Mail/Associated Newspapers)

Martin O'Meara was photographed and filmed at Buckingham Palace on 21 July 1917 when he was presented with his Victoria Cross medal by the King.

Martin O'Meara being presented with his Victoria Cross by King George V at Buckingham Palace. (British Pathé)

Martin O'Meara at Buckingham Palace on 21 July 1917, prior to receiving his VC medal from King George V.

He is wearing his VC ribbon on his chest above his pocket, suggesting that the photograph was taken before he received the medal. 'Faithe Jones)

The portrait of Martin O'Meara taken outside Buckingham Palace was the last photograph taken of him. No photographs of him from July 1917 onwards are known to exist, although it is quite possible that he was photographed whilst at Lemnos during the late 1920s or early 1930s during a social function or excursion. Several photographs of his funeral in December 1935 were published in Perth newspapers; no original photographs are known to exist.

Martin O'Meara's funeral procession at Karrakatta Cemetery (Mirror, 21 December 1935, p.1)

A firing party from the Royal Australian Artillery fires a volley over the grave of Martin O'Meara. Rev John Fahey DSO is partly visible at the right side of the photograph. (Daily News, 21 December 1935, p.1)

Martin O'Meara's casket on a gun carriage at Karrakatta Cemetery. (Daily News, 21 December 1935, p.1)

Small collectable cards were included in packets of cigarettes sold in Australia and other places during much of the early twentieth century, and they featured a wide range of subjects. Several tobacco companies produced card series featuring First World War Victoria Cross recipients, and Martin O'Meara was included in at least two card series in Britain and Australia.

Cigarette card showing a portrait of Martin O'Meara.

Whilst the portrait shows some resemblance to Martin O'Meara, no evidence has been found to confirm this. If it is actually O'Meara it is likely to have been taken sometime between 1900 and 1910.

It is part of a series of cards depicting Australian VC recipients printed by Melbourne company Sniders and Abrahams. (AWM RC09121)

Cigarette card showing a portrait of Martin O'Meara.

An image of a VC medal has been superimposed on a recoloured version of a photograph of him taken at Wandsworth in September 1916.

It is part of a series of cards depicting Australian VC recipients printed by British company Gallaher Ltd. (Author)

Bibliography

Primary Sources

Army Museum of Western Australia

AMWA: PD909 Elverd WA

Australian War Memorial (AWM)

AWM4: First World War Unit War Diaries (for Australian units and formations mentioned).

AWM7: Troopship Records 1914-1918 War (for the *Ajana* and *Arawa*).

AWM8: Unit Embarkation Rolls 1914-18 War (for the men and Australian units mentioned).

AWM9: Unit roll books, 1914-18 War (for the men and Australian units mentioned).

AWM25: Written Records, 1914-18 War:

449/3 VC Winners Furlough to Australia.

707/9 Parts 239-243 16th Battalion Routine Orders.

707/9 Part 562 4th Machine Gun Company Routine Orders.

741/1 Precis of a Lecture on Organisation and System of Training and Scouts and Patrols for Trench Warfare.

861/9 Parts 143-147 16th Battalion Field Returns.

877/1, Courses of Instruction at Imperial School of Instruction, Zeitoun January-May 1916).

AWM28: Recommendation Files for Honours and Awards 1914-18 AIF War (for a number of the men mentioned).

AWM32: AAMC Units in Australia (14, No.24 Australian Auxiliary Hospital).

AWM38: 3DRL 606/54/1, Bean papers – Diary, July - August 1916.

AWM38: 3DRL 606/140/1, Bean papers – Notebook, August 1916.

AWM93: 7/4/639, O'Meara M. Sgt VC Trophies and Relics for Exhibition.

AWM133: Nominal Roll of Australian Imperial Force who left Australia for service abroad, 1914-1918 War (for the men and Australian units mentioned).

AWM 1DRL/0428, Australian Red Cross Society Wounded and Missing Enquiry Bureau files, 1914-18 War (for the men and Australian units mentioned).

AWM 2DRL/0280, Marshall Way.

AWM 3DRL/2316, War Letters of General Monash: Volume 1: 24 December 1914 to 4 March 1917.

Irish Bureau of Military History (BMH)

BMH: Witness Statements WS1017 (Gordon Cassidy), WS1323 (Martin Needham), WS1605 (Rev Eugene Nevin), and WS1606 (Patrick Hegarty)

National Archives of Australia (NAA)

NAA B2455: First Australian Imperial Force Personnel Dossiers 1914-20 (for the men and Australian units mentioned).

NAA K89: G29/247, Mental Homes – HQ Correspondence [care of Repatriation Patients].

NAA MP367/1: Department of Defence - General Correspondence:

500/1/349, Purchase of Stromness Mental Cases Treatment 5MD.

556/33/51, Victoria Cross winners - Furlough to Australia.   .

NAA PP13/1: Pension Files, 1914/1018 War and Boer War (C5474, O'Meara Martin VC).

NAA PP645/1: Medical and hospital files of Veterans (M5474, Martin O'Meara VC).

NAA PT1675/1: NN, Woodman Point Quarantine Station Admissions.

National Archives of Ireland (NAI)

Census records for 1901 and 1911 (available online <http://www.census.nationalarchives.ie/>)

NAI: CS/HC/PO/4/91/7832, Probate Martin O'Meara

State Records of South Australia (SRSA)

SRSA GRG7/2: Application by nominee for assisted passage previously paid for by nominator in South Australia.

State Records Office of Western Australia (SROWA)

SROWA Series 34, Consignment 3403 (Item 1938/1078 Probate File – Martin O'Meara).

SROWA Series 675, Consignment 752 (Item 1919/2359 Claremont Hospital for Insane – Select Committee, Item 1923/2561 Claremont hospital; for insane alleged victimisation of employees who gave evidence before select committee).

SROWA Series 1771, Consignment 1120, Items 116 to 153 Male Patients Day and Night Registers for 1919 to 1926.

SROWA Series 4500, Consignment 1120 (Item 27: Patient Admissions Register (Claremont Mental Hospital, Military Personnel Only)).

SROWA Series 4700, Consignment 2961 (Item 1: Report – Royal Commission on Lunacy).

SROWA Series 4701, Consignment 2962 (Item 2: Transcript of Evidence – Royal Commission on Lunacy).

The National Archives of the UK (TNA)

TNA: WO 95/1852/2, 7 Suffolks War Diary, 1916.

TNA: WO 95/1603/1, 18th Field Ambulance War Diary, August 1914 – September 1919.

Newspapers and Journals

Advertiser (Adelaide SA)

Australian (Perth WA)

Border Mail (Mount Gambier SA)

Brisbane Courier (Brisbane QLD)

Bunbury Herald/Bunbury Herald & Blackwood Express (Bunbury WA)

Camp Chronicle (Midland Junction WA)

Collie Mail (Collie WA)

Daily Herald (Adelaide SA)

Daily Mail (Perth WA)

Daily Mirror (London UK)

Daily News (Perth WA)

Echuca and Moama Advertiser and Farmers' Gazette (Echuca VIC)

Evening News (Sydney NSW)

Geraldton Guardian and Express (Geraldton WA)

Great War (London)

Irish Press (Ireland)

Kalgoorlie Miner (Kalgoorlie WA)

King's County Chronicle (Ireland)

Midland Tribune (Ireland)

Mirror (Perth WA)

Nenagh Guardian (Ireland)

Nenagh News (Ireland)

Register (Adelaide SA)

Southern Times (Bunbury WA)

South Western Advertiser (Perth WA)

Sunday Mirror (Perth WA)

Sunday Mirror (London UK)

Sunday Times (Perth WA)

Transcontinental (Port Augusta SA)

W.A. Record (Perth WA)

West Australian (Perth WA)

Westralian Worker (Perth WA)

Books, Reports and Journal Articles

Bean, C.E.W. (1941): *The Official History of Australia in the War of 1914-1918: Volume I – The Story of ANZAC: The First Phase*, Angus and Robertson, Sydney.

Bean, C.E.W. (1941a): *The Official History of Australia in the War of 1914-1918: Volume III - The A.I.F. in France 1916*, Angus and Robertson, Sydney.

Bean, C.E.W. (1941b): *The Official History of Australia in the War of 1914-1918: Volume IV - The A.I.F. in France 1917*, Angus and Robertson, Sydney.

Bean, C.E.W. (1941c): *The Official History of Australia in the War of 1914-1918: Volume V - The A.I.F. During the Main German Offensive 1918*, Angus and Robertson, Sydney.

Bean, C.E.W. (1942): *The Official History of Australia in the War of 1914-1918: Volume VI - The A.I.F. During the Allied Offensive 1918*, Angus and Robertson, Sydney.

Bean, C.E.W. (2014): *ANZAC to Amiens*, Penguin, Melbourne.

Butler, A.G. (1943): *The Australian Army Medical Services of the War of 1914-1918*: Volume III, Australian War Memorial, Canberra.

Chataway. T.P. (revised and edited by Goldenstedt, P.) (1948): *History of the 15th Battalion Australian Imperial Forces*, William Brooke and Co., Brisbane.

Christenson, R. (Ed.) (1988): *To All My Dear People – The Diaries and Letters of Private Hubert P. Demasson 1916-1917*, Fremantle Arts Centre Press, Fremantle.

Commonwealth of Australia (1918): *Facts and Extracts for Speakers, Organisers, and Recruiters*, Director-General of Recruiting, Melbourne.

Dennehy, J. (2013): *In a Time of War: Tipperary 1914-1918*, Merrion, County Kildare.

Doherty, R. & Truesdale, D. (2000): *Irish Winners of the Victoria Cross*, Four Courts Press, Dublin.

General Staff (1917): *Instructions for the Training of the British Armies in France (Provisional)*, HMSO, London.

Gill, I. (2008): *Bloody Angle: Bullecourt and beyond: 16th Battalion A.I.F. 1914-19*, GEON Advance Press, Bassendean.

Heberle, G. (1997): 'Timber harvesting of Crown land in the south-west of Western Australia: an historical review with maps', in *CALMScience*, Volume 2 Number 3 (pp.203-224).

Hesketh-Pritchard, H. (1920): *Sniping in France: With Notes on the Scientific Training of Scouts, Observers and Snipers*, Hutchinson & Co., London.

Hogan E. (1878): *The Description of Ireland and the state therof as it is at this present in Anno 1598*, M.H. Gill & Son, Dublin.

House of Commons (1852), *The Census of Ireland for the Year 1851 – Part 1 Showing the Area, Population, and Number of Houses by Townlands and Electoral Division – County of Tipperary (North Riding)*, HMSO, Dublin.

Jeffery, K. (2000): *Ireland and the Great War*, Cambridge University Press., Cambridge.

Keech, G. (2011): *Pozières*, Pen & Sword Military, Barnsley.

Kildea, J. (2007): *Anzacs and Ireland*, University of NSW Press, Sydney.

King, S. (2012): *A Lorrha Miscellany*, Seamus J. King, Ireland.

Lawriwsky, M. (2007): *Hard Jacka: The Story of a Gallipoli Legend*, Mira Books, Chatswood.

Legislative Assembly of Western Australia (1919): *Report of the Selection Committee of the Legislative Assembly on the Claremont Hospital for the Insane*, Perth.

Longmore, C. (1929): *The Old Sixteenth*, History Committee of the 16th Battalion Association, Perth.

MacDonagh, M. (1917): *The Irish on the Somme*, Hodder and Stoughton, London.

McLachlan, M. (2007): *Walking with the ANZACs: A Guide to Australian Battlefields on the Western Front*, revised edition, Hachette, Sydney.

Martyr, P. (2014): 'More than Ordinary Care: Martin O'Meara VC', 5th Frederick Bell VC Memorial Lecture, Cottesloe WA, 14 November 2014.

Martyr, P. & Davison, S. (2015): 'The trouble with Martin O'Meara', *Australasian Psychiatry*, 23(5), pp.536-9.

Mills, J. (1986): *The Timber People – A History of Bunnings Limited*, Bunnings Limited, Perth.

Mills, J. (1988): 'The 'Teddy Bears': a history of the South West Timber Hewers Cooperative, Western Australia', in Frawley, K. J. & Semple, N. M. (Eds.): *Australia's ever-changing forests: Proceedings of the First National Conference on Australian forest history*, Australian Forest History Series. Special Publication No. 1, Department of Geography and Oceanography, Australian Defence Force Academy. Campbell, ACT: University of New South Wales, University College, ADFA, Department of Geography and Oceanography.

Pedersen, P. (2003): *Hamel*, Pen & Sword, Barnsley.

Pedersen, P. (2012): *ANZACs on the Western Front: The Australian War Memorial Battlefield Guide*, John Wiley & Sons, Milton QLD.

Richards, R. (1993): *Murray and Mandurah: A Sequel History of the Old Murray District of Western Australia*, Shire of Murray and City of Mandurah, Perth.

Richards, R. (2003): *The McLarty Family of Pinjarra*, J.D. McLarty, Perth.

Sands & Dougall (1912), *South Australian Directory for 1912*, Sands & Dougall, Adelaide.

Serle, Geoffrey (Ed.) (1988): *Australian Dictionary of Biography*, Volume II 1891-1939 Nes-Smi, Melbourne University Press, Carlton.

Simington, R.C. (Ed.) (1934): *The Civil Survey A.D. 1654-1656 County of Tipperary Vol. II*, Stationery Office, Dublin.

Simms, J.G. (1989): 'The Cromwellian Settlement of Tipperary', *Tipperary Historical Journal*, No.4, Tipperary Historical Society, Thurles.

Staunton, A. (2005): *Victoria Cross: Australia's finest and the battles they fought*, Hardie Grant, Melbourne.

Wahlert, G. & Linwood, R. (2014): *One Shot Kills: A History of Australian Army Sniping*, Big Sky Publishing, Sydney.

Wigmore, L. & Harding, B.A. & Australian War Memorial (1963): *They Dared Mightily*, Australian War Memorial, Canberra.

World Health Organisation (2012): 'Risks to Mental Health: An Overview of Vulnerabilities and Risk Factors', Geneva.

Index

www.ingramcontent.com/pod-product-compliance
Lightning Source LLC
Chambersburg PA
CBHW021047090426
42738CB00006B/218